Environmental Law in Israel

Environmental Law in Israel

Sixth Edition

Richard Laster
Dan Livney

This book was originally published as a monograph in the International Encyclopaedia of Laws/Environmental Law.

Founding Editor: Roger Blanpain
General Editor: Frank Hendrickx
Volume Editor: Kurt Deketelaere

Wolters Kluwer

Published by:
Kluwer Law International B.V.
PO Box 316
2400 AH Alphen aan den Rijn
The Netherlands
E-mail: lrs-sales@wolterskluwer.com
Website: www.wolterskluwer.com/en/solutions/kluwerlawinternational

Sold and distributed by:
Wolters Kluwer Legal & Regulatory U.S.
920 Links Avenue
Landisville, PA 17538
United States of America
E-mail: customer.service@wolterskluwer.com

ISBN 978-94-035-1457-4

e-Book: ISBN 978-94-035-1467-3
web-PDF: ISBN 978-94-035-1477-2

This title is available on www.kluwerlawonline.com

The Authors

Professor Richard Laster (born 8 July 1944 in Richmond, Virginia, USA) received his BA in 1966 from the University of Virginia, his JD from the University of Richmond, his LLM from Harvard Law School and his LLD from the Hebrew University, Faculty of Law, Jerusalem.

Professor Laster is a member of the Virginia Bar Association, the Israel Chamber of Advocates, the International Council of Environmental Law and the International Academy of Environmental Law.

From 1973 to 1979, he was the legal advisor to the Environmental Protection Agency in Israel. From 1979 to 1989, he was a partner in the law firm of Laster & Zisquit, and since then, he has been with the law firm of Laster & Gouldman. Among his numerous other functions, he is a professor of Environmental Law and Policy at the Faculty of Law of Hebrew University, where he still teaches. Until 2012, he also taught at the School of Geography and the School of Environmental Sciences of the Hebrew University. He has served as Chairman of the Committee for Revision of Noise Regulations (1984–1990), Chairman of the Israel Environmental Law Association (1990), Founding member of the International Academy of Environmental Law, Member of the International Association on Water Quality (AIDA), Secretary of the Israel Society for Ecology and Environmental Quality Sciences (1992–1998, 2000–2006), Chair of the Society for Health Education in Israel (since 1990), Member of the Israel Chamber of Advocates' Committee on Environmental Law and Chair of the Steering Committee for the Kidron/ Wadi Nar Basin Master Plan. He has published extensively on environmental law, environmental issues and pollution-related health problems in Israel.

The Authors

Dan Livney (born 20 December 1957 in Philadelphia, Pennsylvania, USA) received his LLB in 2002 and his MBA in 2003, both from the University of Manchester. He is a member of the Israel Chamber of Advocates, and he has been working at the law firm of Laster & Gouldman since 2003. He is a lecturer at the Ono Academic College and the Peres Academic Centre. His work focuses mainly on environmental law on the local, national and international levels. He served as legal advisor to the Yarqon and Kishon River Authority Master Plan teams. He has published in numerous journals mainly in the field of international water law. He is active in promoting environmental education in Israel and the Palestinian Authority. He is also an organic olive farmer and member of Kibbutz Gezer.

Table of Contents

List of Abbreviations

CDM	Clean Development Mechanism
CER	Certified Emission Reduction
CERCLA	Comprehensive Environmental Response Compensation and Liability Act
CIS	Countries of the Former Soviet Union
CITES	Convention on International Trade in Endangered Species of Wild Fauna and Flora
DNA	Designated National Authority
EEZ	Exclusive Economic Zone
EPS	Environmental Protection Service
GDP	Gross Domestic Product
IEC	Israel Electric Corporation
ILA	Israel Land Authority
ILS	Israeli Shekel
ISA	Israel Securities Authority
IUED	Israel Union for Environmental Defense
JNF	Jewish National Fund
JWC	Joint Water Committee
K.T.	*Kovetz Hatakanot* (this is the Hebrew version of the regulations. There is no official translation of Israeli regulations in English)
L.S.I.	*Laws of the State of Israel* (this is the official English translation of Israeli laws up to 1987)
NGO	Non-governmental Organization
NIS	New Israeli Shekel
NRA	National River Association
OECD	Organisation for Economic Co-operation and Development

List of Abbreviations

P.D.	*Piskei Din* (this is the official publication of the judgments of the Supreme Court. The publication is in Hebrew)
P.G.	*Palestine Gazette* (this is the official publication of ordinances during the British Mandate (1920–1948). Reference is to the English version of the Gazette)
P.O.	Palestine Ordinance (these are laws passed by the Mandate government before the formation of the State of Israel)
PRTR	Pollutant Release and Transfer Register
S.H.	*Sefer Hahokim* (this is the Hebrew version of the laws, cited where no official English version exists)
USD	US Dollar

General Introduction

Chapter 1. General Information

§1. Geography and Population

1. For a relatively small country (20,000 square kilometres), Israel has a surprisingly large variety of geographical regions.[1] It features almost everything from desert to alpine characteristics.

The most influential factor in determining the country's topography is the Syrian-African rift, which runs north to south along the eastern part of Israel, from the Kinneret,[2] along the Jordan Valley and the Arava Valley. The surrounding area is divided into longitudinal strips, the coastal plain, the hills and the Jordan Valley. Horizontally, Israel is divided into the Negev Desert in the southern half, the Galilee and Golan hills in the northern third, and the central plains rising up to Jerusalem in between.

Most of the rock in Israel is composed of marine sediments. Limestone can be found in the Negev, the Judean Hills and the Galilee. Chalk and softer rock can be found around the hills, while volcanic rock, particularly basalt, is common in the Golan, the Galilee and the south.

Due to varied landforms, the climate differences in various areas of Israel are very pronounced, though certain features are common to the whole of the country. Israel is in the Mediterranean zone (28 –33 degrees latitude). The rainy season is short, and in the summer, there is no rain for six months. There are moderate variations in the length of days and nights and very short transitional seasons. The intensity of the sun, which is always high (35 degrees on 22 December, 82 degrees on 21 June), aided by clear skies in summer and often in winter, makes Israel a warm country. Temperature variations are caused by geographical position, altitude, marine influences and wind direction. The average annual temperature in the hills is 17ºC, in the coastal plain 20ºC, and in the Jordan Valley 25ºC. January is the coldest month, with temperatures often going below 0ºC in the hills, though not much lower. August is the warmest month with temperatures reaching as high as 40ºC in the warmer areas.

---

1. The information in this chapter comes mainly from the following sources: The CIA World Factbook, the Israel Department of Statistics, The Environment in Israel, Fourth Edition, Joyce Whitman (1988); Environmental Quality in Israel, The Ministry of Environment, Report # 16 (1990); The Environment in Israel, Shoshana Gabai, ed., The Ministry of Environmental Protection, Jerusalem (2002); Israel Central Bureau of Statistics (CBS).
2. Also known as the Sea of Galilee.

The distribution of rainfall is uneven, increasing from south to north and from east to west.

The annual average rainfall in Eilat is 22 millimetres, 656 millimetres in the Judean Hills, and 947 on Mount Hermon. Seventy per cent of the rain falls from November through February, January being the wettest month. Snow falls almost every year but only on the hilltops and for very few days.

The composition and density of the vegetation are determined by the following: (1) The position of Israel on the meeting point of three continents and two oceans, resulting in a wide variety of species (3,500 species, compared to 1,700 in England and 1,500 in Egypt); (2) the dry Mediterranean climate, causing plants to adapt themselves by decreasing water loss, increasing absorption facilities and growing in a rainy season cycle; (3) the influence of man's destruction of woodland over thousands of years for domestic and public use and during the many wars in the area.

Israel is one of the two countries in the world to end the twentieth century with more trees than it had at the start. This is even more remarkable in light of the fact that the country is 40% desert.[3]

Farm products depend very much on the micro-climate. Citrus trees, which require irrigation, grow in humid regions; vines grow on the hills and foothills and the coastal plain, while olives grow on the hills, as they require little or no irrigation. Cereals and industrial crops grow mostly in the north and to a lesser extent in the Negev, as they can grow in heavy soils.

According to initial climate change scenarios, increased rain intensity combined with a reduction in overall precipitation will increase surface run-off, soil erosion, and salinity, leading to desertification.[4] The Negev ecosystems may replace the Mediterranean ecosystems in Israel.

2. As of December 2022, the population of Israel stood at 9.656 million people, comprised of 2.037 million Arabs, 7.106 million Jews and 513 thousand others.[5] Since the early twentieth century, large numbers of immigrants have arrived from different countries, speaking different languages and having totally different cultures. In the past, the State has often directed these immigrants to outlying towns and districts, a policy that has had its own special impact on the country.

Israel's population at the time of its establishment in April 1948 numbered 806,000 residents. The population doubled in size from 1948 to 1959 and doubled once again between 1955 and 1975. The population continued to grow rapidly, mainly due to the waves of immigration in the 1970s from the Countries of the Former Soviet Union (CIS) and in the 1990s from Ethiopia and the CIS. Between 1972 and 1979, 179,930 immigrants arrived in Israel from the CIS. Between 1990 and 2000, 815,962 immigrants arrived from the CIS and 41,856 from Ethiopia. In recent years, immigration has significantly decreased. In 2017, there were 26,357

3. Jewish National Fund, www.jnf.org (last visited 26 Apr. 2023).
4. Israel Second National Communication on Climate Change, Submitted under the UN Framework Convention on Climate Change, Ministry of Environmental Protection, November 2010.
5. Israel Central Bureau of Statistics, Press Announcement No. 426/2022' published on 29/12/2022.

immigrants to Israel.[6] But recently immigration from both Russia and Ukraine has increased, due to the war between the two countries. Between March and October 2022, 44,283 immigrants arrived in Israel from Russia, Ukraine and Belarus.[7]

The population growth rate in Israel is 2%, a rate that has remained consistent over the past decade.[8] Normally, this large increase is only found in developing countries; therefore, in light of the fact that Israel is considered a developed country, this rate of population growth is an anomaly. According to the Central Bureau of Statistics, the population in 2035 is expected to reach 11.3 million persons. The effect, of course, is felt in the environmental infrastructure.

Israel's government policy encourages both immigration and population growth. The Ministry of Immigrant Absorption provides new immigrants with economic benefits upon their arrival, including housing grants and loans, tax benefits on the purchase of household items and cars, grants for initial living expenses, income insurance and student grants.[9] The National Insurance Institute of Israel (Bituach Leumi) provides child allowances for families with children. These benefits are paid directly to the families and are given regardless of need. The previous policy provided increasing benefits per child for larger families. The present policy pays similar amounts per child born after 2003.[10]

The large increase in population, together with an increase in the standard of living, has had serious impacts on the country's infrastructure and natural resources. Household water consumption had increased from 698 million cubic metres in 2003 to 758.5 million cubic metres in 2008, then decreased back to 684 million cubic metres in 2009. The drop in household water consumption is due to water-saving advertising campaigns, higher water tariffs and the use of water-saving devices in many households due to several years of drought. The domestic water consumption in 2019 reached 89.1 cubic metres per capita per year.[11] This figure has remained constant over the past decade.

Electricity production in 2020 rose by 0.6% in relationship to 2019. This increase is a result of a 1.9% increase in extreme weather events (mainly in the summer and between seasons), and a decrease in economic activity of 1.3% due to COVID-19.[12] It appears that in the coming years, climate change will cause a continued increase in electricity consumption.

---

6. Israel Central Bureau of Statistics, 4.4 Immigrants by Period of Immigration, country of Birth and Last Country of Residence, published on 16.08.2018.
7. Dr Eliahu Ayala, Immigration Statistics from Ukraine and Russia During 2022, Knesset Center for Information and Research, 12 Dec. 2022.
8. Israel Central Bureau of Statistics, 2.12 Sources of Population Growth, published 04.09.2018.
9. Ministry of Immigrant Absorption website: www.moia.gov.il/Moia_en/HomePage.htm (last viewed 6 Apr. 2023).
10. Present government payments are 164 NIS for the first child, 207 NIS for the second, third and fourth child, and for the fifth child and more 164 NIS. Figures from the Israel National Insurance Institute, www.btl.gov.il (last visited 6 Apr. 2023).
11. Israel Water Authority, https://www.gov.il/he/departments/water_authority/govil-landing-page (Last viewed 6 Apr. 2023).
12. Noga – The Israel Independent System Operator Ltd., production and consumption summary for 2020.

There were 3.84 million motor vehicles in Israel in 2021, an increase of 4.4% compared to 2020.[13] The number of vehicles per 1,000 people has reached 406 in 2021, a number still considered small relative to many countries in Europe and North America.[14]

Israel is ranked the 29th most densely populated country in the world, with 434 people per square kilometre.[15] Density and settlement structure varies greatly from one region to the other. The Tel Aviv metropolitan area has a population density of 8,440 people per square kilometre, 100 times the population density of the southern district.[16]

§2. Legal and Political Structure

3. Until the end of World War I, Palestine, including present-day Israel, was a part of the Ottoman Empire. Turkish rule was followed by British rule, which lasted until the establishment of the State of Israel on 14 May 1948. When British rule superseded Turkish rule, the colonial administration kept intact the laws and customs that were extant. Only those areas of law found inadequate were replaced by British law. With the establishment of the State of Israel, whole areas of Ottoman and British law were retained so as not to overly disrupt the social fabric of the country. These British and Ottoman laws (called Ordinances) were gradually replaced so that no Ottoman legislation remains in force in Israel today. Also, most pieces of British legislation have been replaced, updated (into what is called a New Version) or consolidated with Israeli amendments (in what is known as a Consolidated Version).

4. Israel, like Britain, has no written constitution. Unlike Britain, however, the Israeli legislative body, the Knesset, has passed a series of *Basic Laws* with the hope that these laws will someday form a written constitution. There are currently thirteen *Basic Laws*, including those for the Judiciary, the Legislature, the President, and the Government. There are two Basic Laws concerning human rights which were both passed in 1992: The Basic Law: Freedom of Occupation; and The Basic Law: Human Dignity & Liberty. There is no Basic Law protecting the environment or Israel's natural heritage, although a few versions have been proposed in the Knesset, the most recent in 2001.[17] In 2004, the Supreme Court held that the Basic Law: Human Dignity and Liberty, which protects basic human rights, does not include the right to an environment of reasonable quality.[18]

The Basic Law: Judicature[19] requires that courts follow precedents of higher courts. While the Supreme Court itself is not bound by law to precedent, even its

13. Central Bureau of Statistics, Press release 111/2022.
14. *Ibid.*
15. Israel Central Bureau of Statistics, sources of population growth, 2020.
16. Central Bureau of Statistics Population Density per District, 2020.
17. Proposed Knesset Law No. 2991, 26 Mar. 2001, Basic Law: The Environment.
18. High Court 4128/02, *Israel Union for Environmental Defence v. The Prime Minister of Israel* et al.
19. Basic Law: Judicature, 38 *Laws of the State of Israel* (this is the official English translation of Israeli laws up to 1987 (L.S.I.) 101.

own, in the lower courts, precedent is respected and compelling. The courts are allowed to follow other sources of law, taking into consideration the principles of freedom, justice, equity and peace found in Jewish tradition. This rather vague reference to Jewish tradition does not bind Israel's judges to Jewish law.

5. There are three tiers of courts: the Supreme Court, the District Court and the Magistrates Courts. Magistrates and District Courts deal with civil suits and criminal cases. Jurisdiction before these courts is determined by the size of the claim and by the severity of the punishment. The District Court also serves as an appellate court for the Magistrates Court. The Supreme Court functions both as an appellate court and as a High Court of Justice. In this latter capacity, it deals with administrative and constitutional issues, exercises judicial review over the other branches of government, and gives relief in matters where no other court has jurisdiction. In order to relieve the caseload of the Supreme Court, the Court of Administrative Matters was created in 2000.[20] Acting through the District Court, the Court of Administrative Matters hears appeals of decisions of local planning authorities (not regional or national), claims of damages resulting from public tenders, and also certain administrative petitions and appeals. There are also specialized courts: religious, military, juvenile, labour tribunals, traffic, etc.

Of interest to environmental law practitioners is the operation of the Water Court or Water Tribunal. The Water Tribunal was created under the Water Law, discussed in Chapter 3, *infra*. The Tribunal is composed of a panel of three: a District Court judge who presides over the panel, and two representatives of the general public. The Water Tribunal sits on all matters referred to it by the Water Law and the Drainage and Floods Control Law. Appeals from the Water Tribunal are to the Supreme Court.

6. Israel is a parliamentary democracy with a President, a Parliament and a ruling government. The functioning of these bodies is briefly described hereunder.

7. *Parliament*. As stated earlier, the Parliament – the Knesset – is the supreme legislator.[21] Another important power it holds is the approval of the government's budget. The Knesset ratifies international treaties and elects the President. Elections to the Knesset are held every four years. The country is composed of one constituency, and the elections are proportional. Citizens vote for a party list, which is identical throughout the country.

8. *The President*. The President has mainly ceremonial status and is chosen by the Knesset once every seven years. The President's role[22] includes appointing a Member of Parliament to form a government, signing laws and granting pardons. The President also receives the credentials of foreign diplomats and signs international conventions ratified by the Knesset.

20. Court of Administrative Matters Law, 2000 *Sefer Hahokim* (this is the Hebrew version of the laws, cited where no official English version exists) (S.H.) 1739, 190.
21. Basic Law: The Knesset, 12 L.S.I. 85.
22. Basic Law: The President, 18 L.S.I. 111.

9. *National and Local Government.* The government rules only so long as it has the confidence of the Knesset.[23] A member of the Knesset, capable of forming a majority of Knesset members, serves as the Prime Minister. From the founding of the State, all governments have been coalition governments, as no single party has yet had an absolute majority. The Prime Minister, usually the leader of the largest party, appoints ministers from his/her party, while ministers from other coalition parties are selected by their parties. The government's taking office requires the approval of the Knesset, which can, at any time, adopt a vote of no-confidence. Likewise, the Prime Minister has the power to disperse the Knesset, with the approval of the President.

Local governments in Israel are divided by law, into cities, local councils and regional councils. This structure was originally created during the Mandate period and has been maintained until today.[24] The difference between the structures is determined by the Minister of the Interior. He/she is granted the power to grant municipal status to an area so designated by him/her in an order. Normally, a city in Israel is composed of at least 20,000 residents, but there are exceptions to this rule. A local council is a small town, whereas a regional council is composed of rural villages, including kibbutzim and moshavim. A kibbutz is a voluntary collective society, whose aim is equality and cooperation in production, consumption, social welfare and education. On a moshav, members own their land but may own certain property collectively. In the elections for the regional councils, a head of the regional council is elected along with representatives of each village, who represent their village in the regional council. The Minister of the Interior can also decide to create local committees within local councils which contain more than one town or village. With over 300 local authorities operating in Israel, setting an environmental policy to be implemented by the local authorities is extremely difficult. While the elective process is independent, local authorities are dependent on the central government in several areas. The State provides funding to the local authorities, both in the form of general grants and earmarked income. The national government finances the majority of the local authorities' budget for education and social welfare. State services, principally in the areas of education and welfare, comprise more than half of the local budget and an even higher proportion of the personnel employed by the local authorities. The Minister of the Interior supervises the activities of the local authorities and is primarily responsible for the approval of their budgets and examination of their bylaws. Also, the planning process, an extremely important environmental task, places the local authority under the supervision of a higher planning authority controlled by the central government.[25]

---

23. Basic Law: The Government, 22 L.S.I. 257.
24. Local Councils Ordinance (new version), Order of Local Councils (Regional Councils), 1958, Municipalities Ordinance (new version).
25. Website of the Israel Ministry for Foreign Affairs, www.mfa.gov.il/mfa/government/branches%20of%20government/executive/israeli%20demo cracy%20-%20how%20does%20it%20work#local (last visited 26 Apr. 2023).

§3. Economic Characteristics

10. Israel has a mixed economy, basically capitalistic but with strong government intervention. For three decades after the creation of the State of Israel, the Labour Party held the reins of power. They believed in socialist economic principles, the ideals of worker's rights, minimum wages, nationalized health service, the importance of agriculture and farm communes (kibbutz) and strong labour unions. As time went on, however, the deficiencies of centralization began to show. There was too much government patronage, a bloated, inefficient labour force, heavy currency controls and an extremely heavy tax burden. This led to a change in government, which provided for a freer economy.

In 1977, the right-wing Likud party wrested control of the government from the Labour Party. Some changes were made, but the government-directed economy was maintained. Since then, the two parties have headed the government at various times, with both slowly dismantling the centralized economy. Foreign currency control ended in the latter part of the 1990s, and the budget deficit was reduced to 3% of the Gross Domestic Product (GDP) by 2003. Israel recorded a budget deficit of 2.15% of GDP in 2016, and 4.5% in 2021.[26] The year 2022 ended with a government surplus of ILS 9.8 billion, the first yearly surplus since 1987. But it is important to note that Israel has a government debt of ILS 1 trillion.[27]

The government privatization campaign has reduced and eliminated subsidies on basic commodities and is continuously selling public companies to the private sector, including Bezek, the national telephone company, and the national airline, El Al. The present government is carrying out further reforms in reducing government involvement in the economy, working towards reducing both the budget and taxes.

Sandwiched between the Arab Spring and Occupy Wall Street, Israel's social protest movement erupted in June 2011. After the removal of price controls on cottage cheese, an Israeli staple, the price rose 75% within a year. An ultra-orthodox man infuriated with the price rise, set up a Facebook page urging consumers to boycott cottage cheese for one month in protest. Within days, thousands joined the boycott, which expanded to protests against an economy where many families cannot keep up with the rising cost of living, now higher than in Europe and North America. The protests initially involved hundreds of thousands of Israelis, but by the 2013 elections, had all but died out. They did have an effect on the outcome, with two protest leaders becoming Knesset members of the Labour Party, and a new party called *Yesh Atid* ('There is a Future'), which promised to aid the struggling middle class, winning 19 of the 120 Knesset seats.

In light of the protests and the ensuing Knesset inquiry, which found a lack of competition and monopolization in the food industry, in 2014, the Knesset passed the Law for Promoting Competition in the Food Industry, meant to lower prices through increased competition. Whether the messages of the social protest movement will have a lasting effect on the Israeli economy remains to be seen.

---

26. https://country.eiu.com/article.aspx?articleid=1201752103&Country=Israel&topic=Economy&subtopic=Fo_1 (last visited 14 Apr. 2023).
27. Ynet news website. https://www.ynet.co.il/economy/article/rjx4vz3qi (Last visited 6 Apr. 2023).

In the ten years since the protests and until the outbreak of COVID-19, the cost of living index didn't change. In 2020, COVID-19, coupled with a Parliamentary crisis with four elections within two years (2019–2021) had a devastating effect on the economy, With the ending of the COVID-19 quarantine, the economy bounced back. Prices of basic goods again began rising while housing costs rose at an annual rate of 20%.

In 2021, the GDP was USD 488.5 billion, with an annual growth rate of 8.6%. In 2021, the GDP per person was USD 52,171, placing Israel amongst the twenty largest economies in the world.[28]

11. While GDP is an accurate measure of the well-being of societies and countries, these policies may overlook or even aggravate other problems, like environmental problems and social inequality. Some improvements in today's quality of life may come at the expense of future generations and their available resources. In order to address these problems, the Ministry of Environmental Protection has developed indicators for well-being, sustainability and resilience to provide the public and decision-makers with information on the country's social, economic and environmental status. This provides the tools to better debate national priorities and agendas. In accordance with a government resolution, nine government ministries are preparing proposals on quality-of-life indicators that will measure well-being, sustainability and resilience.[29] This report is based on the Organisation for Economic Cooperation and Development (OECD) Compendium of Well-Being Indicators.[30]

12. The Ministry of Environmental Protection has also begun addressing the issue of environmental inequality. Weaker local authorities in the minority sector, especially in the Arab and Bedouin communities, suffer from many environmental problems and lack the funds to address them. An amendment to the Maintenance of Cleanliness Law enables the Ministry of Environmental Protection to allocate operational budgets to weaker local authorities without the usual requirement for matching funds.

13. Outside of Israel, one often hears of the Kibbutzim, Israel's famous communes. Yet, the population of the Kibbutzim is less than 2% of the country's population. In fact, the agricultural sector as a whole provides work for less than 3% of the country's population. However, the yields are tremendous due to intensive agricultural practices which affect the environment. Israel is a world leader in developing agricultural technology and new plant species as well as the attended water technology. Kibbutzim account for 34% of the agricultural production in Israel. Kibbutzim, however, do not operate only in the agricultural sector. Over the years, they

---

28. https://forbes.co.il/e/israel-is-among-the-top-20-global-economies-in-gdp-per-capita-for-the-first-time/ (Last visited 6 Apr. 2023).
29. *Ministry of Environmental Protection, 'Well-being Indicators for Israel'*, April 2014.
30. *OECD Better Life Initiative, Compendium of OECD Well-Being Indicators*, OECD 2011.

have diversified into industrial production; at first it was in the processing of agricultural products, and today in all fields of industrial activity, from plastics to lens making. The Kibbutz movement's share in Israeli industry amounts to 10% of total industrial production.[31]

14. As a whole, industry in Israel is extremely diversified, especially for a small country with few natural resources. On the coastline, one finds Israel's ports possessing facilities for oil refineries and electric power generation. Moving inland into the cities, one finds heavily polluting industries for the making of pesticides, chemicals, and electroplating as well as less polluting industries such as diamond cutting. The fastest growth rates are to be found in the high-tech sector, which accounts for more than two-thirds of the industrial production of the country.[32] Over 6,900 start-up companies have been founded in Israel over the past decade out of which 4,105 have survived the first year.[33] Several international high-tech companies have research and development facilities in Israel, including Google, Intel, Motorola, IBM, Microsoft, Alcatel, 3Com and Facebook, which opened an office in Israel in March 2014. Intel and Motorola also manufacture advanced products in Israel. One hundred Israeli companies are traded on US exchanges, representing the second-largest number of foreign firms appearing on the US stock markets (after Canada).[34]

15. In 2010, Israel gained entry into the OECD. The process required the government not only to provide access to its inner workings but also to make changes in its policies. OECD membership exposes Israel to comparisons with other countries, and recommendations for policy changes in health, education and the environment based on economic efficiency and worldwide standards. The OECD Working Party on Environmental Performance reviewed Israel's environmental performance at its meeting in June 2011 and approved forty-one recommendations on how Israel's performance could be improved.

§4. Social and Cultural Characteristics

16. Israel's cultural life is very much influenced by its geographical characteristics. Being a warm country, much of the daily activity is held outdoors. Along the coastal plain, people go out for a stroll on the beach or sit and chat in outdoor cafes.

31. Kibbutz Industries Association (Last visited 6 Apr. 2023).
32. Ministry of Foreign Affairs, 'Sectors of the Economy', https://www.gov.il/en/Departments/General/economy-sectors-of-the-israeli-economy (last visited 26 Apr. 2023).
33. http://www.calcalist.co.il/local/articles/0,7340,L-3617486,00.html (last visited 14 Apr. 2023).
34. The Complete List of Israel Stocks Trading on the US Market, As of 27 Mar. 2023. https://topforeignstocks.com/foreign-adrs-list/the-full-list-of-israel-adrs/ (Last visited 6 Apr. 2023).

Much of the activity at home takes place on the porch or the balcony. Going outdoors provides relief and change, especially in the hot summer. This is changing with the advent of air conditioning, now found in 93.2% of the homes in Israel as of 2019.[35]

Israel's history, culture and religion make for a strong attachment to the land. The size and climate of the country provide easy access to parks and nature reserves, enabling Israelis to hike often, all year round and all around the country. This natural affinity for hiking is encouraged and sponsored by the Society for the Preservation of Nature, Israel's oldest and largest nature society. Trails are marked everywhere, making the hike easier for travellers.

Israel's most famous hiking trail is the Israel National Trail, inaugurated in 1995. It winds along the entire north-south length of the country, a total of 1,009 kilometres. National Geographic includes it in their list of the World's Best *Grail Trails*, describing it as connecting 'to something that often gets lost in all the headlines – the sublime beauty of the wilderness of the Middle East'.[36]

Israel has 140 kilometres of beaches along the Mediterranean coast and 14 kilometres on the Red Sea. The warm climate allows these to be enjoyed all year round. The country's major economic and commercial activity is also on the same stretch, including ports, power stations, desalination plants and the country's major population centres. This puts heavy environmental pressure on the beaches and coastal waters. The rising ocean levels, changes in ocean currents and building close to the water edge are all causing destruction to Israel's coastline. The Government has appropriated funds to protect the coasts, but not enough to effectuate real change. There is also concern about a tsunami possibly reaching Israel's coast. The Government set up a panel of experts to prepare data concerning the likelihood and possible damage of a tsunami disaster.

Tourists are attracted to Israel's warm weather, friendly population, enticing beaches, and numerous historical and religious sites. The climate allows tourism year-round, and the Israeli economy enjoys significant revenue from tourists visiting the country. Tourism is heavily dependent on the political and security situation, and has seen sharp rises and falls over the years as a result.

§5. Main Environmental Problems

17. Israel's geography and population distribution, together with its climatic conditions, lay the basis for its major environmental problems.[37] A compact country, over half being semi-arid and three-fourths of its population living along the coast, is a recipe for the environmental problems set out below.

35. Central Bureau of Statistics, Standard of Living- Yearly Statistics for Israel 2022- Number 73, Chart 7.8.
36. https://www.nationalgeographic.com/adventure/article/worlds-best-grail-trails (last visited 7 Apr. 2023).
37. Information for this section comes mainly from the following publications: *Environmental Quality in Israel* and *The Environment in Israel* from the Ministry of Environmental Protection, and *Vital Signs* from the World Watch Institute/Heschel Center.

The Ministry of Environmental Protection has published its latest report on the 'State of the Environment in Israel: Data, Indicators and Trends.' The report presents long-term trends in the areas of demography, air quality, energy production and consumption, transportation, climate change, water and wastewater, seas, streams, biodiversity, open spaces, contaminated land, waste, noise, and radiation. Among the major concerns is the conversion of open landscapes into other land uses.

18. Air Pollution. The number of cars on the roads has increased dramatically, from 1 million in 1990 to 3.84 million in 2021.[38] Thus, transportation is the main source of pollution in Israel's largest cities. In addition, there is pollution from the power plants and industry. With most of the population centres being along the coast, urban sprawl causes traffic jams, filling the greater Tel Aviv area with smog and air pollution. It has been government policy, since the 1980s, to encourage the use of private vehicles as the main source of transportation.[39] The percentage of people using public transportation in Israel is low, reaching only 30%.[40] One reason for this is the government's income from taxes on the purchase of new vehicles and from the sale of gasoline. The government receives approximately 10% of its annual tax revenue from vehicle sales, fuel taxes and licensing. Revenue from these taxes (in real terms) increased by more than 50% between 2000 and 2009. In 2009, they accounted for about 3% of GDP and 10% of total tax receipts, among the highest shares in the OECD.[41]

In certain cities like Haifa, pollution from cars adds to that created by industry. Together, these pollutants get captured in the Haifa air due to the effects of its topography – rolling hills that come down almost to the coast. Compounding the problem is an inadequate mass transit system, based mainly on buses rather than railways and subways.

Israel is now converting some of its coal-fired power plants to gas. For example, the Tel Aviv power plant switched from coal to natural gas in 2006. This trend is being augmented due to the discovery of gas fields in the Mediterranean near Israel's coast. The energy sources for electricity production as of 2019 are 63.7% natural gas, 30.3% coal, 1.5% fossil fuels and 4.5% renewable sources.[42] As of 2021, the percentage of renewable energy sources rose to 8.2%.[43]

Electricity consumption rose from 41.4 billion kilowatt-hours in 2001 to 72.8 billion kilowatt-hours in 2020.[44] This equals electricity consumption per capita of 7539.35 kilowatt-hours. The distribution of electricity is divided into public and commercial consumption (33%), residential (30%), industrial (20.5%), East Jerusalem and the Palestinian Authority (7.6%), water pumping (5.8%), and agricultural

38. Central Bureau of Statistics, Press release 111/2022.
39. M. Epstein, *It Pays to Pollute in Israel 1: Air Pollution from Transportation*, in *Vital Signs 2001 – The Environmental Trends Shaping our Future, World Watch Institute* 170 (R. Frumkin & D. Khenin ed. on behalf of the Heschel Center, Kvutzat Eretz V'Teva (Hebrew)).
40. https://www.ynetnews.com/articles/0,7340,L-4267768,00.html (last visited 7 Apr. 2023).
41. OECD Environmental Performance Reviews: Israel 2011 Assessment and Recommendations, p. 2.
42. Central Bureau of Statistics, Energy Balance Sheet 2019.
43. Israel Electricity Authority, Report on the Status of the Electricity Sector for 2021.
44. Knesset Center for Research and Information, *Report on Electricity Sector in Israel*, 14 Feb. 2022.

(3.1%).[45] All five of Israel's major fossil fuel power plants are located along the coast near the major population centres adding further air-polluting emissions. This, together with vehicle pollution, has led to severe violations of air quality standards.

Studies have shown a correlation between air pollution and lung diseases in Israel, especially among school-age children, as well as a suggested connection between air pollution and premature deaths.[46] Every year 2,500 people die from air pollution, half of them from transport-related pollution. According to Israel's Minister for Environmental Protection, 'It's a problem of national proportions – five times greater than the number of car accidents, one hundred times more than terror incidents!'[47] Air pollution levels in Israel are significantly higher than in Western Europe and endangering children's health in most of Israel's cities.[48] The high volume of lung diseases is also related to the high amounts of dust that naturally occurs in Israel, to which cling pollutants emitted by mobile and stationary sources.

There are also special pockets of air pollution. For instance, the above-mentioned report noted that largely due to a large number of industrial plants, children in the Haifa Bay area are exposed to substantially more pollution and suffer significantly higher rates of illness than other Israeli children. In the northern Negev, a cluster of polluting factories was put there essentially to reduce air pollution in the central part of Israel. An incinerator for hazardous waste was constructed that can handle 20,000 tons per year. This is an example of attempts to reduce one type of pollution and create another, a clear example of pollution transfer from solid waste to air pollution.

19. Water Quality. Water quality matches air quality as one of Israel's most pressing environmental problems.[49] Israel's founding fathers recognized the country's scarce and scanty water resources. They decided, therefore, to capture all sources of freshwater, tap the limited groundwater resources and tie in the Kinneret, Israel's only freshwater lake, into one water grid. This engineering approach to Israel's water resources has prevented water shortages, as in Jordan, but it has had deleterious effects on the environment. All the headwaters of natural flowing streams flowing towards the Mediterranean were captured. The streams dried up and turned into carriers of untreated sewage. The Kinneret underwent increased salinity as the level of the lake fell and saltwater springs flowed into the lake. These springs were, therefore, captured and directed around the lake, pouring directly into the lower Jordan and reducing its quality. Groundwater pumping along the coast was not sufficiently controlled, and ocean water began seeping inland.

As the engineering approach determined the use of Israel's water, so did intensive agriculture the fate of Israel's soil, which in turn led to further pollution of its groundwater. The combination of these events has brought Israel's water system to a situation whereby the supply of water in Israel's aquifers has dwindled. As the

---

45. *Ibid.*
46. A.I. Goren & S. Hellmann et al., *Health Survey among Schoolchildren in Tel-Aviv-1991* (Israel: The Institute for Environmental Health, The Ministry of Environmental Protection May 1994) (Hebrew).
47. *Israel Environment Bulletin, Israel Ministry of Environmental Protection,* Vol. 43 (March 2017), p. 3.
48. Seeing the Child, Report by the Coalition for Public Health, 2009.
49. H. Gvirtzman, Water Resources in Israel (Jerusalem: Keter Publishing 2002) (Hebrew).

supply dwindles, the ocean encroaches further into the groundwater, and the quality of the groundwater deteriorates. This is exacerbated by heavy doses of chemicals and fertilizers, as well as untreated sewage and garbage dumps above the ground. During the years 1990–1991, Lake Kinneret could not meet the demand, and the supply of water from its limited resources was stopped to protect the lake from further environmental damage. Beginning in the year 2000, the water crises reached such proportions that the Kinneret reached its lowest point in thousands of years. The government began a mad scramble to build water desalination plants, but the crisis could have been avoided had the government introduced conservation processes, reduced agricultural use of freshwater and introduced desalination earlier, as had been suggested by several scientific reports and numerous government reports, including the Knesset Committee of Inquiry on the Israeli Water Sector (2002) and the National Inquiry Committee on Management of the Water Sector (2010).

It is difficult to even contemplate the effect of the water shortage on the Kinneret, and the Dead Sea as well (*see* paragraph 99 for a full description of the legal situation of the Dead Sea). The Dead Sea, the world's lowest lake, is dropping a metre each year due to a lack of inflow and a high evaporation rate. Besides the shrinking of a unique natural treasure, this rapid drop has resulted in the appearance of sinkholes, damage to the area's ecosystem, washing out of bridges and roads, and economic damage to the area's tourist industry. The government appointed a committee to study the effects of such evaporation and determine future scenarios and options.[50,51] The report was submitted to the government and its methodology provided a basis for additional committees to consider the future of the Dead Sea. it has adopted some recommendations related to the lower portion of the Dead Sea, but no action has been taken to increase the flow of water from the Jordan River.

Israel geared up to meet the challenge of creeping seawater into the aquifer and drying up of its rivers by rapidly building desalination plants along the coast. These plants are now supplying over one-third of the annual water use, and they have changed the way the water system is operated. At one time, the National Grid flowed north to south, but with desalination plants in the south, the water can flow in different directions. Israel now has the capacity to meet all its water needs and is contemplating letting streams flow and letting more water flow from the Kinneret into the Jordan River. A pipeline was completed in 2022 to allow the pumping of desalinated water from the coast to the Kinneret. This will allow better regulation of the level of the Kinneret, and ensure Israel is able to uphold its agreement to supply water to Jordan. This additional source of water also reduces the tension between Israel and the Palestinian Authority, both using the same natural water sources. Once a cause of conflict, Israel can now afford to let the Palestinians draw more groundwater for their use, as Israelis rely more on desalinated seawater.

50. Israel Government Decision No. 2863, 5 Jan. 2003. The authors were members of the Committee. *See also*: E. Raz, The Dead Sea Book (in Hebrew), Israel Nature Reserves Authority, 1993.
51. I. Gavrieli et al., 'The Impact of the Proposed "Peace Conduit" on the Dead Sea: Evaluation of Current Knowledge on Dead Sea-Sea Water Mixing', Geological Survey of Israel, Report GSI/23/2002, Jerusalem 2002.

20. Noise. It is estimated that about 25% of the population in Israel is disturbed by noise nuisances, a higher percentage than any other environmental nuisance.[52] The greatest source of noise pollution comes from vehicles. Israel's largest international airport is located in the centre of the country, surrounded by several communities, all suffering from noise pollution from the take-off and landing of aeroplanes. There are also air force bases situated close to populated areas. Other major sources of noise pollution are air conditioners, construction work and trains.

21. Sea Pollution. Israel is blessed with a 195-kilometre coastline along the Mediterranean Sea, and a small but important coastline at the Gulf of Eilat-Aqaba in the south. As in all marine states, Israel suffers not only from its own pollution but also from pollution engendered by other oceanic riparian countries, both on the Mediterranean and the Red Sea. Pollution in the Gulf of Aqaba-Eilat is mainly due to the major port facilities in Aqaba and Eilat. To this can be added the ever-present pollution of oil from tankers as well as boat traffic in the Mediterranean Sea and the Red Sea. As oil pollution has been reduced due to technology and international agreements, coastal pollution has increased in the Mediterranean.

22. Solid Waste. The amount of solid waste produced increases by 1.8% a year, which almost directly reflects the increase in population. The amount produced today is 5.3 million tons a year, which averages out to 1.7 kilograms per person daily. The composition of Israel's residential solid waste by weight is 30% organic materials and garden waste, 37% paper and carton products, 18% plastic, 2% metal, 1% glass, 3% textile, 2% disposable diapers, 6% building waste and 1% other materials.[53] The amount of building waste is estimated at 6 million tons per year, not including 3 million tons of excess fill, which contains a large percentage of building waste.[54]

From the establishment of the State in 1948 until the 1990s, the treatment of solid waste consisted of discarding and burying. Beginning in the 1990s, a major effort was made to close the hundreds of unsanitary landfills and build new, modern landfill sites.[55] This has not reduced the amount of solid waste, but it has encouraged the proper handling of solid waste with its attendant encouragement of recycling. National Plan No. 16, 1989, established three central refuse sites, sixteen local sites, one temporary site, one emergency site, one site for dangerous substances (at Ramat Hovav in the Negev) and seven waste treatment sites.[56] The last unauthorized site was closed in 2003. The plan met with resistance from the local authorities in the

---

52. I. Fidelman, Everyday Noise Nuisances-Comparative Survey, Knesset Center for Research and Information, November 2008.
53. Ministry of Environmental Protection, Figures for Waste in Israel. https://www.gov.il/en/departments/ministry_of_environmental_protection/govil-landing-page (last visited 7 Apr. 2023).
54. *Ministry of Environmental Protection, Recycling Building Waste in Israel*, December 2011 (Hebrew).
55. Nazareth Court of Appeals, 671/97 '*Kibbutz Merhavia v. State of Israel-Ministry of Environmental Protection*', *Takdin* 97, No. 4, 425.
56. M. Korach *Waste Treatment in Israel*, in *Vital Signs 2001: The Environmental Trends Shaping our Future, World Watch Institute* 178 (R. Frumkin and D. Khenin eds on behalf of the Heschel Center, Kvutzat Eretz V'Teva (Hebrew)).

Negev region, where the major new waste sites were planned. They felt they were paying the price for the 'NIMBY' approach of others.[57] Today, five modern landfills are handling most of the waste. Each of these sites is looking for new ways to treat solid waste instead of landfilling. One is doing RDF (waste to energy), another is composting and a third is doing biogas. All these new methods are encouraged by the Ministry of Environmental Protection. But it became apparent through the years that attempts at composting organic waste were unsuccessful. Without separating waste at its source, the organic matter separated later at waste sites was unusable for agricultural purposes. As a result, the Ministry of Environmental Protection is writing regulations for separating organic waste at its source.

Due to Israel's compact size, there are difficulties finding appropriate landfills for solid waste. Furthermore, with the population concentrated along the coast, there is now a need to haul solid waste inland for disposal by burial in specified landfill sites. In addition, not enough care has been taken in the past to choose solid waste sites that do not have an effect on Israel's groundwater sources.

With the Ministry of Environmental Protection's policy to close unsanitary landfill sites, there has not been a parallel policy to reclaim the land that has been polluted by the 'pirate' sites. These sites, left in their present condition, cause groundwater pollution, and in some cases, air pollution from methane release. According to the Ministry of Environmental Protection, there are some fifty-three sites that require reclamation. But reclamation has been carried out at only ten of them, and those were relatively small sites. The Ministry puts the cost of reclamation at USD 120,000–USD 130,000 per dunam (one-fourth acre). They admit that little will be done until funding is provided while acknowledging that inaction creates a serious safety and environmental time bomb.

Approximately 24% of solid waste is recycled, a very small percentage in comparison to other OECD countries. In 2011, the Knesset passed a law to encourage recycling, putting the responsibility on the local authorities and the producers. To date, the law's aims have not been actively pursued. The Ministry of Environmental Protection set a recycling goal of 50% by the year 2020, a goal that was not met. There is a clear need for the Ministry of Environmental Protection to develop markets for raw materials which comprise much of Israel's solid waste.

The National Planning and Building Board adopted the Waste to Energy policy guidelines that outline an Integrated Waste Management Strategy between materials recycling and energy recovery. The top aim of the 2030 plan includes the reduction of landfilling to a rate of 26%, the promotion of recycling to a rate of 51% and energy recovery to a rate of 23%. The sorting of all municipal waste in materials recovery facilities, the streamlining of the waste market for waste treatment, and developing energy recovery facilities and recycling plants are necessary milestones in this endeavour.[58]

Dangerous Substances. In ranking Israel's environmental problems, dangerous substances rank together with air pollution and water pollution as one of Israel's

57. High Court 453/98 *City of Beersheva et al., v. Government of Israel et al., Piskei Din* (this is the official publication of the judgments of the Supreme Court. The publication is in Hebrew) (P.D.) 52 (2) 13.
58. Ministry of Environmental Protection, *Waste Facts and Figures.*

major problems. Yet, the seriousness of the problem has not been recognized. Israel is suffering from soil pollution from abandoned industrial plants as well as ground pollution from underground storage tanks seeping and leaking chemicals and petroleum products into the groundwater, Israel's main source of drinking water. Unlike air pollution, there is no serious database for monitoring dangerous substances in the water and food supply in Israel. This subject suffers from a lack of coordination among responsible bodies. Yet studies show that Israeli children are widely exposed to organophosphate pesticides; levels of dimethyl metabolites are high compared to other international populations; and fruit consumption is associated with higher urinary DAP levels. Using urinary DAP concentration data, a recent study found that a portion of the children studied may be exposed to OP pesticides at levels above those considered safe.[59]

23. Asbestos waste from Israel's only (now-closed) asbestos cement plant in Nahariya in western Galilee has been found in the area, in adjacent communities and villages, as well as in waste disposal sites around Israel.[60] Before its dangers were explained to the public, the material was used extensively for roofing and other construction uses, pipes, and water tanks. A large amount of asbestos cement products are still in use in army bases due to the large numbers of pre-fabricated and older structures. The main law regarding asbestos is the Law for Prevention of Nuisances from Asbestos and Harmful Dust, published in 2011. Due to massive publicity, enforcement of regulations, and intensive action by the Ministry of Environmental Protection, asbestos pollution has been largely treated.

24. Ecosystem Protection. Israel's geographical limitations and population growth require advanced environmental awareness and planning to protect its open spaces, natural resources and rich biodiversity. Unfortunately, in many cases development and economic considerations are given preference over environmental considerations. For example, although 25% of Israel's land is preserved as nature reserves and national parks, the majority is in the desert regions, with only 3% of the centre and northern areas preserved. Despite Israel's advanced technologies in the fields of water and energy have not translated into joining the world's effort to address climate change. There is evolving long-term ecological and social research (LTSER) steered by the Israel Academy of Sciences. This programme, when expanded, will serve to create a database of information on the health of Israel's ecosystems.

Ecological corridors connect different types of open landscapes, providing conduits for the passage of animals and plants in a fragmented landscape. National Outline Plan 35 for building, development and protection (*see* paragraph 154) emphasizes the principle of contiguous open spaces as well as the protection of areas with high ecological and landscape sensitivity.

---

59. Tamar Berman, Zohar Barnett-Itzhaki and others, Organophosphate Pesticide Exposure in children in Israel: Dietary Associations and Implications for Risk Assessment, Environmental Research, September 2019.
60. Environment in Israel, 2002, Ministry of Environmental Protection, 185.

Recently, several cities in Israel have embarked on initiatives to increase urban biodiversity. Tel Aviv has joined thirty cities worldwide in this effort.

Chapter 2. Basic Principles of Environmental Law

25. Israel has no single environmental law, nor are the environmental laws of Israel grouped under the control of one minister. From 1948, Israel's founding, until 1989, there was also no central environmental ministry. In 1972, the first governmental organization for the protection of the environment was established. Called the Environmental Protection Service (EPS), its main role was to coordinate government activities in the environmental field. It was given no statutory power. Only in 1989 was a Ministry of Environmental Protection established with authority over numerous laws. As a result of this late start, the Ministries of Interior, Agriculture, Transportation and Health as well as the Water and Sewerage Authority have responsibility for more environmental laws than the Ministry of Environmental Protection.[61]

26. During the 1950s, 1960s and 1970s, most laws passed dealt with the environment from two main vantage points:

(1) Abatement of nuisances and protection of public health.
(2) All-encompassing legislation for a particular natural resource, for example, water, nature reserves and forests.

The abatement of nuisances approach expanded the rights of persons injured by an environmental nuisance. Yet the approach did not allow for environmental planning and the prevention of future environmental nuisances. Not until Israel's Planning and Building Law was passed in 1965 was an attempt made at overall planning to protect the natural environment. Yet even this attempt only hinted at the protection of the environment and was never sufficiently used for this purpose until the passing of the Environmental Impact Statement Regulations in 1982.[62]

All-encompassing legislation for the protection of a natural resource can be found in the Water Law of 1959. This is one of the world's earliest pieces of progressive legislation for the protection of a natural resource. The law nationalized all water sources of Israel, broadly defined to include surface water, groundwater, sewage and run-off, and prohibited any form of pollution. Unfortunately, the law was never fully enforced to protect the environment, but it still represents a fine example of early environmental legislation for the protection of a single natural resource. Another example is the Clean Air Act of 2008. It serves as a vehicle for reduction in air pollution by granting the Minister of Environmental Protection power over individual stacks, fuel quality, transportation patterns and a host of other tools.

In time, the increasing number of Non-governmental Organizations (NGOs) has helped bring about an improvement in environmental quality in Israel. Part of this increased activity is due to the legislation entitled the 'Law for the Abatement of

61. E. Choshen & R. Laster, Environment, Administration, and Law in Israel: Government Ministries (in Hebrew), 41 (Jerusalem: The Jerusalem Institute for Israel Studies 2005), p. 41.
62. *Kovetz Hatakanot* (this is the Hebrew version of the regulations. There is no official translation of Israeli regulations in English) (K.T.) 4307, 502.

Nuisances (Citizen Suits 1992)'.[63] This law is modelled on the American legislation enabling citizen suits, which appears in individual pieces of legislation in the United States such as the Clean Air Act and the Clean Water Act. These acts enable individual citizens who have been injured, or citizen-based NGOs, to bring an injunction against a polluting entity. Israeli law first requires the NGO to petition the Minister of the Environment to abate the nuisance, or the ongoing pollution. The Minister has sixty days to act. If he/she fails to do so, the NGO may then apply to the court in the Minister's stead and ask for an injunction against the polluting entity. The use of this strategy has been expanded and, as will be seen in individual chapters on air and water pollution, the NGOs have acted so in numerous instances when a Minister has failed to use his/her powers.

63. S.H. 1394, 184.

Chapter 3. Historical Background

27. Israel was a British protectorate from World War I until 1948. During that time, the British Mandate instituted laws and institutions to abate nuisances and protect public health. Mandate-period regulations were based on the British approach to environmental protection, extant at that time: a general planning law,[64] prevention of nuisances which could cause spread of disease,[65] collection and discharge of sewage outside municipal limits,[66] control of the supply of drinking water at a defined quality[67] and preventing the creation of foul odours.[68]
There was also an early attempt to nationalize Israel's water sources because of the very real threat of water scarcity,[69] but this administrative attempt[70] never was successful.

28. The British system of law is mainly framework legislation, to be filled in by ministerial regulations and interpreted by the courts. This was the system adopted in Israel after the Mandate, with some modifications. A real change from the common law approach was in the Mandate authority's adoption of tort law.[71] This law expanded certain common law rights but limited others. Like all tort legislation, it had a significant impact on the growth of environmental law in Israel.

29. The British Mandate left Israel with a strong judicial system, a budding administrative system and a desire for a parliamentary system of government. When Israel achieved its independence from the British Mandate, the provisional government preserved major pieces of British Ordinances. This included several pieces of early environmental legislation, the Tort Ordinances mentioned above; the Public Health Ordinance,[72] the Forests Ordinance,[73] the Soil Conservation Ordinance,[74] and the Pharmacy's Ordinance.[75] All of these ordinances remain in effect today.

---

64. Town Planning Ordinance of 1921, *Palestine Gazette*, No. 36, 1; Town Planning Ordinance of 1936, *Palestine Gazette* Suppl. I, No. 589, 153.
65. Public Health Ordinance, 1940, Palestine Ordinance (these are laws passed by the Mandate government before the formation of the State of Israel) (P.O.) 1065, Suppl. I, 239.
66. Municipal Corporations (Sewerage, Drainage and Water) Ordinance, 1936, P.O. 560, Suppl. I, 1.
67. Public Health Ordinance, 1940, P.O. 1065, Suppl. I, 239.
68. Public Health Ordinance, P.O. 1065, Suppl. I, 239. *See also* Safeguarding of Public Water Supplies Ordinance, P.O. 711, Suppl. I, 185.
69. Palestine (Amendment) Order in Council, P.O. Suppl. I-I, 66. *See* Draft Ordinance to Provide for the Control of the Drainage of Surface Water in Palestine and Matters Connected Therewith, 1941, P.O. 1146, Suppl. I, 1189.
70. *See* R. Laster, *The Legal Framework for the Prevention and Control of Water Pollution in Israel*, Ministry of Interior, Environmental Protection Service, 6 (1976).
71. Civil Wrongs Ordinance (New Version), 2 L.S.I. (NV) 5.
72. Public Health Ordinance, 1940, P.O. 1065, Suppl. I, 239.
73. Forest Ordinance, P.O. Suppl. I, 1.
74. Soil Erosion (Prevention) Ordinance 1941, P.O. 1944 Suppl. I, 37.
75. Pharmacist's Ordinance 1921.

Chapter 4. Role of Governmental Institutions in the Shaping and Administration of Environmental Law and Policy

Role of Government Institutions-Introduction

30. At the creation of the State, there were no governmental institutions established for the protection of the environment. There were, however, governmental ministries and institutions with environmental roles. Even today, after the establishment of the Ministry of Environment (now called the Ministry of Environmental Protection) in 1989, there remain numerous governmental institutions at the national, district and local levels responsible for the protection of the environment.[76]

The following is an explanation of government departments to be found under the different ministries' responsibilities. One caveat to the reader is that due to Israel's changing political scene, government institutions are often switched from ministry to ministry, especially following an election. Therefore, the institution mentioned, which is under the responsibility of a certain ministry, may change following the next elections.

§1. Ministry of National Infrastructures, Energy and Water Resources

I. Water Authority

31. Until the creation of the Ministry of Environment, the single most powerful environmental department in Israel was the Water Commission. The Commission was established within the Ministry of Agriculture with the passage of the Water Law in 1959.[77] The Water Law nationalized the water resources of Israel, held in trust by the State for the benefit of the public. At the same time, the Water Law created the position of Water Commissioner to 'manage the water sources of Israel'. The Water Commissioner, now known as the Director of the Water & Sewerage Authority, has almost unlimited authority to prevent pollution and control the supply of water. Parallel to these provisions, the Minister of Agriculture was authorized under the original Water Law to determine water quality for all sources; that is, drinking, sewage, surface and groundwater. Since the passage of the Water Law in 1959, this approach of one minister being responsible for all aspects of water use and misuse has changed dramatically, as will be explained in Chapter 3 – Water Pollution.

76. R. Laster & E. Choshen, *The Roots of Environmental Administration in Israel* (Jerusalem: The Jerusalem Institute for Israel Studies 2003); R. Laster & E. Choshen, *Environment, Administration, and Law in Israel: The Central Administration* (Jerusalem: The Jerusalem Institute for Israel Studies 2004).

77. 13 L.S.I. 173.

With the creation of the Ministry of Infrastructure in 1998 (now known as the Ministry of National Infrastructures, Energy & Water Resources), the employees of the Water Authority were placed under the aegis of the Ministry of National Infrastructures. It must be noted, however, that while the Minister of National Infrastructures has the overall authority for the Water Law, the Director of the Water Authority has independent legal powers granted specifically by law. In addition, the Director is appointed by the government, not by the Minister. The concept behind the Water Law is that the Water Authority sets water policy, distribution, use and reuse, whereas the Director of the Authority executes that policy. The Director has used his/her role chiefly to regulate the water supply and has done little to protect water sources or assure nature's needs for water. In an attempt to change this, a 2004 amendment to the Water Law requires the Director to take into account nature's water needs and to produce an annual report stating the amount of water supplied to nature.[78]

32. National Authority for Water and Sewerage. A 2006 Amendment to the Water Law created a National Authority for Water and Sewerage.[79] The duties of the 'revamped' Water Authority include regulation and development of the water sector, executing water policy and promulgating rules and regulations concerning water production, supply, quality, prices, usage and incidents harmful to drinking water. The law is an attempt to remedy fragmentation in the water sector but leaves power over drinking water quality in the hands of the Minister of Health, power over pollution control with the Minister of Environmental Protection and power over drainage and flood control with the Minister of Agriculture and the Drainage Authorities. The Authority's board is composed of a government-appointed Director, the Director Generals of four ministries (Agriculture, Environment, Interior and Natural Infrastructure, and Energy & Water), the budget director of the Finance Ministry and two representatives of the general public.

The amendment also creates extraction fees, paid according to the amount of water extracted. The fees are not uniform, but rather reflect the deficit of the region and nation, and can differ according to location and sector. The fees are updated annually by the Director of the Water Authority.

33. In 2010, the government passed a decision authorizing legislation for the creation of a government authority for drainage and soil conservation in the Ministry of Agriculture. This decision, coming only four years after the reorganization of the Water Commission, highlights the government's flip-flop attitude on administrative policy. The Water Authority created in 2006 was designed to reduce fragmentation in the water sector. The new drainage authority aims to reduce the Water Authority's presence in the management of surface water and will reduce coordination of the water sector. It should also be noted that the Ministry of Interior,

78. Water Law (Amendment No. 19) (allocation of water to natural resources and landscapes), 2004 S.H. 1948, 436.
79. Water Law (Amendment No. 22), 2006 Arts 124(k)–124(w), S.H. 2057, 331.

responsible for the Planning and Building Law, has increased planning responsibility within the planning authorities, thereby reducing the power of the Water Authority.

§2. Ministry of Agriculture and Rural Development

I. Department for Soil Conservation and Drainage

34. The Soil Erosion (Prevention) Ordinance,[80] first promulgated by the British Mandate Government, remained in force after the creation of the State of Israel and enabled the Minister of Agriculture to protect the land from soil erosion. This was a very serious problem in the early history of Israel.[81] The law established the Department of Soil Conservation in the Ministry of Agriculture. Since its establishment, the Department has done an admirable job in the area of soil erosion, but it has not utilized its powers to deal with the more difficult problems of groundwater pollution or pollution from run-off.

Recognizing the vacuum due to the government's failure to protect the land from soil erosion, the Shikma Besor Drainage Authority requested the permission of the Minister of Agriculture to be granted the powers of a soil conservation authority. The Minister acquiesced to this request and the power was granted in 2004.[82] Since then, all of the eleven drainage authorities have become soil conservation authorities as well.

A major shift in the power structure occurred in 2022 with the Ministry of Agriculture muscling in on the Drainage Authorities. The Ministry pushed through a major change in the Drainage Law (amendment number 7) to give the head of the Department of Soil Conservation, Drainage and Environment, the power to remove the director general of a particular Drainage Authority if that person fails to meet the Department head's expectations.

II. Plant Protection

35. In recognition of Israel's heavy reliance on 'progressive' methods of agriculture, the government passed a Plant Protection Law in 1956.[83] This law created the Department of Plant Protection and Inspection Services in the Ministry of Agriculture.[84] The Department's early function was to ensure that the agricultural sector received an abundance of plant protection devices, including pesticides, herbicides

80. Soil Erosion (Prevention) Ordinance 1941, P.O. 1944 Suppl. I, 37.
81. *See* H. Kendal, *Village Development in Palestine During the British Mandate* (1949).
82. Decision No. 29/04 of Shikma Besor Drainage Authority, 22 Nov. 2004. The decision was given the approval of the Minister of Agriculture in December, 2004.
83. 10 L.S.I. 75.
84. 13 L.S.I. 173.

and fungicides. Over time, the emphasis of the law changed to include environmental factors and problems of toxicity. Today the Department of Plant Protection has the power not to approve any chemical which may harm the agricultural environment.

The Department is also responsible for monitoring and preventing plant diseases as well as for the import and export of agricultural produce. The Department, however, is seriously limited in manpower and budget. It has little capability to enforce its own legislation due to this handicap. The Department is also caught in a dilemma. On the one hand, it must promote the agricultural sector, sometimes at the expense of the environment. Yet, it is also mandated to protect the environment to the detriment of agricultural 'progress'. This balancing act does not bode well for the environment, because the agricultural sector is far more vocal and its problems far more immediate.

III. Drainage Authorities

36. In 1957, the Knesset passed the Drainage and Flood Control Law.[85] This law created a National Drainage Board and Regional Drainage Authorities. The Drainage Authorities are composed of representatives of local authorities in a watershed, as determined by the Minister of Agriculture. The watersheds were purposefully gerrymandered in favour of the agricultural sector. The result was that from 1957 to 1997, twenty-six drainage authorities were created for the small State of Israel. In 1996, the process of reorganization began along basin lines, and the number of drainage authorities was reduced from twenty-six to eleven. The restructuring was a tremendous success – the drainage authorities were energized as they became basin authorities. The eleven drainage authorities have now reduced Israel's serious flooding problems, and have begun investing time and effort in the reclamation of rivers and streams. This effort has been conducted jointly with the Ministry of Environmental Protection, which found the Drainage Authorities to be a reliable platform for stream reclamation.

The Ministry of Environmental Protection approached the Drainage Authorities and requested their willingness to serve as protectors of the environmental aspects of drainage and streams, in addition to their powers as Drainage Authorities. The Drainage Authorities acknowledged their willingness, and all eleven were granted environmental protection powers over streams and rivers.[86] The Drainage Authorities see their future role in environmental protection and not just the prevention of erosion and flood control. This new challenge puts the Drainage Authorities at the forefront of environmental protection and may lead to a true reformation of Israel's water programme by creating River Basin or Basin Authorities instead of Drainage Authorities.[87]

85. 12 L.S.I. 5.
86. Streams and Springs Authorities Order (Granting the Powers of River Authorities to Drainage Authorities), 2003 (Amendment from 1 Jul. 2010 K.T. 6904).
87. *See* Chapter on Water Pollution.

§3. Ministry of the Treasury

37. In 2015, control over Planning and Building was transferred from the Ministry of Interior to the Ministry of the Treasury. The Planning and Building Law was based in part on the British Town Planning Ordinance of 1936. The 1965 Law created three tiers of planning commissions: national, regional and local. These commissions are to engage in positive planning of their sector of control as well as prevent violations of planning decisions. The Local Planning and Building Commission is comparable to the City Council. The Regional Planning and Building Commission is composed of representatives of the national government and local authorities in the region, with a majority of its members being representatives of ministries. The National Planning Council is a multifaceted body made up of over thirty members. It is composed of representatives of governmental ministries, local authorities, environmental and professional groups such as the Society for the Protection of Nature, architects' associations, and others.

38. Although the planning commissions are autonomous bodies, the Minister of the Treasury exercises power over their decisions. First, the Minister appoints the chairman of the Regional and National Planning Boards. Second, the Planning Boards at the regional and national levels often act on the advice of their professional staff, who are employees of the Ministry of the Treasury. Finally, the Minister receives most major plans for approval.

39. The National Planning and Building Council has the authority to approve district outline plans and makes recommendations to the government regarding national outline plans and other issues of national importance concerning building and planning. Since the Environmental Revolution of the 1970s and increasing environmental awareness, the National Planning Council has slowly changed into a body which encourages environmental protection in Israel. During the 1990s, the National Planning Council appointed several professional staffers to develop national plans for Israel's future. One of the master plans was a vision for the year 2020. That plan encourages development within existing cities while maintaining development-free open spaces between them. In addition, the National Planning Council began the process of reviewing Israel's water sources and ordered two professional committees to develop plans for the protection of Israel's water resources. The committees produced a National Outline Plan for Rivers and Drainage (National Outline Plan 34B-3), a major effort to protect stream contours and better plan for surface water management. In addition, the National Outline Plan 34B-4 provides a planning framework for collecting surface water and infiltration and protection of groundwater.

Unfortunately, the government of Israel has tried to emasculate some of the ideas of the National Planning Council, and the *yin and yang* of government policy and planning have not encouraged long-range environmental planning. The most recent effort is the legislation to revamp the entire planning law to reduce public involvement in the planning process.

In fact, the government has, in some cases, taken power away from the national and district planning councils by creating special planning boards for special interest groups. In the year 2002, the government decided that schemes of national infrastructure, normally debated under the auspices of the National Planning Council, would be removed from their authority in order to operate more efficiently.[88] This law created a new National Infrastructure Board to determine, with little time allotted for debate, the construction of railroads, highways, power plants and other large projects with a severe environmental impact, without requiring any serious environmental inspection. The law requires that a plan, which is submitted to the National Planning Board, be reviewed within a period of seven days, thereby giving lip service to the concept of environmental assessment, with no concern for the real environmental impact of the project. On the other hand, legislation promoted by the Society for the Protection of Nature in Israel successfully lobbied for a change in the Planning & Building Law to create a Coastal Planning Committee to review all coastal building plans (*see* paragraph 98).

An additional special planning board was created in 2011 through the Law for the Planning and Building Process to Increase Residential Building (Temporary Order). The purpose of the law is to bring down the high price of apartments of different sizes and types by increasing the supply. The law establishes six regional planning boards with the powers to approve residential building plans through a speeded-up process, including zoning changes. The Minister of Environmental Protection complained that the fast-track process does not provide adequate attention to environmental considerations. The law had an original life of two years and was extended in 2013 for an additional twenty-two months. In 2014, the Knesset created a new planning board to speed up the planning and building of homes for young couples. The new law, titled the Law for Building in Designated Areas, enables the new planning board to speed up the building of large complexes with 30% of the homes designated for long-term rentals.

The National Planning Council has developed a new National Plan, called National Outline Plan No. 1, for the entire country. The idea behind this plan is to streamline and simplify the planning process by combining the approximately fifty different national plans and the hundreds of partial plans, each concerned with a different topic, into one plan. The plan gives more power to the planning authorities, reduces public involvement and, by definition, reduces environmental protection. As can be seen from the above, over the last ten years, the Government has tried to reduce the public's involvement in planning, with a view that the public only slows down the planning process.

§4. Ministry of Interior

I. Introduction

40. The Ministry oversees the licensing of businesses and is the 'parent' of all local authorities. Local authorities in Israel include municipalities (normally towns

88. Planning and Building Law, 1965, ss 6A–6F, National Council for the Planning of National Infrastructure, Amendment No. 60, 2002.

of over 20,000 people), local councils and regional councils. The laws for the creation of municipalities, and local and regional councils give the Minister of Interior broad power to decide which village or combination of villages will be a municipality, local council or regional council.

The Ministry's control over the purses of the local authorities gives it power over the local authority's policy and implementation. It is well known that local authorities remain the key players in any environmental protection programme and the Ministry of Interior, through its power of the purse, can dictate government policy to local authorities once that policy has been set. The Ministry uses its power quite often in areas of solid and liquid waste, transportation and land use.

II. Local Authorities

41. The 255 local authorities in Israel are empowered to act as the first line of defence against environmental degradation. They are responsible for protecting the public from nuisances, preventing health hazards, controlling planning and building at the local level, building and maintaining sewerage works, water supply and treatment systems, and collecting and disposing of solid waste.[89] Local authorities are closely supervised by the Minister of Interior, who budgets their operations, approves their bylaws and supervises their hiring policies.

For the most part, the local authorities are responsive to the needs of environmental protection. There are fifty local authorities with environmental units or departments in operation, staffed by experts in the fields of noise and air pollution, solid waste and environmental education. These local units work closely with the Ministry of Environment.

However, most local authority environmental units are ill-equipped to handle complicated environmental problems or problems that extend beyond municipal boundaries. In addition, they work at the grace of the mayor, and if s/he has an interest in a project detrimental to the environment, they will hardly intervene. This has led to the establishment of Associations of Towns for Environmental Protection (*see* paragraph 42 below). The Associations, although composed of local authorities, are less politicized than the local authority environmental units, since they have independent sources of income.

In 2005, the Knesset passed an amendment to the Cities Ordinance[90] requiring every local authority to create a committee for the environment. In 2010, the Knesset passed a law to encourage local authorities to enforce national environmental legislation. One of the methods chosen to encourage local enforcement of environmental laws is by enabling the local authorities and the Associations of Towns to receive the funds collected from fines for an environmental violation. The idea was to have a monetary incentive for environmental protection; to date, however, the reception to the law has been lukewarm.

---

89. *See*, e.g., Municipalities Ordinance (NV), 1964, 1 L.S.I. (NV) 247; Local Councils Ordinance (NV), 1965, 1 L.S.I. (NV) 315.

90. Cities Ordinance (Amendment No. 97) (Committee for the environment) S.H. 1984, 216.

III. Associations of Towns

42. Since the 1980s, regional authorities responsible for environmental protection have developed in Israel. There are presently ten such Associations of Towns throughout the country. An Association of Towns for Environmental Protection is composed of representatives of local authorities in its region.[91] Local authorities, as previously defined, include municipalities, local councils and regional councils. Normally, the governing body of the Association of Towns is composed of one representative of each local authority member of the Association.

Associations of Towns for Environmental Protection maintain a professional staff of employees trained in environmental protection; for example, air pollution, water pollution, noise control, agricultural waste, planning and environmental education. The Associations operate Israel's network of air quality monitoring stations, which is connected to the central monitoring network operated by the Ministry of Environment.

Like local authorities, Associations of Towns are created by the Minister of the Interior, who supervises their bylaws and personnel. Unlike local authorities, the Associations are regional in nature and less affected by local politics and political patronage. This gives them an impetus to work exclusively for the benefit of the environment.

In 2008, the Associations of Towns Law was amended to require environmental associations to enforce environmental laws in their jurisdiction. Before that amendment, the Associations worked through their members, that is, the local authorities. After the amendment, the Association supersedes the local authority for the enforcement of environmental legislation. The Associations operate a major portion of the national grid for the monitoring of air pollution.

In recent years, a new type of Association of Towns has been created by the Ministry of the Interior called '*Eshkolot*' (in English 'Clusters'). *Eshkolot* serve the purpose of economic streamlining and increased economic development, by bringing together several municipalities within a region for certain sectors. *Eshkolot* projects include joint tenders for waste collection, veterinary services, alternative energy, information services, tourism and more.

§5. Ministry of Health

43. The Ministry of Health operates to protect the environment primarily through the Public Health Ordinance.[92] Under the Ordinance, the Ministry established regulations for the quality of both drinking water and treated sewage water used in agriculture. Through its power under the Drug Ordinance,[93] the Ministry has promulgated regulations controlling the use of dangerous substances.

91. The Associations are located in the following regions (from North to South): Northern Galilee, Haifa, Hadera, Tel Aviv, Southern Judah, Ashdod-Havel Yavneh and Ashkelon. They operate under the Association of Towns Law, 1955, 9 L.S.I. 4.
92. Public Health Ordinance, 1940, P.O. 1065, Suppl. I.
93. 3 L.S.I. (NV) 5 (1975).

The Ministry also gained control over the protection of the environment through the business licensing process,[94] which normally requires the Minister's approval of business operations.

The Ministry of Health, however, historically viewed its role through the eyes of the medical doctor or the sanitation engineer, its two key regional operatives. This prevented the Ministry from taking an active environmental role during the 1970s and 1980s because when an environmental problem approaches proportions where there are health effects, correcting the problem requires tools outside the Minister's powers. With the establishment of the Ministry of Environmental Protection, large sections of authority, once granted to the Ministry of Health, were transferred to them.

§6. Ministry of Environmental Protection

44. Before 1973, the responsibility for the environment was divided among several ministries. In 1973, the EPS was created, functioning first as a branch of the Prime Minister's office, and later as part of the Ministry of the Interior. A separate Ministry of Environmental Protection was created in December 1988. In general, the Ministry of Environmental Protection sets the government's environmental agenda. The Ministry has been granted responsibility in the following areas: air and noise pollution, sea pollution, solid waste, hazardous substances, environmental planning, blight and litter. In addition to these general areas, the Ministry is responsible for determining the quality of natural water sources. The Minister of Environmental Protection also has ministerial responsibility for the Yarqon, Kishon and Beer Sheva River Authorities, the Nature Reserves and National Parks Authority, the Ariel Sharon (Ayalon) Park, the Environmental Services Company, and the Government Corporation for Mediterranean Coastal Cliffs Preservation.

The administrative structure of the ministry is divided into seven main divisions: Natural Resources; Local Authorities, Education & Community; Industry & Licensing; Enforcement; Planning & Policy; Administration & Human Resources; and Overseeing Regional Offices. The Ministry operates through a central office in Jerusalem, six regional offices and sixty-two local units throughout the country; although these local units are staffed by employees of the local municipality and have divided loyalties (*see* paragraph 41 – Local Authorities). In the Ministry's office sits an environmental scientist who also directs research projects which the Ministry feels are important for the future of the environment in Israel.

The Ministry has joint authority with other ministries in a number of other areas. It has representatives on the district and national planning commissions, on the inter-ministerial pesticide labelling committee and on the Water Authority. The Ministry has also been granted the power to stipulate environmental conditions in the process of licensing new or existing businesses. This power is practically unlimited in scope, limited by common sense and the fear of the Supreme Court, sitting as a

94. Licensing of Businesses Law, 1968, 22 L.S.I. 232.

High Court of Justice (discussed later). There is also no requirement that the conditions for environmental protection incorporated in a business license be parallel to the existing regulations.

§7. Ministry of Housing and Construction

I. Israel Land Authority

45. Ninety-three per cent of the land in Israel is in the public domain; that is, either the property of the State, the Jewish National Fund (JNF) or the Development Authority. The Israel Land Authority (ILA)[95] is the government *agency* responsible for managing this land, which comprises 4,820,500 acres. 'Ownership' of real estate in Israel usually means leasing rights from the ILA for forty-nine or ninety-eight years.

As landowner, the ILA could require those occupying the land, its 'tenants', to manage the land in such a fashion as to protect the environment. Since each tenant must contract with the ILA, a clause for the protection of the environment could be included in such a contract. To date, however, the government has not made use of this mechanism. In 2009, the Knesset passed an amendment to the ILA Law of 1960. The amendment restructures the ILA and allows people to own their property outright, rather than lease it from the ILA, and makes the organization subordinate to the Construction and Housing Ministry. Its purpose is to change the ILA from a landowner to a land regulator. Although the ILA has not used its inherent powers to protect the natural environment as a landowner, as a regulator, there will probably be less incentive.

95. Israel Lands Administration Law, 1960, 14 L.S.I. 50. Israel Lands Authority: http://land.gov.il/en/Pages/AboutUs.aspx (last visited 9 Apr. 2023).

Part I. Pollution Control

Chapter 1. General Law

46. Israel has little general environmental legislation. There are three interrelated laws that have formed the axis for pollution control since the 1960s: the Planning and Building Law, 1965; the Licensing of Businesses Law, 1968; and the Abatement of Nuisances Law, 1961.

§1. The Planning and Building Law

47. As mentioned previously, the Planning and Building Law is based on British Mandate legislation from 1936.[96] The law gives extraordinarily broad powers to planning authorities to protect the environment. For those unfamiliar with the law, the following statement can serve as a general axiom: no one, not even the government, can move a grain of dirt in Israel without planning approval. Planning approval can be a tortuous process. For new projects, it involves proper planning, publication, citizen's involvement, an open hearing for objections and an environmental impact statement process for significant projects.

The Planning Commissions are practically unlimited in their power to require background information on the natural environment to be changed by a proposed plan. They also have broad leeway in rejecting, accepting or amending proposed plans in the interest of protecting the environment and public health. The Planning Commissions are also empowered to make positive plans; that is, to plan certain areas for amenities, public open spaces, industrial parks, etc. The National Planning Board may even determine population dispersal requirements, new towns, the creation of ports, highways and airports, flight patterns, etc.

The Commissions may also determine that no industry will be built in an area unless it prevents additional pollution. Since planning approval includes not only new enterprises but changes to existing ones, a Planning Commission can require an existing industry to update its equipment to prevent pollution when that industry requests planning permission to expand its enterprise. In essence, the Planning Commissions have the power to prevent environmental degradation in the macro by proper national, district and local outline plans, and in the micro by planning approval of industrial, residential and transportation networks.

---

96. *See* M.D. Gouldman, *Legal Aspects of Town Planning in Israel* (Jerusalem: Institute for Legislative Research and Comparative Law 1966).

With the proper exercise of their powers, the Planning Commissions could have made Israel an environmentalist's dream. Since Israel is far removed from such a dream, the question arises as to the effectiveness of the Planning Commissions. They have only been sporadically effective. Regarding very large industrial projects, care has been taken during the past twenty years to require an environmental impact assessment (EIA) followed by strict pollution control, modern technology and supervision. For medium and small industrial enterprises, the Planning Commissions have been less effective in the protection of water sources, proper road planning and the protection of parks and streams.

Here, ideology clashes in an atmosphere reminiscent of the Coliseum. It is a credit to the country that the lions do not always win. Since the Planning Commission is a microcosm of the country, pressure for development clashes with sustainability. There are also clear periods of high and low tides, normally following a large influx of immigrants. The Knesset also 'confuses' the system by its constant meddling, enacting shortcuts to speed up the process when the vital essence of long-range planning is deliberation and debate. One example is the government's decision to build several 'temporary' villages for the resettlement of some of the former Israeli residents of the Gaza Strip in the summer of 2005. The largest of these villages, comprising 350 homes, was built on the last remaining open sand dune area on the southern coastal plain of Israel. The final 'blow' to environmental protection using the Planning and Building Law is the legislation proposed by the Prime Minister's Office in 2010. This legislation removes some of the decision-making powers of the District Planning Commissions by giving some control of local planning to the local authorities. Unfortunately, local authorities have fallen prey to developers and if this trend continues, Israel's environmental amenities will be heavily reduced. In addition, as stated in an earlier section, two planning committees have been created since 2010 to speed up the planning process and reduce the value and impact of the environmental analysis of each project. Finally, a new plan to speed up the renovation, destruction and rebuilding of individual buildings is rendering havoc in the planning process. Hundreds of houses are adding floors in a sped-up process, without the requisite infrastructure being put in place. This means that more and more homes will be built in the inner city, without the requisite parks, schools, parking lots and proper entry and exit to the area.

§2. The Licensing of Businesses Law

48. All is not over, however, with the planning approval. Actually, where businesses are concerned, planning approval is only the beginning. Once an enterprise has been built, it must obtain a licence to operate, granted by the local authority. The lists of businesses requiring licences are found in regulations promulgated by the Minister of the Interior. Depending on the purpose of the regulations, they are subject to additional approval by the Ministries of Health, Environment, Labour, Agriculture and Public Security. These categories include business licences meant to ensure proper environmental conditions and prevent harm and nuisances (Ministry of Environmental Protection), prevention of danger to the public (Ministry of

Public Security), the safety of those on or near the premises of the business (Economics Ministry), providing for the public health including reasonable sanitary conditions (Ministry of Health) and the prevention of animal diseases and pollution of water resources by pesticides, fertilizers or medicines (Ministry of Agriculture).[97] The Minister of the Interior alone may list types of businesses requiring licences in order to ensure compliance with the laws concerning planning and building, and fire prevention.

One permitted criterion for granting a new licence is that the industry meets environmental criteria as determined by the local authority, with the approval of the departments of Health and Environment. These special criteria are included in the licence and may be updated from time to time, presently every six months. In practice, however, the special criteria are not updated every six months, but at intervals dictated by changing processes, technology, or dictates from the Ministry of Environmental Protection.

The licensing process is a further check on new enterprises with planning approval as well as on established enterprises. By enabling a local authority to change the special conditions in a licence every six months, if needed to protect the environment, the business licence is a powerful weapon in the hands of local authorities. It enables them to demand improvements in equipment and processes to prevent environmental degradation.

The Licensing of Businesses Law has effectively prevented total disregard of environmental amenities. But its effectiveness depends on the local authority's determination to demand special conditions in the licensing process. As local authorities vary, as the quality of their staff and inspections vary, and as the strengths of political heads of local authorities vary, so too varies the enforcement of this law and its clause protecting the environment.

In order to reduce local political influence, the Minister of Environmental Protection reviews the process and has also pressed the Ministry of the Interior, responsible for the law, to pass regulations. Several regulations have been passed pursuant to the law, including regulations on the disposal of hazardous waste, hazardous industrial plants, transfer stations for waste, pest control, industrial effluent treatment, and sanitary conditions in gas stations. These regulations will be described in the following chapters. Several regulations have been passed describing the different types of businesses which require licences.[98]

Regulations passed in 2000 by the Minister of the Interior require businesses to provide plans of the surrounding area in which they are located and of the business itself, including water and sewerage lines, refuse removal, smokestacks, fire prevention equipment, placement of gas and fuel supply, and other dangerous substances.[99]

---

97. Licensing of Businesses Law, 1968, para. 1.
98. Regulations for the Licensing of Businesses (Businesses Requiring Licenses) 1973; Regulations for the Licensing of Businesses (Businesses Requiring Licenses) 1995; Order for the Licensing of Businesses (Businesses Requiring Licenses According to Other Laws) 1974; Order for the Licensing of Businesses (Businesses Requiring Licenses) 1995.
99. Regulations for the Licensing of Businesses (General Orders) 2000.

§3. The Abatement of Nuisances Law

49. If the planning process fails and the Licensing of Businesses Law does not remedy the failure, there is still an additional line of protection: the Abatement of Nuisances Law, 1961,[100] or as it is more popularly called the 'Kanowitz Law'.[101] As its name implies, the Abatement of Nuisances Law aims to reduce an already existing nuisance, one that somehow slipped through the planning and licensing process.[102] In reality, there are too many of these slip-ups, and the Kanowitz Law is ill-equipped to handle all of them.

Since the Abatement of Nuisances Law is Israel's oldest, most popular and most maligned piece of environmental legislation,[103] it will be discussed here and again in the chapters concerning air and noise pollution, although its importance has been curtailed with the passage of the Clean Air Law. Until the passage of the Clean Air Law, it was Israel's defence mechanism against air, olfactory and noise pollution.

The Kanowitz Law forbids anyone to cause unreasonable air, olfactory or noise pollution. The law does not define, however, air, olfactory and noise pollution. It places this responsibility with the two ministers originally appointed to administer the law: Health and Interior. In 1985, administration was transferred solely to the Ministry of the Interior, and in 1989 to the Ministry of Environmental Protection.

The law got off to a very inauspicious beginning. Soon after the law was passed, some members of the public appealed to the High Court of Justice to require the Ministers of Health and the Interior to define air, olfactory and noise pollution.[104] The Court granted the appellant's request and required the ministers to publish regulations that would give meaning to the law. Regulations were passed. But not long after, another appeal was made to the Supreme Court demanding the need for further regulations.[105] Again the Supreme Court granted the appellant's request, and again, further regulations were promulgated.

The above illustrates the Ministers of Health and the Interior's lack of enthusiasm in administrating the law. In fact, the number of criminal suits against violators of the law during its administration by the Ministers of Health and Interior can be counted on one hand. But other provisions of the law have been exploited. First of all, the law allows private citizens to sue those violating its terms. It even broadens the scope of torts legislation to encourage such suits. Many such suits have been filed asking for remedies, varying from injunctive relief to damages.[106]

Second, the law allows private citizens to bring criminal suits in those cases where the government fails to do so. Not only does the law encourage suits brought

---

100. 15 L.S.I. 52; *see also* 1 Is. L. Rev. 462 (1966).
101. Named after the member of Knesset who proposed the bill.
102. According to para. 9 of the Abatement of Nuisances Law, every license required by law for running a business is conditional on the upholding of the Abatement of Nuisances Law.
103. *See* Gerald M. Adler, *'Legal Supervision Control of Industrial Air Pollution in Israel'*, Conference on Law & the Environment, Technion Institute of Israel, at 11, (1972) (Hebrew); but *see* Kretzmer, '*Judicial Conservatism v. Economic Liberalism: Anatomy of a Nuisance Case*', 13 Is. L. Rev. 13 298 (1978): 298.
104. *Hillel Oppenheimer v. Ministers of Health and Interior*, P.O. 21 (1) 309.
105. *Peranio v. Ministers of Health and Interior*, P.D. 26 (1) 809.
106. Examples include a claim for damages and injunctive relief due to noise and odours from a supermarket loading area (Case No. 002289/01-Tel Aviv District Court); injunctive relief for noise from

by private citizens, but it also allows the ministry administering the law's terms to issue enforcement orders against an individual polluting factory. These orders can require the factory to employ certain devices or refrain from certain practices to prevent pollution of the environment. Failure by the factory to abide by these orders exposes it and its personnel to criminal sanctions.

The law was given new life when the Ministry of Environmental Protection took over its administration. One of its first acts was to amend the law's provisions by increasing enforcement powers. Another was to promulgate new regulations or update old ones. Unfortunately, however, the Minister of Environmental Protection has failed to continue the legislative process and prefers working through another section of the law which allows individual treatment for the industry. The section enables the Ministry of Environmental Protection to require polluters to meet individually designed standards. The procedure was meant for exceptional cases but is implemented in place of standardized environmental controls.

There have been various regulations promulgated since the law's inception. These regulations include ambient permissible levels for noise and air pollution,[107] as well as car emission standards.[108] There are as yet no regulations for permitted noise levels from vehicles and trucks.

The Kanowitz Law supplies legislative support for command and control regulation. The law enables the Minister of Environmental Protection to promulgate ambient standards for olfactory, noise and air pollution, and follow this regulation with emission standards. Only in noise control, however, is there a panoply of regulations. This law was modified with the passing of the Clean Air Law, which is discussed below.

Aside from the lack of regulation in certain areas, the law itself has serious drawbacks. It contains no provisions for soil or water pollution. The law can be effectively used by the government to reduce an existing nuisance, but not as a planning tool to prevent future ones. Finally, the law does not enable effective airshed and watershed management. For these reasons, the provisions for protection against air pollution were removed from the Kanowitz Law with the passage of the Clean Air Law.

Despite the Kanowitz Law's drawbacks, if used together with the Planning and Building Law and the Licensing of Businesses Law, it could be an effective tool for the control of existing nuisances. According to the provisions of the Licensing of Businesses Law, no licence can be granted unless the licensee meets the requirements of the Kanowitz Law and its regulations. This means that a business must meet standards laid down in regulations, in addition to criteria set out in the business licence. In actual fact, with the dearth of emission standards, the provision has little effect on business practices *(see also section 196-The Law for the Prevention of Environmental Nuisances (Citizen Suits), 1992).*

---

a pub (Case No. 2899/01-Haifa District Court); the right to cancel a rental contract to an artist's studio due to noise and odours from a neighbouring factory (Case No. 000193/00-Nazareth District Court).

107. *See*, e.g., Regulations for the Abatement of Nuisances (Air Quality), 1992, K.T. 972; Regulation for the Abatement of Nuisances (Unreasonable Noise), 1990.

108. Regulations for the Abatement of Nuisances (Air Pollution from Vehicles on the Road), 2001.

§4. The Law for Environmental Protection (The Polluter Pays) (Amendment of Laws)

50. The Law for Environmental Protection (The Polluter Pays), 2008 is an attempt by the Knesset to eliminate the economic advantages of polluting. It amends thirteen environment-related laws at once by changing three elements. First, it increases the maximum fines and prison terms allowed under each law. Second, it allows the court to impose even larger fines and prison sentences for crimes committed that cause or may cause severe environmental harm. Third, it allows the court to impose fines that reflect the damage caused and the economic benefits or profits gained from the act, on top of any other fine imposed. The thirteen environmental laws amended cover air, water and soil pollution, solid waste, dangerous substances and non-ionizing radiation.

§5. The Law for Environmental Protection (Emissions and Transfers to the Environment: Mandatory Reporting and Registration)

51. The Law for Environmental Protection (Emissions and Transfers to the Environment – Mandatory Reporting and Registration), 2012 was passed for the purpose of increasing transparency concerning environmental information, encouraging factories to decrease emissions and transfer of pollutants and waste to the environment and aiding decision-makers, researchers and policy makers in making sustainable decisions based on environmental justice. The law requires industries to report emissions and transfer of pollutants and waste to the environment. It establishes a public registry for this information, accessible to the public at all times.

The Pollutant Release and Transfer Register (PRTS or MIFLAS in Hebrew) publishes data on 114 pollutants released into the air, water, sea and soil or transferred offsite for treatment and disposal from 500 factories, power plants, landfills, transfer stations, sewage treatment plants, desalination plants, agricultural facilities for animal raising and more. On the Ministry website, a map with all 500 plants supplies information concerning each one, enabling a search according to facility, sector, pollutant, group of pollutants, location and medium. Information is also available concerning each facility, including the name, the type of activity and the contact details. The Registry also publishes an annual report that supplies information about all of the pollutants released from each installation.[109]

109. Ministry for Environmental Protection website.

Chapter 2. Air Pollution

§1. Stationary Sources of Air Pollution

I. Legislation

52. The Clean Air Law. In 2008, the Knesset passed a modern law for the reduction of air pollution in Israel: the Clean Air Law. During the years 2011 to 2015, the law's provisions slowly came into force, affecting various branches of industry. Regulations establishing air quality standards entered into force in May 2011 and updated regulations in January 2015. Previous to the law, responsibility for the control of air pollution was scattered amongst several ministries, including Transport, National Infrastructures, Economy, Treasury and Environment. The law concentrates many of these responsibilities under one ministry, the Ministry of Environmental Protection.

The law forbids unreasonable air pollution and gives the Minister of Environmental Protection the power to promulgate regulations defining what unreasonable air pollution is and the steps for prevention. The law requires the Minister of Environmental Protection to prepare a national plan for the reduction of air pollution and publication of air pollution forecasts and administrative remedies for air pollution prevention in real-time, including measurable reduction amounts and timetables. Major industrial polluters require emission permits, which are assessed according to the type and amount of pollution. They must use the best available technology to prevent air pollution. Local government is also required to act to limit and reduce pollution. During extreme pollution occurrences, the Minister of Environmental Protection must declare a pollution alert for the affected area and require immediate action by the local authorities. Recent regulations were promulgated by the Minister of Environmental Protection to limit air pollution from gas stations, requiring monitoring equipment, fume prevention, and other pollution prevention requirements.[110]

The Clean Air Law adds an arsenal of power to the Minister of Environmental Protection. More importantly, the law empowers the head of the air pollution department of the Ministry with powers normally bestowed on a minister. The head of the department controls the licensing of each smokestack in Israel, which, in essence, empowers him/her to determine the configuration of any new factory in Israel. In addition, the head of the department is empowered to issue administrative fines, without resort to the courts, for violations of the Law.

II. Enforcement and Control

53. The Reading D Power Plant. During the 1950s and early 1960s, there was little activity in the field of air pollution control. This was true even after the passing of the Abatement of Nuisances Law in 1961 because the law did not define

110. Clean Air Regulations (Prevention of Air Pollution and Odours from Gasoline Stations), 2017.

permitted levels of air pollution. Israel's first major clash of environmental and developmental interests occurred over a particularly large source of air pollution, an oil-fired power plant. The following description of the clash provides the reader with insight into air pollution prevention and control measures in Israel in the late 1960s.[111]

In 1965, the Knesset passed the Planning and Building Law and required all new enterprises, including government enterprises, to obtain planning approval prior to establishment. Immediately after the passage of the law, the Israel Electric Corporation (IEC) filed a plan for a new power plant in northern Tel Aviv. The plant was to adjoin three previously existing plants named after Lord Reading of England: Reading A, B and C. It was to be appropriately called Reading D. When the IEC plan was filed with the District Planning Commission, the representative of the Ministry of Health objected. He demanded that air pollution studies be done, claiming that adding a power plant of 500 megawatts to the Tel Aviv area was an environmental mistake.

The objection of the Planning Commission did not find favour with the then Ministry of Development and the government. When the government discovered that planning approval was delayed, it went into action. Even though the print on the Planning and Building Law was hardly dry, the government passed specific legislation to plan and build the Reading D power plant.[112] The legislation was pushed through the Knesset in record time. It enabled the government to bypass the Planning and Building Law and build and operate the power plant under the watchful eyes of three ministers: Health, Interior and Development. These ministers were to ensure that the power plant would not be too much of a nuisance.

A small, but vocal, group of environmentalists in Tel Aviv refused to accept this *fait accompli*. Even though the power plant had not yet been built, a civil action was filed under the provisions of the Kanowitz Law. The complaint charged that the operation of the power plant in Tel Aviv would cause unreasonable air pollution. The plaintiffs sought an injunction to prevent the power plant from being built. After losing in the Magistrates Court, winning in the District Court and fighting a counter-appeal in the Supreme Court, the Tel Aviv residents won the first leg of the battle. The Supreme Court held that the Kanowitz Law enables a private citizen to bring an injunction against a potential air pollution nuisance.[113] The case was remanded to the Magistrates Court for a final hearing. Unfortunately, the plant had been partially built before the hearing began.

The citizens then requested an injunction against the operation of the partially built power plant. The Magistrates Court held that the citizens had the right to enjoin the operation of the plan. No injunction was issued, however, pending the appeal of the IEC to the District Court, where the lower court's decision was upheld.[114] Again, the IEC appealed but the case became moot in the Supreme Court[115] because the power plant had already begun operation.

---

111. *See* R.E. Laster, *Reading D: Planning and Building or Building and Then Planning*, 8(4) Is. L. Rev. 481 (October 1973).
112. The Tel Aviv Power Plant Law, 1967, 21 L.S.I. 141.
113. *Israel Electric Co. v. Oded Avissar*, 1969, 23 P.D. II 314.
114. *Avissar Oded v. Israel Electric Co.*, 1970, 75 P.M. 3.
115. The Supreme Court compromise agreement was never published.

This case study is presented to prove several points. First, the forces of development were powerful enough in 1965 to cripple new environmental legislation. Second, the citizens who refused to accept this fact found refuge in the courts. Third, the Kanowitz Law could be used to prevent a potential future nuisance, not simply to abate an existing one. This lesson was not lost to the government, as will be seen in the next citizen's battle against another significant air polluter.

54. Hadera Power Plant. The next large power plant to be built in Israel was planned for the area between Tel Aviv and Haifa, near the town of Hadera. The plant was designed to operate on fuel oil, however, in 1978, the National Planning and Building Board decided to convert its operation to coal. With the plan before the National Planning Board, environmental forces went into action.

First, the local population of Hadera demonstrated against the plant's site. Second, the head of Israel's Environmental Protection Service appeared before the National Planning Board and demanded that an environmental impact statement be prepared and filed with the National Planning Board, even though not required by law. Finally, there was pressure put on the Ministry of the Interior to create an Association of Towns for Environmental Protection for the Hadera region to supervise the plant's operation, once built, and to prevent environmental degradation, once in operation.

This time, the government did not pass special legislation to bypass the Planning Law and Building Law. In 1978, working within the confines of the Planning and Building Law, the National Planning Board required the IEC to file an environmental impact statement as designed by the EPS. In 1979, the National Planning Board recommended and the Ministry of Interior created, an Association of Towns for Environmental Quality in the Hadera area to oversee the power plant's operation.

Finally, the plan, as approved, established environmental guidelines to prevent air and other types of pollution, including noise and sea pollution. The National Planning Board even went so far as to limit the power plant's total emissions to no more than one-half of the ambient air pollution standard for SO_2 as laid down in regulations under the Kanowitz Law.

Two watchdog groups were empowered to enforce the Planning Board's decision. The first was a permanent committee of the National Planning Board to ensure that the plan would be executed. The second was the Hadera Association of Towns for Environmental Protection. The government, under pressure from the EPS, purchased air quality monitoring stations for the Hadera Association of Towns to enable the Association to monitor air quality in the region. The National Planning Board, with government approval, established a permanent epidemiological study team to determine the long-term effects of the power plant on the Hadera population and its agricultural produce in the surrounding area. To date, no danger to health or agriculture from the power plant has been shown.

The Hadera Power Plant solution was a clear victory for environmentalists. The requirement of an environmental impact statement, air pollution control measures and watchdogs to monitor air quality, served as a model for later power plants planned and built in Israel.

Of significant psychological importance was the passing of the Tel Aviv Power Plant (Cancellation) Law of 1994.[116] As discussed above, a power plant situated in Tel Aviv in the late 1960s (and still functioning today, although it has been converted to natural gas) was designed and built over objections from the Tel Aviv community. Its erection was enabled due to the passing of a special law which bypassed the Planning and Building Law which had only recently been enacted. For years the Tel Aviv Power Plant Law of 1967 served as a disgraceful example of anti-environmental legislation. Its cancellation in 1994 marked a milestone in the annals of Israel's environmental law; that is until it was replaced with similar protective legislation for the Dead Sea Works (*see* paragraph 99, *infra*, The Dead Sea).

In 2000, the Minister for National Infrastructure decided to significantly enlarge the existing coal-fired power plant in Ashkelon. Once again, a decision was made by the National Infrastructures Committee (the controversial fast track for major infrastructure projects that bypasses many of the established environmental and public overview safeguards). The National Infrastructures Committee held a one-day public hearing on the issue in late January 2008 that was closed to the media. NGOs were given a few minutes to represent the public interest. Several environmental groups, concerned citizens as well as the Ministers of Health and Environment fought the decision. Over 20,000 objections were filed with the National Infrastructure Committee, but nevertheless, the project was approved. In spite of the approval, environmental groups made an administrative appeal to the High Court of Justice in an attempt to stop the project.

A major area overexposed to air pollution exists in Haifa Bay. There, a combination of an active port, the petrochemical industry and meteorological conditions produce the highest rate of cancer in Israel. Public pressure has been relentless to force the government to intervene to reduce pollution burdens, resulting in some of the most successful environmental cases in Israel. The first major case against one of Haifa's notorious polluting industries, Haifa Chemicals, was filed by the Union for Environmental Defence (Adam, Teva V'Din) for its pollution of the Kishon River. There the court fined the company heavily for its actions and enabled the creation of a pollution fund. In a case brought by the government for a single air pollution incident in 2005, the oil refineries in Haifa were fined the single highest fine ever levied for pollution in the history of the country. The Ministry of Environmental Protection issued specific instructions to the Haifa Bay oil refineries for the prevention of air pollution in 2006 and again in 2009, as allowed under the Kanowitz Law. This is to be achieved by reducing pollution from the stacks, as well as from indirect sources of pollution. In 2021 an inter-ministerial committee decided that all petrochemical industries in the Haifa Bay area must close within a decade.

55. Enforcement Controls under the Clean Air Law. The law contains several mechanisms for the control of air pollution levels. The Minister of Environmental Protection may appoint air pollution inspectors with police powers. The head of the air quality section of the Ministry of Environmental Protection can write administrative orders against polluters, ordering them to immediately cease polluting and to

116. S.H. 1466, 150.

shut them down completely in the event of non-compliance. The law also provides for substantial fines and possible imprisonment against polluters.

In tandem with enforcement controls, the Clean Air Law mandated the passage of a national pollution reduction and prevention programme for the years 2012–2020. The government adopted the programme in 2013, after several challenges by the Ministry of Finance. The goal is to establish future policies for the reduction of pollution from transportation, industry, energy and households in order to reach target values.

III. Summary: Stationary Sources of Air Pollution

56. In the above description, one gets a flavour of the prevention and control of a large stationary source of air pollution. In fact, potentially large sources of air pollution have been controlled through the Planning and Building Law. For existing stationary sources, air pollution has been controlled and even reduced through enforcement orders issued under the Kanowitz Law. Enforcement orders or personal decrees, as they are sometimes called, were proposed by the EPS and issued against Israel's major stationary air polluters in the 1980s. Enforcement orders are permitted under the Abatement of Nuisances Law, but it was contemplated that they would be issued from time to time against certain factories and not used as an alternative to regulations. The Abatement of Nuisances Law empowers the Minister of Environmental Protection to promulgate regulations in the command and control format so well known. The Minister, however, has done little to promulgate regulations and instead has issued personal decrees or enforcement orders against some thirty industrial sources of air pollution in Israel. This is done on a piecemeal basis without an overall strategic plan being developed. The result is that Israel has failed to promulgate regulations or set emission standards for most types of domestic industry. The Clean Air Law was passed in order to remedy this situation and to bring Israeli *legislation* and administration in line with Europe and North America.

It has been argued that this piece-by-piece strategy is used by the Ministry because it is easier to apply than to develop overall regulations. The result, however, is that quite unlike countries in Europe and the United States where emissions from stationary sources have been reduced since the 1980s, Israel has seen little or no reduction in total air emissions over the same period. Pressure from the Ministry on the IEC has had its effect, however. It also does not hurt that the IEC is a public monopoly. Beginning in 2004, the IEC began converting its older plants to operate on natural gas instead of oil. Coupled with the air quality standards required by the Clean Air Law, there has been improvement in Israel's air quality in recent years from stationary sources. It will be interesting to see, however, as small gas-fired power plants are being scattered all over the country, what the long-term effects will be. There certainly has not been a robust programme for off-the-grid solar installations, in spite of the fact that Israel is a country with sunshine most of the year.

§2. Air Pollution from Vehicles

57. Air pollution from vehicles has replaced stationary sources as the major source of air pollution for certain pollutants such as hydrocarbons, carbon monoxide, lead and ozone. In addition, particulate emissions from diesel trucks, buses and cars have added particles with health risks to humans and this has caused an added risk of cancer among Israel's population. Studies have shown that along major thoroughfares, the amount of air pollution in Israel exceeds the standards set for air quality in areas such as Tel Aviv, Haifa, Jerusalem and Ashdod.

The only significant reduction of air pollution from vehicles can occur when a country makes a principle decision to require land use controls in order to reduce the most popular mode of transportation, the vehicle. Israel has moved against the trend in other countries and, during the 1980s and 1990s, encouraged vehicle use, culminating in a major decision, in the late 1990s, to build a toll road through the centre of the country, which would encourage further vehicle traffic. The road was built in spite of objections from all the health and environmental factions in Israel.[117]

There is no doubt that a country can more easily control air pollution production from stationary sources than from individual vehicles. There is a tiny ray of hope, however, in that the government has constructed a high-speed rail link from Jerusalem to Tel Aviv and the coastal areas of Israel. In addition, the government built the first phase of a light-rail transit system for the city of Jerusalem, while the Tel Aviv subway is in the construction phase. This shows that the government does understand the need for rail transportation as a way of reducing vehicle pollution in urban centres. But with the government depending on large amounts of taxes from vehicles, the incentives keeping the public dependent on private cars are hard to resist. In 2016 and 2017, the government collected ILS 80 billion (USD 23 billion) in taxes from car owners, through purchase taxes, gasoline taxes, and other related taxes.[118] Just vehicle purchase taxes and fuel taxes comprised 12% of the total government income from taxes in 2016.[119]

Air pollution from vehicles is controlled under separate pieces of legislation:

> Transportation Regulations[120] and the Clean Air Law. Control of emissions under the Transportation Regulations is done at the source – that is, for new vehicles – and at the annual licensing test for used vehicles. The new Clean Air Law transfers power over vehicle emissions standards and fuel standards to the Ministry of Environmental Protection. There are air pollution control

---

117. For example, Case No. 4128/02 High Court of Justice, *Israel Union for Environmental Defence v. Prime Minister of Israel* et al., The Israel Union for Environmental Defence (IUED) appealed to the High Court of Justice, demanding that an environmental impact statement be carried out on the road as a whole, rather than piece-meal. The appeal was rejected.
118. *See* article (in Hebrew)-'Milking of Taxes by the State: 80 Billion Shekels in Two Years From Taxes On Vehicles' https://www.globes.co.il/news/article.aspx?did=1001148932 (last visited 9 Apr. 2023).
119. Ministry of Finance report from 2015–2016, Part A: State Income from Taxes and Fees.
120. *See*, e.g., Regulations for the Abatement of Nuisances (Air Pollution from Vehicles), 1963, K.T. 1794.

regulations based on American or European standards for new vehicles, depending on their place of export.[121] Since Israel does not manufacture cars, this standard is an acceptance of fact, rather than a statement of policy. Israel is too small a market to demand import controls to reduce air pollution. For used cars, the annual licensing test requires cars to be tested for carbon monoxide only. Cars operating on diesel fuel are checked annually, and there is an on-the-road-test for black smoke.[122] In 2009, the Minister of Environmental Protection promulgated regulations for the reduction of pollution from vehicles as required by the Clean Air Law, including publication of emissions and energy requirements of vehicles. These figures must accompany all advertisements of vehicles. The regulations must be in line with established emissions requirements in the developed world and the recommendations of international organizations, including the EU. Additional regulations for vehicular pollution were promulgated in 2012 and updated in 2018, establishing legal limits for pollution from diesel, gasoline and gas-powered vehicles and incorporating air pollution testing as part of the annual vehicle inspection procedure.

A criminal procedure order[123] provides for the imposition of immediate monetary fines (similar to parking tickets) in lieu of an appearance in court. The order is intended to provide for efficient enforcement of the regulations on pollution from vehicles on the roads. The fines relate to five categories of vehicular emission violations, largely relating to smoke and carbon monoxide emissions.

In 2015, new rules were issued by the Ministry of Environmental Protection for existing heavy vehicle fleets. The provisions set an average emissions target for a fleet of vehicles, such that by 2018, heavy vehicles will meet the EUR 4, EUR 5 or EUR 6 emission standards. The rules affect some 12,000 vehicles, which is about a quarter of all heavy vehicles in Israel.

In addition, the Association of Towns for the Haifa general region published a local bylaw for tests for air pollution from vehicles in order to reduce the increasing rate of air pollution in this area.[124] Both the government regulation and the Haifa regulation require tests for vehicles with gasoline or diesel motors. The gasoline regulations control the emission of carbon monoxide, while the diesel regulations require a reduction in particles produced. Both regulations refer to vehicles already in use.

Tel Aviv has also published requirements that gas stations in the Tel Aviv area must carry low-sulphur diesel fuel for diesel-operated engines.

In addition to the above regulations, the Ministry of Environmental Protection issued a personal order, under the Abatement of Nuisances Law, against Israel's two major bus cooperatives. This order required the two major bus cooperatives to reduce pollutants by switching to low-sulphur fuel (city diesel), with a content of 0.005% sulphur. The order also required the two cooperatives to scrap old buses and

---

121. Transportation Regulations, 1961, s. C, Art. 10A(1).
122. K.T. 5751, 837. Reference is made to s. 15.03 of the Council or CFR 40–86, or 88/76 EEC.
123. *The Criminal Procedure Order (Finable Offences – Air Pollution from Vehicles on the Road)*, 2001.
124. General Association of Towns (Haifa Region) (Air Pollution from Vehicles) (By-law 2001).

increase the monitoring of buses in order to meet the requirements. The bus companies would monitor themselves under previous regulations promulgated by the Ministry of Environmental Protection. The decree further required a reduction of omissions of nitrogen oxides and hydrocarbons.

The Ministry of National Infrastructure added its power to the Ministry of Environmental Protection by promulgating an order forbidding the production, import and marketing of diesel fuel that is not low in sulphur.[125] The Clean Air Law transfers power over types, ingredients, quality of fuels and fuel additives, to the Minister of Environmental Protection, to be carried out in consultation with the Minister of National Infrastructure.

In 2009, Israel's first green tax reform came into force. For the first time, purchase tax rates on vehicles are linked to the emission rates of five pollutants.

§3. Case Law

58. The Ministry of Environmental Protection's activity regarding air pollution has been extremely limited. The Ministry claims that air pollution is currently their biggest challenge and that the reason for their inactivity is that air pollution is difficult and expensive to test, unlike water, for example.

There are few landmark cases with respect to air pollution. The major landmark case of Reading D has already been discussed previously. A second category of cases mentioned also led to the promulgation of regulations under the Kanowitz Law. These cases come in two forms. The first required the minister authorized to promulgate regulations under the Kanowitz Law to do so for ambient air pollution.[126] The second required the ministers to publish regulations for emission standards.[127] Other air pollution cases concern citizens' suits against major polluters, as well as public[128] and private[129] criminal suits. The following are a few examples from the Israel courts.

In Rogen and Others against the State of Israel and Others T. A. 15485/82, residents near the Tel Hashomer Hospital brought an action against the hospital to stop pollution from one of the hospital's chimneys. The court held in favour of the plaintiffs and the hospital was required to replace its smoking chimney.

Another case is the Oil Refineries against the State of Israel (Authorized Appeal) T. A. 68/82. In this criminal case, the Magistrate's Court of Haifa found the oil refineries to be in violation of the Kanowitz Law regulations for air pollution from their industry premises, and they were fined. The refineries appealed the case, arguing that the flames which come from oil refineries are needed to burn off the extra oil otherwise there will be a risk of an explosion in the refineries. They argued that they

125. Vehicle Operation Order (Engines and Fuel) (Low Sulfur Diesel Fuel), 2003.
126. *Oppenheimer v. Minister of Health and Interior*, P.D. 21 (1) 309.
127. *Peranio v. Ministers of Health and Interior*, P.D. 26 (1) 809.
128. *State of Israel v. Oil Refineries, Ltd.*, Criminal Com. 4338/79, Magistrate's Court Haifa, 31 Dec. 1981; Criminal Appeal 43/81, Haifa District Court, 25 Dec. 1981; Appeal Request 62/82, Supreme Court, 7 Dec. 1982; *State of Israel v. Nesher*, Criminal Com. 1628/80, Magistrate's Court Haifa, 1 Jan. 1981.
129. *Yitzhak Eren v. Mekorot*, Criminal Com. 1469/71, Magistrate's Court Rehovot.

met the conditions of the Kanowitz law by using the best available technology. Their appeal was rejected, and the Court held they must take new steps to reduce air pollution.

Recent cases reflect a trend less tolerant of polluters, especially those that reap financial benefits through pollution. A bakery and its directors were found to have caused air pollution over an extended period of time in violation of the Kanowitz law, and the air pollution regulations promulgated under the law.[130] In his decision, the judge declared it time for the courts to move from talk to action in response to serious crimes being committed against the public from poisoned air, poisoned soil, and all the existing poisonous substances. He claimed that he was certain that the area residents suffered and are still suffering from health problems due to breathing polluted air. In response to the defendants' plea for leniency due to financial difficulties, he stated that what the defendants were really saying was that due to their (the baker's) lack of funds, the area residents had to suffer physical damage, illnesses and even death. A polluter has to choose either to stop polluting or suffer the legal consequences. Similarly, the Tel Aviv Magistrate's Court stated that the common view today sees environmental crimes as serious infringements of the law.[131] Since the crimes committed by the defendant were done for economic gain with disregard for the environment, a heavy punishment would show the defendant that his/her actions had caused severe harm and distress to society.

In 2007, an NGO named 'Air to Breathe' brought suit against the City of Tel Aviv claiming that the City was not using the powers granted to them to supervise and enforce environmental standards against diesel-powered vehicles.[132] They, therefore, asked the Court for a long list of remedies including declarative orders and orders to carry out and desist as well as damages caused by the pollution. The Magistrate's Court rejected their claims holding that the national or local government cannot be seen as 'a cause of a nuisance' as described in the law for the Prevention of Nuisances.

In 2012, the head of the air quality section used his authority under the Clean Air Law to fine the Jerusalem Bus Station operators for non-compliance in improving the air quality in the bus station. An appeal to the District Court in its function as the Court of Administrative Matters in 2014 was overruled and the authority of the head of the air quality section to levy fines was upheld, although the court reduced the fine by 20%.

According to a report from the Ministry of Health, the residents of Haifa suffer from higher incidences of heart disease, breathing ailments including asthma in children, and cancer than the rest of Israel.[133] The Ministry recommended approving the expansion of the Haifa oil refineries on condition that the public health is not affected. The plan was approved without taking these conditions into account. The

---

130. *Ministry of Environmental Protection v. Alumot Holon, Ltd. et al.*, Criminal Case No. 001928/04, Rishon Le'Zion Magistrate's Court, 31 Dec. 2004.
131. *State of Israel v. Khalil Elsayad*, Case No. 005841/07 Tel Aviv Magistrate's Court, 25 Jul. 2009.
132. *Air to Breathe v. City of Tel Aviv*, Case No. 043927/03 Tel Aviv Magistrate's Court, 25 Dec. 2007.
133. Position Paper, Ministry of Health Concerning Illness in the Haifa Bay, File No. 280456316, 15 Dec. 2015.

Supreme Court in 2019 stopped the plans for the expansion of the Haifa oil refinery, requiring an environmental impact analysis and detailed planning before any approval by the planning authorities.[134]

Due to the pollution levels in the Haifa area, there has been a discussion of closing down all industrial activity in the area and converting the area to residential and business by 2030. A decision to close the petrochemical industries was made official by an inter-ministerial committee, especially since it appears to be more attractive financially than continuing refining of oil (*see* section 70 – Legal Action).

The use of class action suits has increased over the years[135] and deters large companies from pollution. A significant case 'Haifa Companies'[136] set the standard for environmental class actions. In this case, a non-profit called Citizens for the Environment filed a class action suit against thirty companies in Haifa.[137] They sued on behalf of the residents of Haifa and surrounding towns suffering from air pollution. The companies filed for dismissal of the class action, using previous precedent to establish their request. The court judge rejected the companies' request and allowed the petitioners to claim for damages, in addition to a petition to abate the pollution. Thus, the judge rejected the companies' claim that each person has to file for damages for their individual claim.

Another case, based on a procedural error, was overturned by the Supreme Court.[138] The court found for the plaintiff, against the 'deep pocket' of the defendants and returned the case to the District Court. In a case against Volkswagen for excessive emissions,[139] a Tel Aviv court allowed a class action case on behalf of all those exposed to the emissions. According to the court, over 11 million people were exposed worldwide to excessive air pollution due to Volkswagen's tampering with the exhaust system to avoid violating gas emissions during the annual test.

§4. COVENANT ON IMPLEMENTING AIR POLLUTION EMISSION STANDARDS

59. In January 1998, the Ministry of Environment and the Manufacturers Association signed the 'Covenant on Implementing Standards on Pollutant Emissions into the Air'. The stated aim of the Covenant is to 'regulate the implementation of emission standards and the mode of cooperation between them in reducing industrial air pollutant emissions and their impact on air quality'. Since no emission standards have been promulgated, the Covenant sets out, in an appendix, the minimum standard which an industry wishing to comply with the Covenant must meet.

134. *City of Haifa v. National Authority for Planning and Building*, Case No. 2605/18, Supreme Court sitting as the Court of Appeals. 125 21 Is. Env. Bull. 4, at 19, Gabbay ed. (Autumn 1998).
135. Yehial Kasher & Eyal Ofer, 'Environmental Class Action Suits, the Israel Forum for Information'.
136. *Ibid.*
137. Class Action suit 165868-07, *Citizens for the Environment, v. Elkon Recycling Center*.
138. Civil Appeal 5638/21, *Roy Galili v. Rotem Import*, published in Hebrew, Nevo-14.1.22.
139. Class Action, Tel Aviv, 756-10-15, *Shlomo Golan v. Volkswagen*, Hebrew, Nevo-28.09.2022.

The Covenant was heralded by the Ministry as a major breakthrough[140] because it is Israel's first example of voluntary compliance with air pollution emission standards. Critics of the Covenant have been less jubilant. They argue that Israel is simply copying other countries and that the Covenant is a publicity stunt. In fact, emission standards set out as an appendix to the Covenant are faulty and outdated. The Covenant is meant to be used as part of a package of enforcement measures and not standalone. Finally, the Covenant was prepared and signed in secret; its contents were made known to the public only as an afterthought, and the enforcement committee created in the Covenant includes no representatives of the public or an environmental NGO. In 2011, it was replaced by the Clean Air Law and its accompanying mandatory standards are now promulgated by the Ministry of Environmental Protection.

§5. International Air Pollution Treaties

60. Montreal Protocol on Ozone Depletion. Israel has signed and ratified the Montreal Protocol on Substances that Deplete the Ozone Layer, including the London, Copenhagen, Vienna and Beijing Amendments. In January 2004, the Minister of Environmental Protection promulgated regulations to implement the provisions of the Protocol.[141] The regulations set restrictions on the production, consumption, import and export of substances that deplete the ozone layer, and establish verification mechanisms for these restrictions. The regulations include restrictions and controls on the sale and usage of methyl bromide, a serious commitment on the government's part in view of Israel's place as the second-largest producer in the world.

61. United Nations Framework Convention on Climate Change. Israel ratified the United Nations Framework Convention on Climate Change (UNFCCC) in 1996. The Kyoto Protocol, requiring countries to reduce greenhouse gas emissions to the levels that were recorded in 1990, was ratified by Israel in 2004. As of February 2005, it became legally binding on Israel and the other parties. Israel is designated as a developing country according to the Kyoto Protocol. The Clean Development Mechanism (CDM) provides for developed parties to implement projects that reduce emissions in developing countries in return for Certified Emission Reductions (CERs). Israel has created a Designated National Authority (DNA) for the CDM under the ministerial responsibility of the Ministry of Environmental Protection. It includes representatives from several ministries and public bodies. The main function of the DNA is to determine whether a proposed CDM project complies with sustainable development criteria.

140. Hazardous Substances Regulations (Implementation of Provisions of the Montreal Protocol), 2004.
141. Israel's submission to the UN Climate Change Convention-Copenhagen Accord, Minister of Environmental Protection, 31 Jan. 2010.

62. Israel committed to reducing per capita GHG emissions by 26% below the 2005 per capita emissions level by 2030. In April 2016, the government passed a national plan aimed at reaching this target.[142]

Israel signed the 2015 Paris Climate Accord on 24 April 2016, committing the country to reduce emissions per person by 26% by the year 2030 in relation to 2005, a 17% reduction in energy usage and a 17% increase in electricity produced by renewable sources by 2030.

63. Protocol on PRTRs. The Pollutant Release and Transfer Register (PRTR), also known as the Kyiv Protocol, is a protocol to the UNECE's Aarhus Convention. Israel acceded to the Protocol on 14 January 2013, reflected in Government Decision No. 5269. Israel's PRTR, called MIFLAS, can be accessed freely on the Ministry of Environmental Protection website (*see* paragraph 51 for a description of MIFLAS).

142. Ministry of Environmental Protection. https://www.gov.il/en/Departments/Guides/reducing_greenhouse_gases_increasing_energy_efficiency (last visited 14 Apr. 2023).

Chapter 3. Water Pollution

§1. Introduction

64. Israel has expansive legislation in the area of water pollution prevention and control, both freshwater, as discussed in the first paragraphs of this chapter, and seawater, which is discussed in section 5, *Marine Pollution*. Through a series of laws dating from the 1950s, the Israeli government has the power to control the use and quality of every drop of water – ground, surface and piped. This is probably the world's first example of legislative overkill in the environmental field: very expansive legislative coverage of the subject with little or no administrative policy on the one hand, nor enforcement on the other.

This chapter will discuss the problem from two vantage points; first, there follows a discussion of the laws relating to water quality, management and control from a national and regional approach. The second vantage point covers those miscellaneous laws that prevent pollution of water sources, for example, drinking water and sewage water. Finally, the chapter closes with a discussion on marine pollution.

§2. Water Quality Management and Control

I. The Water Law 1959

65. Most legal regimes grant the right of ownership over water sources either as a riparian right or as a right of prior appropriation.[143] Once this legislation is in place, general regulations of water flow or quality become a Herculean task. Israel was more fortunate than most Western nations because it inherited the Laws of the Megelle, the Ottoman code of civil laws, which held that water, like air, fire and earth, could not be held in private ownership.[144] From the declaration of the State in 1948 and during the 1950s, the Israeli government published four water laws, which are the envy of those countries in the world wishing to protect their water resources. The first law, the Water Drilling Control Law, was adopted in 1955.[145] This law prohibits the drilling of any well without a licence from the Director of the Water Authority. The law enables the Director to refuse any licence if he/she feels that the licence will cause salinity or pollution of groundwater. The second major law was the Water Measurement Law, also of 1955.[146] According to the law, no water is supplied in Israel, from any source, without first being measured.

143. Water Law, 1959, 13 L.S.I. 173.
144. The Magelle, s. 1235 'Water flowing in the bowels of the earth are not the property of any man'; s. 1237 'Oceans and large lakes are ownerless'; s. 1238 'The many rivers that are no man's property and are not separated into rivulets, i.e., they do not enter into channels that are the property of a recognized group of people, are ownerless ….'
145. Water Drilling Control Law, 1955, 9 L.S.I. 88.
146. Water Measurement Law, 1955, 9 L.S.I. 85.

In the year 1957, the Drainage and Flood Control Law was passed.[147] The act created a National Drainage Board made up of eight members appointed by the government. The country was divided into twenty-six Drainage Boards to prevent soil erosion and promote orderly drainage. In 1997, the drainage boards underwent a serious reformation, to be discussed in later chapters, but the original Act did enable Israel's administrative authorities to protect the country from flooding and run-off. The Drainage Law also allowed the Director of the Water Authority to protect water sources by creating a protective strip around them.

The Water Law of 1959 dwarfed all previous legislation and established a water management programme for all sources of water.[148] The law established a Water Commission headed by a Water Commissioner (today the Water Authority and its Director) who, in the words of the law, is to 'manage the water resources of the country'.

The law's first section sets the tone for the entire law. Clause 1 declares, 'The water sources in the state are public property, subject to the control of the state and destined for the requirements of its inhabitants and for the development of the country.' By this very sentence, all persons who up until that date thought that they had private control over a water source lost such control. In effect, the Water Law nationalized all the water sources of the country for the benefit of the public. Ownership, however, was not vested in the State but vested in the people. Clause 2 defines water sources so broadly as to include every source of water imaginable except falling rain or water evaporation. The definition includes springs, streams, rivers, lakes and other flowing or standing sources of water, whether surface or groundwater, whether natural or conducted, whether the water is flowing or standing perennially or from time to time, including drainage and sewage water.

The subsequent clauses in section 1 grant a limited right to the citizens of Israel to water use. The use must be for a purpose stated in the law: household, industrial, agricultural, business, public works or nature. The use is also conditional on the prevention of salinity increase or overuse. The law abrogates the riparian rights doctrine so prevalent in other countries. A liberal interpretation of the original law would allow the Director of the Water Authority to prevent the over-pumping of ground and surface water. But the Director has failed to use this authority wisely and most of Israel's perennial streams suffered from lack of freshwater intake. To bring the matter to the attention of the Water Authority, an amendment to the law added a new permitted use of water for nature: To maintain and reclaim natural resources and landscapes, including springs, rivers, and wetland habitats.[149]

In short, the Water Law brings all water sources under government control. It also abrogated, overnight as it were, a private citizen's contention that he/she has a right to water from a certain source and of a certain quality. When this contention was formally tested, the Supreme Court held that once the Water Law nationalized the water sources, the private citizen has a right to water, neither from a particular

147. SH 236, 4.
148. Water Law, 1959, 13 L.S.I. 173.
149. The Water Law 1959 (Amendment No. 19) (Allocation of Water to Natural Resources and Landscapes), 2004.

source nor of a particular quality.[150] Following this general declarative section are clauses dealing with water allocation as well as water pollution, prevention and control.[151] In 1972, the Water Law was amended to include an entire section on pollution prevention and control. Yet, even prior to this amendment, the original law empowered the Water Authority to charge any person found polluting a water source with the costs of remediation. If the polluter failed to pay, the Water Authority has the right to remediate and recoup the costs through the tax enforcement process.

The original Water Law appointed the Minister of Agriculture as the Minister responsible for its execution. This was based on thinking, at the time, that Israel would become a State whose economy was based on agricultural production, and in fact, at one time, one-quarter of Israel's economy was based on agricultural production. Since then, however, there has been recognition of the fact that the economy cannot be based on agricultural production, that agriculture's share of Israel's limited water supply has been reduced from its high point of 90% to below 50% today and that the power of the Ministry of Agriculture over water has been reduced. Today, the Ministry of Agriculture remains responsible for the Drainage and Flood Control Law, but the responsibility for Water Drilling Law, Water Metering Law and Water Law was transferred to the Ministry of National Infrastructures, Energy and Water Resources, except for the powers delegated specifically to the Ministry of Environmental Protection under the Water Polluter Amendment of 1972, which will be discussed shortly.[152]

II. Amendment of the Water Law

66. The 1972 amendment to the Water Law came on the heels of international action in the environmental field and environmental legislation in other countries.[153] The 1972 amendment, paralleling the original law's broad definition of water sources, defines water pollution in the broadest possible manner. Essentially, under Israel's Water Law, any change in a water source is, prima facie, pollution. The law goes on to say that it is forbidden to pour a liquid, gaseous or solid substance into or near a water source. This clause, if interpreted strictly, forbids anyone from swimming or sunbathing near a water source, a perfect example of legislative overkill. But that is not all. The amendment empowers the Ministry of Environmental Protection to publish regulations to prevent water pollution in the following

150. High Court of Justice, Case No. 221/64 *Local Council Pardess Hana v. the Minister of Agriculture*; Haifa District Court, sitting as the Water Court, Appeal No. 105/02, *Ben Ezer v. Water Commissioner et al.*

151. Bagatz 221/64, *Pardess Hana v. Minister of Agriculture*, P.D. 24 (4) 533.

152. 26 L.S.I. 7 (1972).

153. The United Nations Conference on the Human Environment, held in Stockholm from 5 to 16 Jun. 1972, was the first global conference on the environment. Many of its decisions subsequently served as international legal precedents, as well as an impetus for enacting national environmental legislation, including Israel.

areas: (1) siting of potential water polluters; (2) the use of certain products or processes, including agricultural produce and the use of fertilizers and pesticides; (3) the production, importation, distribution or sale of any product; (4) the regulation of transport on or near a water source.

In light of the sweeping definition of water pollution in section 20(A) of the amended Water Law, the Minister of Environmental Protection can regulate the State of Israel with the powers granted to him/her under the Water Law. The Minister can determine the siting of factories, their products and processes, and their distribution and sales routes, all for the purpose of preventing water pollution. The Minister can go so far as to regulate transportation around or near any water source, including Lake Kinneret, or stop it altogether. To put it mildly, the Minister has been relaxed with his/her unlimited powers.

67. The 2006 amendment to the Water Law began as an attempt to centralize power over the water system, within the Water Commission, by bringing under one authority power originally dispersed among several ministries. The major substantial change was the transfer of powers from the ministerial level – the Minister of National Infrastructure – to the administrative level – the newly created Water Authority. The Water Authority's controlling committee is composed of the Director, the Director Generals of four ministries (Agriculture, Environment, Interior and National Infrastructures), the budget director of the Finance Ministry, and two representatives of the general public. The amendment does not, however, solve the problem of fragmentation. The Minister of Health still has power over drinking water and sewage effluent quality; the Minister of Environmental Protection has power over pollution control and the Minister of Agriculture over drainage and flood control. As of this edition, the government has approved an initiative to create another authority, this time for surface water and drainage, appended to the Minister of Agriculture.

III. Legal Protection of Water Sources

68. Ministry of Environmental Protection. Until 1991, the Minister of Agriculture used his powers to protect water sources infrequently. In fact, he promulgated only one regulation under the amendment of 1972, forbidding the production of laundry detergents that do not emulsify in water. With the change in authority over the protection of water sources from the Minister of Agriculture to the Minister of Environmental Protection, some major legislative changes have been made in the area of enforcement, control and protection under the Water Law. The following is a brief overview of the major regulations promulgated since 1991 (*see also* section 4. Miscellaneous Water Laws, paragraphs 89–91).

In 1994, the Ministry of Environmental Protection passed regulations to reduce the amount of salt in industrial processes.[154] The regulation reduced the acute problem of salt overload in wastewater treatment plants. These regulations require

154. Water Regulations (Prevention of Water Pollution) (Reduction of Soil Pollution and the Regeneration Process), 1994.

industries to undertake a number of technical steps to bring about salt reduction in the regeneration of ion-exchange in order to reduce the quantity of salt used in the water softening process. In addition, the Ministry of Environmental Protection passed a regulation in 1998 prohibiting salts from being emitted into Israel's water sources. Salt is a special problem in Israel due to salting meat according to religious dietary laws. Additional sources of salts occur in the ion-exchange process from the food, tanning and textile industries, and from hospitals. The regulations call for separating wastewater streams so that the brines are isolated from the rest of the wastewater. The regulations are meant to prevent salt enrichment of municipal sewage, which is an impediment to effluent irrigation.[155]

Heavy metals from industrial sewage are a big pollutant of groundwater and sludge, preventing it from being used in agriculture. Regulations were passed in 2000 in order to reduce the amount of heavy metals polluting water sources.[156] They require pre-treatment of wastewater at the source to within acceptable levels. The regulations set maximum concentration levels for twenty pollutants and prohibit dilution as a method of meeting these standards.

Under the Abatement of Nuisances Law, the Ministry has published several regulations for the purpose of protecting water sources and the soil from land-based oil pollution. One regulation requires appropriate handling and reuse of used oil to prevent damage to the operation of sewage treatment plants.[157] Sellers, users and consumers of oil for lubrication, insulation and similar uses must collect the used oil in specially designated receptacles for subsequent transport and disposal or recycling. In 1997, the Ministry of Environmental Protection published regulations regarding the storage of oil and gas in service stations throughout Israel.[158] In addition, in the year 2000, the Ministry of Infrastructure passed regulations requiring notification of the operation of any gas station within fourteen days of its opening.[159] The report must be filed with the local authority and must include the types of fuels supplied, and the number of storage tanks and pumps operated by the station. This will help reduce groundwater pollution from gas stations. To this were added additional regulations concerning the planning, building and maintenance of fuel pipelines.[160]

An agreement was reached between the oil companies and the Ministry of Environmental Protection for the treatment of soil and water already polluted at existing gas stations. Unfortunately, as of 2014, only 25% of the gas stations where ground pollution was detected had completed soil treatment, and the oil companies have not even completed surveying all of the suspected polluting sites.[161] A 2013 lawsuit filed by the State of Israel against the four major oil companies for not testing gas station tanks for leakage, in violation of the Water Regulations (Prevention of Water

155. Water Regulations (Prevention of Water Pollution) (Prohibition on Discharge of Brines to Water Sources), 1998.
156. Water Regulations (Prevention of Water Pollution) (Metals and Other Pollutants), 2000.
157. Abatement of Nuisances Regulations (Used Oil), 1993.
158. Water Regulations (Prevention of Water Pollution) (Gasoline Stations), 1997.
159. Order for Operation of Cars (Motors and Fuel) (Reporting on Gas Stations), 2000.
160. Water Regulations (Prevention of Water Pollution) (Fuel Pipelines), 2006.
161. http://www.calcalist.co.il/local/articles/0,7340,L-3631023,00.html (last visited 9 Apr. 2023).

Pollution) (Gasoline Stations) 1997, ended with a settlement requiring each company to pay in the vicinity of ILS 0.5 million.[162] The settlement reached between the sides erased the liability charges against officials from the oil companies.

As of March 2016, only 56% of the gas stations in Israel complied with all equipment requirements. A large percentage of the stations not in compliance were from small companies or independent stations.[163]

Another source of ground and water pollution is leakage from sewage pipes. In an attempt to prevent water and soil pollution, regulations were promulgated in 2011 that require adequate maintenance of sewage systems and data collection and dissemination. This includes regular system inspections, measurements of sewage flow amounts, reporting of any changes in amounts or other indications of leakage, updated computerized maps of systems and published procedures for repairing system leakage.[164]

The Public Health Ordinance, 1940, under Chapter 20: Nuisances, defines a 'nuisance' as untreated sewage, or any action that harms the health of the environment. The Ordinance empowers the local authority to notify those causing nuisances on how to remove them. Noncompliance by the polluter is a criminal offence. The Ministry of Environmental Protection has the right under this law to order the local authority to use its power to prevent and remove nuisances. In urgent cases, the Ministry can carry out the local authority's mandate and in situations of inactivity by the local authority, the Ministry can do so on the local authority's account.

Hydraulic fracturing, or fracking, a method of removing natural gas from shale rock through underground blasting with water, chemicals, sand and sometimes heat, has recently become a concern for its potential to harm Israel's water quality as well as the amount of water required. The use of fracking has begun in Israel, although there is no environmental legislation regulating its usage (*see* paragraph 179 *Fracking*).

69. The Ministry of Health. While the Ministry of Environmental Protection has the overall responsibility for sewage treatment, the Ministry of Health maintains the authority to establish standards for wastewater used for commercial purposes. Rules promulgated under the Public Health Ordinance by the Minister of Health specify the treatment required for wastewater.[165] The regulations require secondary treatment of wastewater to a minimum baseline level of 20 milligram/litre BOD and 30 milligram/litre suspended solids in every community with a population exceeding 10,000 people.[166] In 2010, the Ministers of Health and Environment promulgated stricter regulations for wastewater quality, which is of extreme importance in light of the fact that nearly 90% of the wastewater is used for agriculture.[167] Instead of

162. *State of Israel v. Sonol Israel Inc.*, *Delek Inc.*, *Paz Inc.*, and *Dor-Alon Inc.*, Criminal Case (Tel Aviv) 16215–12-10.
163. Analysis of Seal Testing of Fuel Tanks and Pipes in Gas Stations, 2015/2016 Report, Prepared for the Ministry of Environmental Protection by the Faculty of Industrial Engineering and Management, the Technion, 1 Apr. 2016.
164. Water Regulation (Prevention of Water Pollution) (System for Transport of Sewage), 2011.
165. Public Health Ordinance, 1940, s. 62(b).
166. Public Health Regulations (Quality Standards for Wastewater), 1992.
167. *Ibid.*, 2010.

the previous two categories of parameters (BOD and suspended solids), the new standards contain thirty-seven categories. They also contain stricter guidelines for testing, control, publication and reporting, both for wastewater treatment plants and sewage producers. The regulations establish separate standards for wastewater to be used for the irrigation of crops.

The Ministry of Health has also passed regulations for the purpose of protecting sources of drinking water. Under these regulations, no one may drill a well in an area subject to pollution from floods or the flow of wastewater.[168]

Plans for the installation of sewers, purification or treatment plants outside of the jurisdiction of the local authority require ministerial approval.[169]

70. The Ministry of the Interior. Section 2 of the Local Authorities Law (Sewage) empowers the Minister of the Interior to require a local authority to create a sewage system in its area and even outside of its area (whose plans must be approved by the Regional Planning Authority, section 13). The Minister is in charge of carrying out this law and can set regulations regarding the times of use of sewage and the ways in which plans for purification plants can be submitted and approved (section 55).

71. The Ministry of Transportation. Section 60(11) of the Ports Ordinance (New Version), 1971, empowers the Minister of Transportation to publish regulations regarding the 'prohibition of pollution of port water, a waterway, a river fit for sailing, or any place on land from where the pollution can reach a river, a waterway or a river fit for sailing'.[170]

72. The Director of the Water Authority (Previously the Water Commissioner). Under the 1972 amendment to the Water Law, the Director of the Water Authority was granted additional powers to prevent water pollution. First of all, if the Director of the Water Authority finds that an enterprise requires discharge of sewage from its premises, he/she may order that enterprise to prepare a sewage plan.[171] The plan can be as broad or as narrow as the Director of the Water Authority determines. It can include the effluent quality levels to be achieved and a time schedule for achievement. If a polluter fails to prepare the plan so ordered or fails to carry it out, the Director of the Water Authority may bring an action in court to execute the plan or carry it out at the expense of the polluter.

Even an enterprise improving the quality of water must be licensed by the Director of the Water Authority. This permission is essential because, as stated above, any change, even an improvement in the quality of a water source, is defined as pollution. In addition, the Director of the Water Authority may diminish or cut off the supply of water to a polluting factory. He/she may require a polluting factory to pretreat its sewage or use certain processes to improve the quality of its sewage.

168. Public Health Regulations (Health Conditions for Wells for drinking water), 1995.
169. Local Authorities' Ordinance (Sewage), 1962, s. 13.
170. *See also* para. 71 *Rivers and Streams.*
171. 26 L.S.I. 7 (1972) at s. 20E. A person who has under his control any polluter, the operation of which requires the disposal of sewage therefrom, upon the order of the Water Commissioner, will submit for his approval a scheme detailing the mode of sewage disposal.

The Director of the Water Authority is authorized to delegate certain powers under the Water Law to local or regional parties, including Drainage Boards. He/she has done so with relish. As will be seen in the discussion of regional water authorities below, the Director of the Water Authority has delegated his power to require polluters to stop pollution and prepare sewage plans to most Drainage Boards in Israel, to some local authorities and to several Associations of Towns for Environmental Protection.

IV. Enforcement of the Water Law

73. A legal survey of water litigation in Israel, carried out by the authors together with students from the Hebrew University, revealed that the number of court cases concerning water throughout Israel's history is small. We found 520 court cases from 1948 until 2015, with the numbers increasing yearly. For example, we found only 16 court cases concerning water between 1957 and 1970, and 119 from 2013 to 2015. This coincides with a steady increase in court cases in general. The majority of recent cases concern criminal cases of water pollution as well as civil cases regarding water prices, the right to water and torts. We also noticed a jump in water litigation when relevant laws were passed or significantly amended. This trend points to an interesting historical fact. At the founding of the State, the distribution, supply and purification of water were prerogatives of the national and local government. Since the passage of the Associations for Water and Sewerage Law, the number of cases filed against the Associations increased exponentially. There is obviously a connection between the willingness of people to sue the government as opposed to their increased willingness to sue semi-private water companies.

It is no secret that the Director of the Water Authority has used very few of the water protection powers granted to him under the law. Between 1999 and 2005, only thirty warrants were issued by the Water Commission, an embarrassingly low amount considering the state of water in Israel.[172] There is no doubt that there is great difficulty in enforcing performance orders against municipalities, but this does not excuse the total lack of enforcement. The Director of the Water Authority's approach is one of understanding and cooperation with polluters, rather than enforcement. Violators are aware of this leniency and are, therefore, inclined to continue polluting. In a court case brought by the environmental NGO Adam, Teva V'Din in the Water Court, the Water Authority was criticized by the presiding judge for showing an interest only in the wake of legal action.[173]

Nor can one find a reason to exculpate the Ministry of Environmental Protection for its failure to publish stream and lake quality standards. This has had a detrimental effect on all the streams and lakes in Israel.

74. Legal Action. The Water Law of 1959 allows any person who has been directly injured as a result of an act of water pollution as described in Article 1A,

172. Interview with Shirley Babai, Legal Division, Water Project, the Israel Union for Environmental Defence, Tel Aviv, 3 Nov. 2005.

173. *Adam Teva V'Din v. Government Authority for Water and Sewage,* 14047-06-15 Water Court.

or a local authority within whose jurisdiction the offence has been committed, or listed NGOs to register a criminal complaint as stated in Criminal Procedures (Consolidated Version) Law, 1982.[174] For example, in 1997, one of Israel's environmental NGOs, the Israel Union for Environmental Defense (IUED), filed a private criminal suit against Haifa Chemicals, Inc. and others.[175] The sides came to a court-recognized compromise, whereby Haifa Chemicals would install a sewage treatment facility and obey the agreed-upon pollution standards.

In an attempt to change the approach of the Director of the Water Authority, the IUED filed two lawsuits against groundwater polluters.[176] One was against the Israel Military Industries for groundwater pollution in Jerusalem, and the other was against factories in the Mishor Rotem industrial area in the Negev. They included the Director of the Water Authority as a defendant, demanding that he invoke his powers to prevent water pollution under section 20(R) of the Water Law. Both cases were settled out of court.

The Abatement of Environmental Nuisances (Civil Action) Law, 1992, empowers citizens to file civil environmental lawsuits on behalf of themselves or non-profit organizations of which they are members, in cases of environmental pollution or nuisances. The law places three types of legal remedies at the disposal of the citizen: restraining orders, prevention of recurrence orders and corrective orders. The law does not allow monetary remedies. In addition, the law gives standing to environmental groups. Innovative use of the law was provided by a newly formed NGO in Tel Aviv in order to enhance the quality of the Yarqon River. In 2001, a suit was filed in the Magistrates Court of Tel Aviv against the Ministry of Environment and the Yarqon River Authority for not adequately cleaning up the river.[177] In fact, the original concept of the law was not to attack the government ministries' response to regulation but to act instead of the government to attack the polluters themselves in order to get a clean-up order against the polluter. The Magistrates Court's judge did not understand the finite ramifications of the law and allowed the suit to go forward. In the meantime, additional municipalities and regional and local authorities were added as defendants in the suit in order to get a wide sweep of the number of defendants, who, according to the suit, were responsible for either polluting or not preventing pollution of the Yarqon. The case ended in a compromise agreement, with the local and national government authorities agreeing to support the efforts of the Yarqon River Authority to reclaim the river.

A similar suit was filed against the Ashdod Association of Towns, alleging mismanagement of a waste dump that went up in smoke and caused serious air pollution for several days.

The Ministry of Environmental Protection has been active in filing suits against local authorities for polluting water sources with raw sewage. Numerous cases have been filed with fines ranging upwards of thousands of shekels for violation of the

174. Water Law of 1959, Art. 20Y.

175. *Adam Teva V'Din v. Haifa Chemicals, Inc. and Others* 5790/94. Haifa Magistrates Court, unpublished, cited in Fish, 204.

176. *Adam Teva V'Din v. Water Commissioner 102/02, Water Court; Adam Teva V'Din v. Economics Minister et al.*, 2907/06 High Court of Justice.

177. *Greens v. Yarqon River Authority et al.*, Tel Aviv Magistrates Court 119663/01.

law.[178] The Ministry regards this action as one of its biggest achievements in enforcement because today, unlike in 1990, most of the country is connected to sewage treatment plants.

A 2012 criminal appeals court upheld the conviction of a poultry hatchery for endangering groundwater.[179] In another case, an appeal to the Supreme Court of a conviction for an illegal garbage dump, which endangered water sources among several other infringements, the Supreme Court declared that:

> Society's increasing need to protect natural resources that are continuously depleting and the recognition of the damage caused to the general public due to pollution of nature and the environment requires lawmakers to establish substantial levels of punishment to those who carry out these crimes, and the courts in turn to enact a policy of stricter punishment towards those criminals.[180]

The Ministry has also filed several suits against dairy farmers for polluting water sources.[181] As a result, nearly all of the dairy farms in Israel are now equipped with infrastructure to prevent pollutant infiltration.

In 2017, in one of the worst ecological disasters in Israeli history, 100,000 cubic metres of *acidic water* poured into the Ashalim stream near the Dead Sea, when the retention wall at the Rotem Amfert Negev plant, a major producer of phosphate fertilizer, partially collapsed. Around 20 kilometres of the riverbed, which is also a popular hiking area, was affected, causing major ecological damage, destroying flora and killing mammals, reptiles and birds despite immediate efforts to pump out the acid water and set up temporary clean water troughs for wildlife. Hikers are still forbidden to enter the area. In a lawsuit, the State, represented by the Minister of Environmental Protection, sued the company responsible not only for reimbursement of costs related to the cleaning of the area and the rehabilitation of the ecosystem but also for damages to compensate the Israeli public to benefit from and enjoy the nature reserve. After bringing a lawsuit in the District Court, the NGO Adam Teva V'Din, together with local residents, reached an agreement with the company whereby production will be transferred to a site that will not endanger the Ashalim stream and the groundwater. The court also fined the company approximately ILS 100 million.

Although the Ministry has brought many suits regarding water, they often decide to settle with the polluter, robbing judges of a chance to bring the polluters to justice by sentencing them to a tougher punishment and requiring them to pay appropriate amounts. This failure of strict enforcement damages the strength of the

178. For example, *State of Israel v. City of Ashdod* 1872/00, *State of Israel v. Hevel Modiin*, Regional Council 2640/00.

179. Criminal Appeal 408/09 *Hasolelim and others v. Ministry of Environmental Protection, Nazareth District Court.*

180. Criminal Appeal 1223/07 *Salah Ali Murshad et al. v. Ministry of Environmental Protection*, Supreme Court, para. 4.

181. Examples include *Ministry of Environmental Protection/Tel Aviv v. Hefer Dairy,* Netanya Magistrates Court 2144–10-09; *Kibbutz Tzuba v. State of Israel*, Jerusalem District Court 7138/03; *State of Israel v. Kibbutz Naan*, Ramle Magistrates Court 001881/04.

Ministry's enforcement arm by setting a precedent whereby polluters feel that they can escape serious punishment by settling and paying a smaller fine.

V. Regional Water Authorities

A. *Introduction*

75. Rivers and Streams. Israel has one major river, the Jordan, and forty-one streams, most of which flow only during rainy periods. The upper Jordan River brings water from Israel's northern border down to the Kinneret (Sea of Galilee), the source of approximately 20% of Israel's water. The streams are of little importance as sources of drinking water, and have, therefore, been neglected and abused. What little water they had was diverted at source, turning them into drainage and sewage canals. For example, the salt springs by the Sea of Galilee were diverted around the entire sea and dumped into the lower Jordan River, leaving that section of the river uninhabitable to most aquatic life. The Yarqon River was once Israel's second major river, but in the 1950s, the springs at Rosh Ha'ayin, the major source of the Yarqon, were diverted, leaving the river high and dry but for the run-off and treated sewage which are now its main component.

76. It is an axiom that proper water management requires a regional watershed approach.[182] The European Water Framework Directive of 2000 takes a holistic and comprehensive approach to water management as it covers the following relevant components of the water cycle; inland surface waters, transitional waters, coastal waters and groundwaters.[183]

There are differences of opinion about the type of organizations needed to protect a watershed, but the need for a law to protect a water source in its natural environment is imperative. This requires control over three elements: stream intake, stream quality and uses and allocation of costs among polluters. Israel today has two different models of regional watershed management operating side by side. The following analyses the models and describes their merits and disadvantages.

B. *The Drainage Authority Model*

77. In the Mandate period, erosion was a major environmental problem.[184] Therefore, with the creation of the State of Israel, one of the first pieces of legislation passed was the Drainage and Flood Control Authorities Law, 1957.[185] This

182. L.A. Teclaff, *Water Law in Historical Perspective*, 1983 (ECEL: Madeira Declaration on the Sustainable Management of Water, April 1999).
183. 'Directive 2000/60/EC of the European Parliament and of the Council establishing a Framework for the Community Action in the Field of Water Policy', commonly known as the EU Water Framework Directive.
184. H. Kendall, *Village Development in Palestine During the British Mandate* 115 (London: Crown agents for the colonies 1949).
185. 12 L.S.I. 5.

law empowered the Minister of Agriculture to divide the country into Drainage Districts. Until 1996, Israel had twenty-six drainage authorities, operating under power vested in them by the Law. These authorities were unable to develop a full range of protective plans for their respective drainage areas because the areas were too small for effective control. In 1996, the twenty-six authorities were reduced to eleven, aligned as much as possible along catchment basin lines.[186]

In each district, a Drainage Board was formed, composed of representatives of local and regional authorities in the drainage area. In addition to the regional Drainage Boards, a National Drainage Board was established to set policy throughout the country. The Drainage Boards were empowered to prevent soil erosion, control the flow of streams and prevent health hazards, yet they were strictly prohibited from handling sewage. At first, this restriction was an asset. The Drainage Boards acted vigorously to prevent soil erosion and flooding. Yet, as time went on, more and more headwaters of streams were captured for household, industrial and agricultural use. This denied the streams of freshwater intake and left them with agricultural run-off and sewage water, but without enough flow to dilute the sewage. Since the Drainage Boards were prohibited from handling sewage, the result was that the Drainage Boards could do nothing to prevent the inflow of sewage and the streams became sewage carriers.

78. The Drainage Boards of Israel have come to recognize that drainage and flood control, while important, does not compare with the need for the protection of rivers and streams for environmental quality. Several drainage boards have begun the process of transforming themselves from drainage boards to river boards. This has been done on a voluntary basis, promoted by the Ministry of Environmental Protection, through a vehicle known as the Rivers and Streams Administration. This administration is a non-statutory body funded by the Ministry of Environmental Protection, using the Drainage Boards as a platform for funding since no other similar bodies exist.

The Rivers and Streams Administration improved several of Israel's streams by creating parks and scenic walkways along the banks of some of the western flowing streams. The Ministry of Environmental Protection realized, however, that without a statutory vehicle, this programme was doomed for failure because it would be attacked by other sources for providing income to non-statutory groups without the proper framework required by Israel's administrative law. The Ministry, therefore, turned to the Drainage Boards to serve as a platform for the transfer of funds. The Drainage Boards then asked the Ministry to give them the authority to renovate streams under the Rivers and Streams Authorities Law of 1965. An order written by the Minister of Environmental Protection in 2003 gave two drainage authorities the legal powers to act as River Authorities.[187] These powers include deciding on the route of a river or stream, maintaining the landscape on the banks or around springs

186. The Drainage and Flood Control Order (Establishing Drainage Authorities) (Amendment), 1996, K.T. 11.

187. Streams and Springs Authorities Order (Granting the Powers of a River Authority to Drainage Authorities), 2003.

(unless found within the boundaries of a national park or nature reserve) and developing these areas for usage as parks, recreation and sport. They are required to create a work plan with the approval of the Minister of Environmental Protection. It must be drawn up with an ecological and environmental perspective of the entire drainage basin within its boundaries.[188] This includes sustainability, role of ecological systems, quality of water sources, and protection of the biological diversity.

In 2005, six more Drainage Authorities were granted the powers of River Authorities by the government and in 2010, the remaining three Authorities. It is too early to determine if the government initiative to create a National Drainage Authority will supplement or complement the eleven Basin Authorities.

The Minister of Agriculture has commissioned the draft of a new bill for drainage and flood control. The proposed law extends the power of the drainage authorities to control all aspects of river basin management, including preventing pollution and protecting amenity uses. The law has yet to be presented to the Knesset for approval.

C. River Authority Model

79. The second model of authority for managing a stream in Israel is the River Authority. The River and Springs Authorities Law of 1965[189] enables the creation of River Authorities: a board composed of representatives of local authorities and riparian users in a defined watershed with the power to handle pollution inflow, drainage, streamflow and quality and amenities along stream banks.

The law was originally under the control of two ministers, Interior and Agriculture because it affected water quality (Agriculture) and the rights of local authorities (Interior). Unfortunately, this dual control doomed the law to cold storage for twenty-five years because the two ministers never agreed on the creation of a river authority. It came out of the closet only after relentless pressure from the Ministry of Environmental Protection, to which control of the law was transferred in 1989.

The first River Authority, established for the Yarqon River,[190] set a model for the next authority established for the Kishon River.[191] Both were created along similar lines, with a large council setting policy and a small directorate executing it. The Yarqon River Authority has been successful in creating a regional plan for the protection of the river, its banks, and a region quite similar to the catchment basin in which it rests; yet the actual borders of the Authority only reach up to 20 metres from each bank.[192] This has not stopped the Authority from developing parks along the Yarqon River for the benefit of the citizens of the Greater Tel Aviv area, Israel's most populated region.

The Yarqon River Authority has successfully reduced pollution in the river. Today, no raw sewage flows into the river, and the purified effluent flowing in is of

188. *Ibid.*, Art. 3.
189. 19 L.S.I. 149.
190. Yarqon River Authority Order, 1988, K.T. 855.
191. Rivers and Springs Authorities Order (Kishon River Authority), 1995, K.T. 6.
192. Yarqon River Authority Bylaw (Protection of Yarqon River and its Banks), 1994, K.T. 607.

much better quality than during the 1990s. The Government of Israel has approved an expenditure for a further upgrade in the quality of purified effluent inflow polluting the river and also requiring that certain amounts of freshwater be released into the Yarqon to protect its water quality.

This model has tremendous benefits, yet the government of Israel does not recognize that a regional water authority cannot operate only within 20 metres of the banks. And without the power to supply water, purify sewage, and do other water-related activities in the basin, the Yarqon River Authority will continue to operate with one hand tied behind its back.

The Kishon River Authority has had similar problems, although it had more sources of pollution than the Yarqon River. In fact, two tragic incidents, in both the Yarqon and the Kishon, raised public awareness of just how dangerous these waters can be. In the Yarqon, there were cases filed against the government of Israel for the death of athletes who were injured or who died when falling from a temporary bridge over the Yarqon River.[193] In the Kishon River, cases have been filed against the government by divers from the Marine Commando Unit claiming that they developed cancer as a result of years of diving in the Kishon River as part of their diving exercises.[194] These two cases have put the spotlight on the Yarqon and Kishon Rivers, and they have enabled the River Authorities in both situations to raise interest and support from both the public and the government, for the needs of these two authorities and the improvement of surface water quality.

The Yarqon River Authority spearheaded a plan to build artificial wetlands which further improve the quality of the purified effluent before reaching the river. The Kishon River Authority has dredged the lower 7 kilometres of the riverbed contaminated for decades by industrial waste and municipal wastewater. The polluted sediment will be biologically treated and become part of a public park.

A third river authority, the Beer Sheva Stream Authority, has been established for the purpose of creating a 1,000-acre park within the city of Beer Sheva and rehabilitating the Beer Sheva Stream and its environs, balancing between nature and recreational uses.[195] It is a hybrid between a river authority and a government project. Upon the completion of the rehabilitation works, the authority will be transferred from the Stream Authority to the City of Beer Sheva.

80. National River Association (NRA). Besides the above-mentioned statutory river administrations, the NRA was established in 1993. Initiated and headed by the Ministry of Environmental Protection and the JNF, the NRA serves as a coordinating body for the numerous agencies which deal with rivers in Israel and oversees restoration of the country's rivers and the preservation and renovation of natural and historical sites along riverbanks. It includes representatives from the Environment, Interior, Tourism and Agriculture Ministries, the Water Commission, the Nature and National Parks Authority, and local authorities adjacent to the rivers. So far, regional river administrations have been set up for the following rivers: Lachish, Zippori,

193. Criminal Case No. 15237/97 *State of Israel v. Micah Bar Ilan et al.*

194. *See* report of the Government Investigation Committee on the Results of Military Activities in the Kishon River and the Surrounding Water on the Health of IDF Soldiers, 2001.

195. *Rivers and Springs Authorities Order (Beer Sheva River Authority) 2011*, K.T. 6796 p. 680.

Ayalon, Taninim, Hadera, Alexander, Soreq, Harod, Na'aman, Besor, and the Lower Jordan. These are in addition to the statutory administrations which already exist for the Yarqon and Kishon Rivers and the Beer Sheva Stream. Master plans have been prepared or are in the process of being prepared for these rivers, and parks have been developed around the Lachish, Harod, Hadera, Kishon, Alexander and Taninim Rivers. As their budget dwindled, the river administrations lost their effectiveness.

D. Kinneret Administration

81. Israel has only one freshwater lake famous for its natural beauty, and historical and religious significance. The lake has not only more than one name, but also has a multitude of uses: swimming, boating, fishing and baptizing, and it is a major source of drinking water.

Control over the lake and its catchment basin is split among numerous bodies. The Kinneret Authority or '*Minhelet Hakinneret*' was established to coordinate government and local activity in the basin. It works alongside and in the same offices as the Kinneret Drainage Authority. The coordination involves all the duties of a lake administration without being designated as such by law. All planning in the lake's catchment basin is coordinated with the Minhelet. The Minhelet fields inspectors to prevent theft of lake aggregates, supervise the operation of tourist facilities along the lake and provide minimum sanitation facilities and trash collection for visitors. The Minhelet supervises fishing and transportation in the lake with the help of the Ministries of Agriculture and Transportation. Finally, the Minhelet receives up-to-date information on the health of the lake from the Kinneret limnological laboratory, which has been monitoring the lake's quality for years.

Previous to 2008, the Kinneret beaches came under the control of five different local authorities. The large number of administrators impeded efficient management and resulted in planning infractions, inflated beach entry fees and deficient infrastructure. They did not have a comprehensive view of the Kinneret's multiple uses and fragile ecosystem. Thus in 2008, the Knesset passed a law creating the Kinneret Association of Towns.[196] It too is run from the offices of the Kinneret Drainage Authority. Its members include representatives from three local authorities, seven government authorities, a representative of the Society for the Protection of Nature and a member of the public in the sphere of nature protection.

There is severe pressure on the Kinneret, and the government will one day have to decide if it wants a lake with a multitude of uses or a multitude of uses without a lake. For example, in 2010, the Minister of Agriculture announced a ban on fishing for two years to protect the dwindling numbers of fish in the lake. But due to

196. Law for Regulating the Management of the Kinneret Coast, 2008, S.H. 2148, 450. Representatives from the government, the five local authorities and public organizations. It has a mandate to regulate the management of the Kinneret coast and to enforce laws protecting the Kinneret. The law also includes an amendment to the Coastal Environment Law which would apply the law to the Kinneret in addition to the Mediterranean and the Red Sea coastal areas.

pressure from local fishermen, the ban was cut down to a four-month annual break during the spawning season of the Saint Peter's fish, the most popular Kinneret species.

§3. Conflicts

I. Introduction

82. In the Middle East, water has been a source of conflict since ancient times.[197] The years have only changed the names of the contestants and their preferred choice of weapons. Conflict over water rights presently exists between Israel and her neighbours, and, within Israel, between the various government agencies responsible for water management.

II. Internal Conflicts

83. Challenges to the Government. Enforcement of water laws and regulations is essential in preserving and improving the state of water in Israel. However, a number of obstacles prevent administrative bodies from carrying out their enforcement role effectively.

84. Fragmented Authority. The original Water Laws of the 1950s empowered the Minister of Agriculture and the Water Commissioner with overall authority over Israel's water resources. This authority left unattended in the Minister's hands, was gradually parcelled out to other public authorities. The Minister of Health gained control over drinking water and wastewater quality. The Minister of Environmental Protection took over from the Minister of Agriculture the power to determine the quality of Israel's national water sources as well as the power to prevent pollution. The local authorities were granted the power to supply drinking water to their residents and transfer wastewater to sewage treatment plants. In 1996, the new Minister of Infrastructure took over from the Minister of Agriculture the power over both the water supply and the handling of sewage. The Minister of Agriculture is left with the power over drainage and flood control.

This diversification of power has not strengthened government control over water resources; it has simply created waste and bureaucratic infighting at the public expense. As a result, the Ministry of the Treasury, responsible for government fiscal

197. For example, 'The Oath of Beer Sheva': Genesis XXI, 25: 'And Abraham reproved Abimelech because of the well of water which Abimelech's servants had violently taken away'. And Abimelech said 'I know not who hath done this thing'. And Abraham took sheep and oxen and gave them to Abimelech and they two made a covenant; Abimelech said unto Abraham 'What mean these seven ewe lambs?' And he said 'Verily these seven ewe lambs shalt thou take of my hand that it may be a witness unto me that I have digged this well'.

'Where for that place was called Beer Sheva because there they swore both of them'.

responsibility, has been looking towards reducing government involvement in the supply and management of water and sewage by transferring this function to private companies.[198]

An example of ministry infighting is the approval of regulations regarding fuel pipelines, whose purpose is to decrease the chance of leaks from fuel pipelines in order to prevent groundwater pollution from gas stations. The Ministry of Environmental Protection and the Water Authority were unable to agree on the division of authority over them, and regulations were not approved. In 2004, the IUED brought suit in the High Court of Justice demanding action by the two authorities. As a result, in 2006, the Minister for Environmental Protection promulgated regulations for minimizing the risk of fuel leaks. The regulations include instructions for building and operating fuel pipelines. These were followed by Water Authority rules delineating procedures to be followed in case of a fuel leak.[199]

85. Legal Enforcement. In order for polluters to take their environmental responsibility seriously and respect the authority of enforcing bodies, judges must make decisions that cause industries and local authorities to take responsibility for their actions. The Water Law of Israel incorporates serious criminal punishment for ones violating the law. These punishments were rarely used from 1959 to the late 1990s. Since then, however, there has been a serious change in the attitude of the government ministries responsible for water polluters and the judges responsible for enforcing the law's provisions.

Since the late 1990s, numerous criminal charges have been filed against mayors of over thirty communities in Israel for allowing untreated effluent to flow from their towns and cities. There have also been a number of cases filed against individuals and companies for pollution of water sources. Some of the fines have reached serious proportions of over ILS 0.5 million.

There is, however, an argument that has been put forth by the Ministry of Environmental Protection that the fines still do not reflect the benefits gained by polluters for their failure to meet basic criteria. Those arguing for heavy fines or even jail sentences point out that Israel has yet to implement the full effects of the polluter-pays principle. The argument here is that as long as a company can make more profit from polluting than from paying the costs of environmental harm, the company will continue to do so. This problem was addressed in the 2008 amendment to the Water Law, as part of the Law for Environmental Protection (Polluter Pays) (Amendment of Laws) ['Polluter Pays Law'], which increased penalties and gave the courts the power to assess fines equal to the economic benefits achieved by polluting. However, time will tell whether judges will use this power to substantially increase fines and penalties for offenders.

86. Water Supply Shortage. Chronic water supply shortages and the ensuing public outcry resulted in not one, but two national inquiries, a Knesset committee in 2002 and an independent inquiry in 2010. Both agreed that the water shortage was

198. *See* para. 88. The Water and Sewerage Companies Act.
199. Water Regulation (Prevention of Water Pollution) (Fuel Lines), 2006; Water Rules (Treatment of Water Pollution from Fuel), 2010.

man-made, and not a result of climate change and less rainfall. A lack of planning and initiative by the national government ignored the writing on the wall. A lack of transparency and public involvement, red tape, and lack of trained personnel exacerbated the situation.

Over the last decade, Israel has built five state-of-the-art desalination plants, supplying 600 million cubic metres of water, almost 40% of Israel's water needs. This has given Israel more room to manoeuvre in years of scant rainfall. But the environmental price tag includes the emission of large amounts of salt and other chemicals to the sea, high energy needs and the building of industrial facilities on precious coastal space. The Law for the Prevention of Sea Pollution from Land-Based Sources, 1988 requires permits for the release of any liquid or solid substance to the sea, including brine and wastewater from desalination plants.

III. External Conflicts

87. Between 1993 and 1995, peace treaties were signed between Israel and Jordan[200] and between Israel and the Palestinian Authority. The treaties have provisions regarding use and misuse of water resources to resolve past conflicts and prevent future ones. According to Article 6, paragraph 4 of the Treaty between Israel and Jordan, the parties agree to search for ways to alleviate water shortage and to cooperate in the following fields: (a) development of existing and new water resources; (b) prevention of contamination of water resources; (c) mutual assistance in the alleviation of water shortages; (d) transfer of information and joint research and development in water-related subjects.

Annex II of the Treaty contains provisions for the implementation of its terms, including mutual obligations to prevent pollution of the Jordan and Yarmouk Rivers, and joint groundwater basins. The agreement contains provisions forbidding unrestricted flow of untreated effluent by either of the parties. It also requires mutual agreement to divert the flow of stream waters. Section 40 of the Agreement between Israel and the Palestinian Authority sets out the principles for cooperation in the management of sewerage and waterworks. To implement this obligation, a Joint Water Committee (JWC) was established to manage water and sewage-related infrastructure in the West Bank. The agreement also obligates each side to take all necessary measures to prevent pollution or degradation in the quality of water resources. The Israel-Jordan agreement has been kept according to the letter and spirit of the law. Israel is obligated to transfer 55 million cubic metres of water a year to the Jordanians because of their very great need.[201]

An agreement signed in 2021 raised this amount to 100 million cubic metres.

At the COP 27 Climate Summit in 2022 in Sharm El Sheik, Israel and Jordan signed a memorandum of understanding (MOU) to move ahead with a water-for-energy deal after an initial examination of the project found it to be feasible. The idea is for Jordan to build 600 megawatts of solar power capacity that would be

200. Treaty of Peace Between The State of Israel and The Hashemite Kingdom of Jordan, 1994.
201. Figures from Israel Water Commissioner, 'Water in Israel, Consumption and Production 2001', December 2002.

exported to Israel. In return, Israel would provide water-scarce Jordan with 200 million cubic metres of desalinated water.[202]

The situation regarding the Palestinians has become much more complex for two main reasons. First, area water sources and flows are interconnected with little relationship to political boundaries. Second, despite several interim agreements, a final agreement was never reached and the conflict between the two sides continues unabated. The Israel-Palestinian agreements call for several joint committees to be established regarding environmental issues, but the only active committee is the JWC. The resolution of conflicts has become much more difficult in the face of continued conflict. Additionally, both sides have opposing interests; whereas the Palestinians want to increase their water supply, Israel wants to protect water sources from pollution and over-pumping while maintaining present extraction amounts. Moreover, although the environment may not be a high priority for the Israeli government, it is even lower down on the priority list for the Palestinian Authority, which prevents ongoing talks and environmental projects on a government level. NGOs and local initiatives have had more success in creating individual instances of participation in this area.

88. Transboundary Pollution. In addition to the normal problems of implementation of water law provisions within the State of Israel, there are serious problems of transboundary pollution. Most of Israel's western flowing streams are polluted not only by sources in Israel but also by factories and cities in the Palestinian Authority (PA). Within the PA, there is only one functioning wastewater treatment plant in El Bireh.[203] Plans for joint sewage purification plants along those streams which affect both Palestinians and Israelis have not been implemented. There has been a movement to face the impasse. A Hebron sewage treatment plant has been approved by the JWC, and the World Bank has agreed to fund it. In the Tulkarm area, Palestinian sewage is treated as it crosses the border. Not all raw sewage flows from the PA to Israel. The raw sewage from the eastern side of the city of Jerusalem flows to the Dead Sea and pollutes the Kidron Valley. Along the way, it also collects raw sewage flows from residents of the Palestinian towns of Beit Jala, Beit Sahur, Bethlehem, Azariya, Obadiya and Doha. The amount of sewage is quite substantial and, therefore, there is an on-and-off debate between Israel and the Palestinian Authority about the construction of a joint sewage purification plant to reduce the pollutant overload of the Kidron. In the past, the cities of Jerusalem and Bethlehem tried to build a joint sewage treatment plant, but the PA rejected the proposal. To date, there has been little progress made, but there is presently work being done to either develop a joint sewage purification plant or individual units. The authors initiated the construction of a pilot neighbourhood wetland system that will prevent water pollution and allow safe reuse of the treated sewage. A larger system is now in the planning stages, capable of treating the sewage of 1,500 people.

---

202. https://www.reuters.com/business/cop/israel-jordan-move-forward-with-water-for-energy-deal-2022-11-08/ (last visited 14 Apr. 2023).
203. O. Tal-Spiro, *Israeli-Palestinian Cooperation on Water Issues, Knesset Research & Information Center*, 5 (February 2011).

But one can say with a great deal of certitude that until the situation is resolved diplomatically, there will hardly be any effective long-term overall solutions for joint pollution problems. This is also true for shared aquifer problems. The JWC makes every effort to improve the coordination between the two parties, but this coordination will still require, in the final analysis, a political solution before the JWC can implement a long-range plan.

§4. Miscellaneous Water Laws

I. Introduction

89. As was noted previously, the Water Law conceptualized total control of the water cycle under one ministry. Over time, however, this concept eroded in the face of pressure from other ministries.

II. Drinking Water Quality

90. Israel's potable water comes from three sources: the Kinneret and its tributaries supply 20%, desalinated seawater almost 40%, and groundwater accounts for the rest. Protection of the Kinneret as a source of drinking water has been briefly discussed above. Protection of groundwater, as previously mentioned, is the responsibility of the Water Authority and the Ministries of Infrastructure and Environmental Protection. The Ministry of Environmental Protection has never published regulations for the quality of ground and surface water. On the other hand, it has published regulations to prohibit the use of certain products and practices to keep the surface and groundwater free from pollution.[204]

While a step forward, none of these methods has been adequate to protect the quality of surface and groundwater from deteriorating during the past twenty years. Today, one finds a cocktail of pollutants in Israel's groundwater due to a lack of proper administration above ground.

During the Mandate period, and immediately afterwards, drinking water was the responsibility of local authorities supervised by health and sanitation officials. This historical fact continued, even after the passing of the Water Law in 1959. In 1970, the Ministry of Health was empowered to promulgate drinking water standards.[205] Standards were published in 1975 and updated again in 1989.[206] In 2000, the Minister of Health signed an amended version of the Public Health Regulations which raise chemical standards for water quality to very stringent levels. Maximum levels for thirty-eight new chemical substances – including pesticides, organic solvents and petroleum products – were set for the first time while existing standards for

204. *See also* para. 64 *Legal protection of water sources.*
205. 24 L.S.I. 107.
206. Public Health Regulations (Sanitary Quality of Drinking Water), 1974; 1989, K.T. 697.

nitrates, lead, cadmium and zinc were tightened. The regulations relate to seventy-five substances and determine sampling frequencies for different tests. Most importantly, they increase the frequency of complete chemical tests from once in ten years to once in three years.

Updated water quality standards were published in 2013 based on the recommendations of an inter-ministerial committee. They include limits and frequency of testing for nearly 100 pollutants. They leave open the addition of magnesium to desalinated water. For now, the regulations only require economic and scientific expert recommendations concerning magnesium and a pilot plant to be set up at one of the desalination plants. Based on these, the Health Ministry now recommends adding 30 milligrams/litre of magnesium to desalinated drinking water, which is the average level found in Israel's natural water sources.

Enforcement of the standards is in the hands of the local authorities with supervision by the Ministry of Health. Actual samples of drinking water are taken frequently for examination to make sure that drinking water quality is maintained. When a source is found polluted, the Water Commissioner is required to find an alternative source of water. Pursuant to the 2001 amendment to the Ordinance for Municipalities (the new version), municipalities have a legal obligation to distribute an annual report to their residents on the quality of the drinking water provided to them. The Minister of the Interior, in consultation with the Minister of Health, has also published rules regarding the manner in which the report is to be circulated. This requirement is important as it allows for scrutiny by the public.

National Outline Plan 34B-4 provides a planning framework for protection of groundwater. For example, the building of potentially polluting facilities in water-sensitive areas requires proof of the actions to be taken that will prevent water pollution and protection of groundwater.

III. Sewage Water

91. Management and control of sewage are divided among several ministries and local authorities. First, it is the responsibility of each local authority to provide basic sewerage services for its inhabitants.[207] This power enables the local authority to collect fees for the planning, building and operation of a sewerage system. It also enables the local authority to sell its piped sewage. Furthermore, the local authority is authorized to build sewage purification plants for reclamation of its sewage. Yet, the actual process of planning, building and operating a municipal sewerage system can require the intervention of five statutory bodies. First, in order to build the system, a municipality must have planning approval from the District Planning Commission empowered under the Planning and Building Law. Second, approval of funding by the local authority and its residents requires the approval of the Minister of Interior. Third, building a sewage purification plant requires the approval of the Ministry of Health, and if the plant is to discharge sewage outside municipal boundaries, also the approval of the Ministry of Infrastructure and the Ministry of Environmental Protection. The destination of purified sewage water may need more than

207. Local Authorities (Sewerage) Law, 1962, 16 L.S.I. 81.

just the approval of the Ministries of Infrastructure and Environment. Israel reuses nearly 90% of its effluent for agricultural usage. If the purified effluent is destined for irrigation or an 'economic use' (undefined in the law), the quality of the effluent is determined by Ministry of Health regulations.[208] If the purified effluent is destined for the sea, the municipality needs approval of the effluent quality and quantity from the committee set up under the Law for the Prevention of Pollution of the Sea from Land-Based Sources, 1988.[209]

The government has adopted the findings of a professional committee, which set strict parameters for the standard of purified sewage to be used for irrigation purposes or released into the nation's waterways. In 2010, the new parameters were promulgated as regulations.[210]

These come on top of existing regulations setting threshold values for salt concentrations in industrial sewage.[211] The regulations aim at reducing the salinity of sewage in Israel, which constitutes a major problem due to the country's use of reclaimed effluents for irrigation purposes. Other regulations establish pH values in order to prevent the pollution of water sources from the impacts of corrosion generated by industrial sewage and limit the volume of wastewater and the concentration of pollutants in it.[212]

IV. Privatization

92. *The Water and Sewerage Companies Act.* Israel's first attempt at privatization of a water service occurred with the registration of the Company for Treatment and Reuse of Sewage in the Hadera River Region. This association, although registered as a private company in the Companies Registry, is actually composed of seven local authorities. It is, therefore, not privatization in the real sense, but an attempt to bring fiscal responsibility to local government management of an area-wide wastewater treatment plant. The result of this innovative approach has been to bring a business-like attitude to water management in the Hadera region. This attitude enabled the creation of a similar corporation for the town of Pardes Hannah-Karkur to privatize the water, sewerage and drainage systems of the town. For the first time in Israel's history, the entire water infrastructure of a local authority was tendered to a concessionaire for twenty years. The regional sewage company for Hadera has also created a regulatory authority that supervises the newly appointed concessionaire and serves as a liaison between the private operator of a public service and the public at large. The privatization of the Pardes Hannah-Karkur water sewage and drainage system has not been successful. Reviewing the original concept created in 1996, the present situation is one of serious conflict between the local

208. Public Health Rules (Purification of Sewage for Irrigation), 1981, K.T. 1357. *See also* Public Health Regulations (Standards for Sewage), 1992, K.T. 1033 and Public Health Regulations (Quality Standards for Sewage and Rules for Sewage Purification), 2010, K.T. 6886.
209. 44 L.S.I. unpublished; S.H. 5750, 250.
210. Public Health Regulations (Quality Standards for Sewage and Rules for Sewage Purification), 2010.
211. Business Licensing Regulations (Salt Concentrations in Industrial Sewage), 2003.
212. Water Regulations (Prevention of Water Pollution) (Metals and Other Pollutants), 2000.

authority and the concessionaire. The conflict seems unbridgeable, and the parties are locked in a legal battle over control of the water sewage and drainage systems. Apparently, the conflict revolves around a total lack of understanding of the concept of a concession vis-à-vis public ownership and operation of a water sewage and drainage system.

Despite this failure, the government, encouraged by the Ministry of the Treasury, finally succeeded in passing a law to enable the privatization of water and sewage systems, entitled the Law for Water and Sewerage Companies Act.[213] The law requires local authorities to create either a local authority company or a private company to own and operate the system. The Ministry of the Interior has overall responsibility for executing the law and has created a new department for water administration within the Ministry.

Supporters of the law claim that it will create efficiencies unheard of in local authorities, and will not only raise the quality of water supply and service to consumers, but it will also reduce the cost. Presently, the local authorities buy water mostly from Mekorot (the national supplier of water in Israel) and sell this water to its residents, thus making a profit. This profit is an important income for the local authority, which it uses in many different areas such as building schools and planting flowers, and not exclusively for water and sewage-related expenses.

Some environmental authorities believe the profit should be used to properly manage the water, which is what citizens are paying for, rather than other projects that are carried out by the local authority for political purposes. Failing to properly maintain the system has caused local authorities to lose water due to leaking pipes. It is hoped that this new law will stop the transfer of fees charged for water and sewage services to other municipal services and employee benefits as well as streamline municipal services. Under the law, profits may only be allocated towards uses that are in line with the company's purposes.

This legislation has caused much debate in Israel. On the one hand, some feel that the Act introduces a progressive idea that may be damaging to the local authority in the short term as it strips them of a source of income. However, it has the potential to benefit local authorities in the long-term because once the company makes enough money, it can give out dividends to the local authority. Moreover, they argue that the company, by law, can sell some of its shares (49%) to people in the private market, thus getting property out to the market, allowing the local authority to still control the company (by owning 51%) and having 49% as income to use in their jurisdiction.

On the other hand, some environmentalists argue against privatization. First, because the water system is a cycle, they believe that the system is better controlled with an integrated approach. This approach requires that the overall authority for the system rests with one government body that will have the flexibility to make changes in the water supply when necessary. They argue that privatization breaks the hydrological cycle by allowing private companies to control water supply and sewage. Additionally, these companies have no incentive to reduce water usage and protect a stream from sewage that they purify. In fact, they tend to encourage water use and purify sewage at the lowest quality allowed by law in order to cut costs.

213. Water and Sewerage Companies Act 2001.

Second, some are ideologically opposed to selling water as a natural resource since the commons belong to everyone and should remain in the hands of the people, held in trust by the State (one of the more important statements of the Israel Water Law).

The Law for Water and Sewage companies grants 180 local authorities the right to privatize their system, with a regulator to oversee the regulation of fees. In England, the system is difficult enough to regulate, where there are ten private water companies. With 180 water companies, regulation will be impossible. Furthermore, no one has proven that the English system of privatization has been successful, except in raising prices. Public English water companies worked successfully prior to privatization, and there was no reason to believe that they would not continue doing so without privatization.

Privatization under the law has begun, but problems have arisen. Local authorities that are not of a certain size may not initiate privatization alone but must do so in collaboration with other local authorities, in order to take advantage of size. But, this condition creates a highly complicated and bureaucratic procedure. Each local authority must put the idea of privatization up for public debate. Then, the local authorities must agree on how to work together. Afterwards, permission must be sought from the government.

Once permission is received, managing a company between local authorities becomes complicated. All local authorities must be consulted regarding decisions made. Additionally, if one city requires more reparation, entailing expenses on behalf of the company, other cities lose profits that they would otherwise receive.

As of 2015, there are fifty-five water and sewage companies operating in Israel. In order to reduce this number, the Water Authority has proposed combining companies into fifteen regional companies/authorities. Those local authorities without companies would be added to the regional companies. The government has approved this proposal, but it has not been implemented. The proposal has also been brought to the Knesset as an amendment to the Law for Water and Sewage Companies but has not been passed into law.

A 2016 amendment to the law gives regional water and sewage companies additional powers, including drainage and flood prevention.[214]

The Water Authority claims that the switch to water companies has resulted in improvements in several areas, mainly in an increase in investment in water infrastructure and water loss reduction. In contrast, a proposal has been raised in the Knesset Interior and Environment committee to cancel the Law for Water and Sewage Companies.[215]

---

214. Law for Water and Sewage Companies, Amendment No. 6 2013 and Amendment No. 10 2016.

215. R. Benita, *Local Authorities in Israel, Background Paper for the Interior and Environment Committee* 34–36 (Knesset Research & Information Center, 17 May 2015). (Prevention) Ordinance (New Version), 1980.

§5. Marine Pollution

I. Introduction

93. Although the Water Law of 1959 is all-encompassing, the Minister of Agriculture never included marine pollution under ministerial authority. Marine pollution remained, for years, the responsibility of the Ministry of Transportation. This responsibility included protection of pollution of the sea by ships and port facilities regulated by the Ports Ordinance. Under pressure from the EPS of the Ministry of Interior, the Ministry of Transportation transferred its power to prevent pollution of the sea from oil to the Ministry of the Interior in 1979. This enabled the Ministry of the Interior to control two significant laws for the prevention of pollution of the sea: the Seawater Pollution by Oil,[216] and the Prevention of Sea Pollution (Dumping of Waste) Law, 1983.[217] With the creation of the Ministry of Environmental Protection in 1988, these laws were transferred from the Ministry of the Interior to the Ministry of Environmental Protection. In addition, the Ministry of Environmental Protection passed regulations in 1999 in order to incorporate the shipboard oil pollution emergency plan of the Barcelona Convention into Israeli law. These regulations prohibit the dumping of oil in waters without a permit.[218]

II. Pollution of the Sea from Oil

94. Israel has had modern legislation to control and prevent sea pollution from oil since 1980, with the passage of the new version of the old ordinance for the prevention of sea pollution from oil. This law requires all sea-going vessels to keep a log book and report every movement of oil from and to the ship. There is a stiff penalty in the law for failure to record the movement of oil. The second major section of the law deals with dumping oil into the sea. The law empowers the Minister of Environmental Protection to order the owners of the ship to take all steps necessary to prevent an oil spill or keep the spill to a minimum. For example, the Minister may order the ship to remain stationary. Once the oil is spilt into the sea, there is absolute liability on the part of the ship's owner or captain for the spill. Both are subject to a fine or imprisonment, or both. In addition, courts are empowered to burden the ship's owner with the cost of clean-up of the spill.

The third section of the law creates an ocean clean-up fund for oil spills. The fund is managed by an inter-ministerial committee. Its function is to receive all fines allocated against ship owners for oil spills and establish and maintain a mechanism for oil prevention, control and clean-up.

216. Seawater Pollution by Oil (Prevention) Ordinance (New Version), 1980, 3 L.S.I. (NV) 122.
217. 37 L.S.I. 127.
218. KT-5968 at 8 (1999).

III. Enforcement and Control

95. The law has been rigorously enforced. A fund has been established for oil pollution and money from this fund maintains a team of inspectors and operators to prevent and cleanup oil spills. Heavy fines have been levied against violators, and clean-up costs have also been levied in certain cases. In 2003 alone, twenty-three criminal investigations were held regarding sea pollution. In addition, Israel has built coastal facilities for bilge water to prevent this type of sea pollution.

In 2018, a ship docked at Haifa Port was convicted of incorrect management of log books and illegal dumping of oil in the sea, as per the Ordinance and Regulations for the prevention of sea pollution from oil.[219] A plea bargain was reached, with fines paid by both the company and two employees.

IV. Prevention of Sea Pollution from Other Sources

96. Up until 1983, Israel had a patchwork of laws dealing with sea pollution from solid waste, sewage and other sources. For the most part, this legislation handled a portion of the problem at a particular source. For instance, the Port's Ordinance prohibited the dumping of refuse in port waters and required boats to use the services of the Port Authority to collect refuse.[220] The Water Law and the Local Authorities (Sewerage) Law were aimed at preventing stream pollution which, in turn, prevents pollution of the sea by sewage. An additional law for the protection of bathing places was intended to protect bathers from the pollution of beaches.[221] None of these laws were effective, however, because they were used mainly to prevent nuisances, not sea pollution. Since 1983, things have changed. In 1983, Israel ratified the Dumping Treaty and made the Treaty's provision a part of Israel's legal framework. The Prevention of Sea Pollution (Dumping of Waste) Law, 1983, requires that all those intending to dump any material into the sea be required to obtain a permit. Permits are to be issued by a permanent inter-ministerial committee established for this purpose under the law.

A person found violating the law's provisions is subject to a fine. In addition, the court is empowered to penalize the offender by requiring him/her to pay clean-up costs, both in finding the waste dumped and in cleaning up the polluted coast.

In 2010, the Transport Minister promulgated regulations concerning the dumping of trash from ships.[222] They forbid dumping trash at sea that is comprised of plastics or harmful materials and put the responsibility for upholding the regulations on the ship's captain. A plan for garbage management is required for every ship, written in a language understood by the crew. Every international journey requires keeping a log that lists every act of waste disposal at sea, by incineration, or disposal in port.

---

219. *State of Israel v. River Elbe Shipping Ltd.*, Criminal Case No. 35323–08-17.
220. Ports Regulations, 1971, K.T. 306.
221. Bathing Places (Regulation) Law, 1964, 18 L.S.I. 170.
222. Ports Regulations (Dumping of Trash from Ships), 2010, K.T. 6854, 604.

97. *The Law for the Prevention of Sea Pollution from Land-based Sources, 1988* is based on the international treaty of the same name. The law forbids the release of any solid or liquid substance directly into the sea, or in any fashion that might indirectly allow it to flow into the sea.[223] The law creates an inter-ministerial committee to grant permits to those requesting permission to dump into the sea. Regulations passed in 2011 allow levies to be imposed on permit holders, based on the types of pollutants discharged and the amounts.[224] Those violating the law's provisions are subject to a fine.

The law even allows private criminal suits against violators when the State fails to act. As in previous sea pollution prevention laws, the court adjudicating the case is allowed to charge the violators of this law with clean-up costs. Regulations under the law have been promulgated by the Ministry of Environmental Protection.[225] These regulations describe the permit process and limit the powers of the inter-ministerial committee with regard to the issuance of permits. The regulations require those requesting a permit to supply complete data on the type of liquid or solid waste flowing into the sea as well as on the site where the waste is to be deposited. In addition, the regulations grant the inter-ministerial committee the power to permit the flow of waste into the sea only if there is no other method of disposal feasible and the polluter has installed the best available technology economically achievable in order to avoid pollution as far as possible.

An important amendment was made to the law in 2005. First, and most importantly, it empowers courts to levy fines higher than those previously allowed. Specifically, the fines may reflect all of the profits the polluter earned by not installing appropriate mechanisms to prevent pollution.[226] Although courts have general authority to give these types of fines, writing them into law makes it declarative, and is an important step towards building recognition amongst the judiciary and industry of the heavy cost of polluting the environment. Second, it grants additional power to the Ministry of Environmental Protection to issue administrative orders and injunctions.[227]

The enforcement powers were further increased as part of the 'Polluter Pays' law, which increased the maximum amounts of fines. In an interesting twist, it does not allow assessing fines lower than the maximum amount prescribed by the law without ministerial permission.

98. *Protection of the Coastal Environment.* Much of Israel's coast has been taken away from the public for other uses, including naval bases, ports, power plants and private interests. During the 1990s, several coastal cities approached the National Planning Council with plans to build marinas. These plans also incorporated building schemes for support services, tourism facilities and vacation homes. As a result, further sections of the coast changed from public to private hands. In a 2002 Supreme Court case brought by the IUED against a company building on the

223. 44 L.S.I. unpublished; S.H. 5750, 250.
224. Prevention of Sea Pollution from Land-Based Sources Regulation (Prevention of Sea Pollution Levy), 2011, K.T. 7031, 1356.
225. Regulations for the Prevention of Sea Pollution from Land Based Sources, 1990, K.T.
226. Law for the Prevention of Sea Pollution from Land Based Sources, 1988, s. 6-6B, S.H. 1256, 118.
227. Law for the Prevention of Sea Pollution from Land Based Sources, 1988, s. 8A, S.H. 1256, 118.

Haifa coast, the Supreme Court stopped the building and required the buildings already erected to be used for tourism and not residential purposes.[228] The court held that the small and dwindling amount of Israel's public coastal area needs to be protected for the common good. Public pressure on the Knesset resulted in the passing of the Protection of the Coastal Environment Law, 2004 for the purpose of protecting and preserving the coastal environment as a unique asset for the benefit of the public. The law extends the coastal area protected from the water to 300 metres inland, prevents building within 100 meters of the coastline and assures an open public right of way along the entire length of the shore. It also gives the Minister of Environmental Protection the right to impose fees and to issue orders to prevent or remove environmental damage to the coastal environment. The Law creates a special planning committee to review all building plans within the 300-metre open space. To date, the committee has applied stringent criteria to keep the coast open to the public. NGOs have been leading the fight to give the public right of way to walk along the coast as well as the beaches of the Kinneret uninterrupted. After a five-year legal battle, the District Court overruled the appeal of Kibbutz Ein Gev on the shores of the Kinneret, requiring the kibbutz to remove fencing and other barriers preventing free access to pedestrians along the shore.[229]

In a 2017 Tel Aviv District Court decision, the court held that the coastline should be measured at a height of 0.75 meters above sea level since the level of 0.00 is underwater most of the time.[230] This was already agreed upon in professional discussions leading up to the passing of the Law for Coastal Protection and was seen as a compromise between 0.00 and 1.5 meters as recommended by some experts. In an appeal to the Supreme Court, this ruling was upheld.[231]

Since Israel has only one lake inhabitable to sea life, artificial fish ponds are used to grow fresh-water fish. A similar intensive method is used to grow fish in the Mediterranean Sea, comprised of floating cages in which fish are raised. In both methods, the concentration of so many fish in such a small area creates large amounts of nitrogen-rich waste. In land-based fish ponds, after the fish are removed, the water is flushed out, while in the Mediterranean Sea, the waste goes directly into the Sea. The latest statistics from the Ministry of Agriculture show that 90% of the fish eaten in Israel are imported. The remainder (11,000 tons) comes from fish ponds and 3,500 tons from the Mediterranean Sea and the Kinneret.[232]

---

228. *Supreme Court Civil Appeal 1054/98, Carmel Coast Vacation and Tourism Ltd. v. Israel Union for Environmental Defence* et al.
229. Nazareth District Court, Criminal Appeal 16147–04-17 *Kibbutz Ein Gev v. Ministry for Environmental Protection.*
230. Tel Aviv District Court, Administrative Appeal 27857–04-14 *Forum for Coastal Protection v. Bat Yam Local Planning and Building Committee.*
231. Supreme Court sitting as a Court of Administrative Appeals, Case No. 9557/17, *Bat Yam Local Planning and Building Committee v. Forum for Coastal Protection.*
232. Ministry of Agriculture report on the fish eaten in Israel, 29 Aug. 2020.

V. The Dead Sea

99. The Dead Sea is truly unique.[233] It is the world's saltiest body of water situated at its lowest spot. It is a part of the Great Rift Valley, extending from the middle of Africa to Syria and Lebanon. Although it sits in the centre of a harsh desert area, its springs are an important stopping point for birds migrating between Europe and Africa.

Since 1960, the Dead Sea is losing about 1.25 meters a year. At one time, the Dead Sea received 1.75 billion cubic metres of water a year, and this amount has been reduced by over 1.25 billion cubic metres a year as a result of the diversion of the sources of Lake Kinneret and Jordan River by Israel and the Yarmouk River by Jordan. In addition to water being diverted before it even reaches the Dead Sea, the Dead Sea Works in both Jordan and Israel use 300 million cubic metres of water a year for mineral extraction, further reducing the amount of water in the Dead Sea.

Due to the falling water level, in 1977, the Dead Sea permanently split into two sections. In the Northern Basin, the water level continues to drop at a rate of 1+ metres per year. The Southern Basin would have dried up had it not been turned into an artificial evaporation pond by the Dead Sea Works in Jordan and Israel. The Southern Basin also serves as a tourist attraction in both Israel and Jordan, with several hotels along the shores. Besides the additional 300 million cubic metres of water used by the Dead Sea Works, they return salts to the Southern Basin floor, thereby raising the level of the seabed and creating a potential risk of flooding for the hotels in the vicinity.

All these factors led the government of Israel to create a blue-ribbon panel of experts to study the future of the Dead Sea. The government's decision required the experts to develop facts and figures related to three scenarios. The first scenario is business as usual, and the Dead Sea continues to recede. The second is a review of the proposed Dead Sea-Red Sea channel or Dead Sea-Mediterranean Sea channel, and its potential effects on the Dead Sea. Finally, the third scenario was to study reduction and diversions from the Jordan River and allow additional flow of water into the Dead Sea to reduce or even stop the rate of recession without building the Red-Dead Canal.

The committee did not include in its output the legal and administrative implications of changes in the Dead Sea and a model for an administrative committee or commission, or other legal entity, which can plan, develop and implement a strategy for the future of the Dead Sea. This must take into account the international aspects of the Dead Sea as well. While recommendations in this direction were made by the legal experts on the committee, political pressure kept them out of the report presented to the government.

Another committee to discuss the future of the Dead Sea published a draft document in 2022. Established according to government decision, initial recommendations include piping water from the Red Sea to the Dead Sea and releasing 100 million cubic metres of water to flow in the lower Jordan River, in coordination with

233. R. Laster, D. Livney & D. Holender, *The Sound of One Hand Clapping: Limitations to Integrated Resources Water Management in the Dead Sea Basin*, 22(1) Pace Envtl L. Rev. (Spring 2005).

Jordan and the international community.[234] The 'Red-Dead Pipeline' was previously proposed in 2013 to convey seawater from the Red Sea through the Arava Valley to the Dead Sea, along with a desalination plant in the Jordanian city of Aqaba. It was approved by Israel, Jordan and the Palestinian Authority, but was never built due to political tensions.

As mentioned above, the Dead Sea Works caused the level of the seabed in the lower part of the Dead Sea to rise exposing the hotels along the shore to flooding and potential damage to their foundations. A case was filed by owners of hotels in the vicinity of the Dead Sea Works, who argued that the Dead Sea Works were carrying on construction not according to the Planning and Building Law and causing them damage.[235] The Dead Sea Works argued that since they held a concession for the area, the hotels were actually on-site at their grace and the Planning and Building Law had no application to the Dead Sea Works' operation within the boundaries of the concession. The District Court of Beer Sheva found in favour of the hotel owners. The Court found that the Planning and Building Law applied to all works carried out by the Dead Sea Company and its affiliated industries. As a result, the government panicked, as it did in the Tel Aviv Power Plant Law, and passed protective legislation to protect the Dead Sea Works from attack under the Planning and Building Law.

The first protective law passed in 1994, is entitled the Dead Sea Concession (Planning and Building) (Emergency Measures for Certain Work) Law, 1994.[236] The law enabled the Dead Sea Works, for several years, to receive a planning commission concession under the Licensing of Business Law for all those activities which it had carried out since the original concession in 1961, without getting planning and operation permission. This protective law lapsed after four years of operation and is no longer in effect. It was followed, however, by an additional law, which remains in effect and is entitled the Dead Sea Concession (Legislative Amendments) Law 1995.[237] This law is an amendment of two of Israel's most important environmental laws: The Planning and Building Law of 1965 and the Licensing of Businesses Law of 1968.

The first portion of the amendment relates to the Planning and Building Law. The amendment makes the distinction between the two types of land developed by the Dead Sea Works: land which is leased and land which is protected. The two types

234. Government Decision No. 3742. The Future of the Dead Sea- Long Term Policy Document, Draft June 2022.

235. Beer Sheva District Court., Civil Appeal 7/92 13/92, *Moria Hotel Ltd. v. Dead Sea Works Ltd* (not published).

236. Dead Sea Concession (Planning and Building) (Emergency Measures for Certain Work) Law, 1994, S.H. 1459, 124.

237. S.H. 1459, 123. 220 S.H. 1505, 128. However, the planning commission cannot reject a request to carry on work on the leased property unless it can show serious damage to the environment or serious health effects from the works. Regarding work to be carried out in the protected areas, a request is first given to the Nature Reserves and National Parks Authority for their approval. If they reject the request, an appeal can then be made to the National Planning Council's Committee of Appeals and the National Planning Commission must then decide this appeal within thirty days. The law requires that the appeals committee takes into consideration the balance between the concessions granted to the Dead Sea Works and the serious infringement on nature and the panorama.

of land actually refer to the property which is within the concession area, but a portion of it, a protected area, is in a nature reserve and a national park. Regarding the land which is leased, the special planning commission is entitled to review a planning request.

The second portion of the amendment deals with the Licensing of Businesses Law of 1968. First, it grants a licence to the Dead Sea Works retroactive to the date of the concession for all works in preparation. Second, the licensing authorities are entitled to set out conditions of the business licence for the concessionaire and the conditions will come into effect for new work to be carried out. Yet, the amendment specifically states that no action can be taken to enjoin the works under the Licensing of Businesses Law unless such action has been approved by the government or a ministerial committee for this purpose. It is quite obvious from this last statement that it would be very difficult for any government minister to enforce a special licensing condition unless the entire government agreed.

Since the judgment in the Hotel Moriah Case in the Beer Sheva District Court requiring the Dead Sea Works to apply for permission to plan and build in the concession area and because they are now required to be licensed, the atmosphere has changed considerably. In addition, the Dead Sea Works has received ISO 14,000 recognition, which requires it to meet Israel's environmental standards. It further requires that the company prepare a five-year plan to improve environmental quality in its operations. This has forced the Dead Sea Works to recognize that it is no longer a state within a state in Israel, and it must abide by the rules and regulations of the country in order for it to retain its status as an ISO 14000 company.

With the growth in health tourism and ecotourism, the State of Israel realizes that the Dead Sea has greater potential for tourist resources than it does for mineral resources. Therefore, the national, district and local authorities involved have begun to recognize the Dead Sea Works' place in proportion to its contribution. Most importantly, there is now recognition of the Dead Sea as a unique natural treasure, which deserves to be protected for future generations. This change is reflected in a government decision from 2012 which requires the Dead Sea Works to remove the salt that has built up on the seabed of the lower part of the Dead Sea. This salt harvesting project will cost an estimated USD 1 billion, of which the Dead Sea Works will pay approximately 75%.

A 2019 Haifa District Court decision held that the Water Law applies to the Dead Sea as well, and therefore the Dead Sea Works must obtain a production licence which restricts pumping quantities and guarantees that water resources will not be harmed, just like any other water producer. The judge also criticized the Water Authority for taking no interest in the activities of the Dead Sea Works and only began to show an interest in the wake of the legal action taken by the NGO Adam Teva V' Din.[238] In 2022, Adam Teva V' Din again brought suit in the Supreme Court (*Bagatz*) demanding the Dead Sea Works pay for the water they use in chemical production.[239] The amount of water used from 2018 to 2020 is valued at ILS 83.544 million.

---

238. Haifa District Court/Water Court, Appeal According to the Water Court, 14047-06-15 Adam Teva V' Din v Government Authority for Water and Sewerage.
239. Bagatz, Adam Teva V' Din v Ministry for National Infrastructure et al (Case not yet published).

VI. Red Sea

100. Eilat is Israel's southernmost city and the only one on the Red Sea coast. It serves as both a major port city and a major tourist area. With a population of only 52,000, its large area makes it Israel's fifth-largest city geographically.[240] Eilat is connected to the rest of the country by only two highways, requiring a four-and-a-half-hour trip to the centre of the country. It's international location, next to both the Egyptian and Jordanian borders, created additional socio-economic challenges. For years Eilat was a central location for refugees fleeing Africa. In 2011 refugees comprised 13% of the population.[241]

Eilat's location raises many challenges, but its desert location and beachfront, opportunities for cooperation with Arab countries and border crossings, large numbers of hotels, it's warm 'exotic' weather for most of the year and it's special VAT tax exemption status have resulted in Eilat becoming Israel's number one tourist destination. In addition, unique nature surrounds the city, including a mountainous desert and coral reefs.

Eilat's coral reefs are the northernmost in the world. In spite of the political tensions between the countries bordering the Red Sea, an international research team has asked UNESCO to declare the Red Sea coral reefs a World Heritage Site.[242] Due to its unique oceanographic and geographic conditions, Eilat's coral reefs are better equipped to withstand climate change in spite of the quickly warming Middle East region.

Eilat has a tourist promenade along the northern beach area of the city. It was approved by a national plan that stipulated that the southern beach area and the beach itself, located alongside the coral reef, remain an open and protected nature area while opening the northern beach area to commerce and tourism. Recently a policy plan was approved, based on building permits given forty years before the present national building plan, allowing a new tourist promenade along the coast of the southern beach area. The policy plan is meant to develop additional tourist facilities, entertainment centres and businesses to attract additional tourists and prevent tourists from preferring neighbouring countries. But the plan disrupts the status quo and led to massive construction in the protected natural areas of the city.

Over 250 scientists, with the support of the Ministry of Environmental Protection, Nature Reserves and Parks Authority, and civil environmental organizations, began protesting against the building plans for the southern beach area.

The Eilat Ashkelon Pipeline Co. Ltd. was established in 1968 as a private company supporting Israeli-Iranian cooperation and received a forty-nine-year licence to pipe oil which expired in 2017. The company was responsible for several environmental disasters, including polluting the Zin Canyon and oil spills in the Evrona Nature Reserve that resulted in severe and irreversible environmental damage.[243] In

---

240. Central Bureau of Statistics, Ombudsman's Report.
241. Ben Hartman, 'Eilat Worries Over Rising Tension With Migrants', The Jerusalem Post, 10 Jun. 2012 (Last visited 19 Apr. 2023).
242. https://www.hayadan.org.il/scientists-call-unesco-save-the-coral-reefs-in-the-red-sea-declared-it-a-world-heritage-site-2304201 (last visited 20 Apr. 2023).
243. Class Action Suit, Beersheva District Court, 49319-12-14, *Levi Pirsak et al v. Eilat Ashkelon Pipeline Co. Ltd. et al.*

order to advance agreements between Israel and the United Arab Emirates, a government company was established in place of the Eilat Ashkelon Pipeline Co. Ltd., called the Europe-Asia Pipeline Company. In 2020, parallel to the normalization of relations between Israel and some Arab countries within the framework of the Abraham Accords, including the United Arab Emirates, an agreement was signed between the new company and the Red-Med company.[244] Under the agreement, Israel agreed to drastically increase the amount of oil transported through the pipeline. This drastically increases the danger to Eilat's coral reef as well as public health, from pollution to air, water and land in case of leakage.[245]

In summary, the tensions between the development and protection of the unique natural surroundings require solutions that balance them. Our position is to leverage the unique characteristics of the city to advance its economy, rather than seeing the two as clashing interests. Decision-makers need to have a long-term integrative vision, rather than focusing on short-term gains.

---

244. Knesset Centre for Research and Information, Environmental Ramifications of the Europe-Asia Pipeline Co. and the Red-Med Co. (24.10.2021).
245. Letter from Attorney Dr Uri Sharon, CEO Israel Ecology and Environmental Sciences Association, to the Ministry of Environmental Protection and the Office of the Prime Minister (24.10.2021).

Chapter 4. Solid Waste

§1. Introduction

101. The treatment of solid waste is normally divided into production, separation, collection, disposal and litter. At each stage of the process, legislation can reduce quantity and nuisances. Israel has little legislation pertaining to solid waste and none with an overall approach, nor does Israel distinguish between industrial and household waste.

In 2021, Israel adopted a strategy which follows the European example of a 'No-Waste' policy – prevent and reduce waste, maximize recycling and reuse, limit incineration to non-recyclable materials, phase out landfilling, and legislate economic incentives to make the circular economy a reality. Unlike Europe, however, this strategy has not been introduced into legislation. Without such legislation, the strategy will itself become solid waste.

§2. Waste Production

102. By 'production' of solid waste, one means the production of material that does not degrade quickly in the natural environment. Good examples of this are products that are made to withstand biodegradation, such as plastics, paints and certain metals. Production of these products increases the burden on those responsible for the collection and disposal of solid waste. Good environmental legislation can prevent production of materials that are not biodegradable if alternative products are available. In addition, good legislation can require the manufacturer or distributor of certain products to reduce the build-up of solid waste by buying back his/her products; for example, returnable bottles found throughout the world. Israel has no requirement for biodegradability of certain items nor does it require production of cans from a single metal or using specific types of plastic to simplify recycling.

§3. Storage and Separation of Waste

103. Once items have been discarded from a home or business, the law can intervene to require proper storage facilities, separation or reduction. Such laws aim to prevent the creation of nuisances and make the polluter pay for the return of returnable items to reduce collection costs.[246] In 1993, Israel passed legislation requiring local authorities to set goals for the reduction and separation of solid waste in houses and at the business place. This legislation has been slowly put into operation; As of 2020, only 22% of the solid waste collected by cities was recycled. In 2011, the Knesset passed new regulations to require extended producer responsibility (EPR) for solid waste. The legislation was sabotaged by the producers until 2021

246. K.T. 5730, 1841.

when a new government was formed and moved the legislation a giant step forward. Legislation requiring proper storage facilities for solid waste disposal at the home and on business premises can be found under the Planning and Building Law under the Licensing of Businesses Law.[247] The special handling of solid waste from industry is treated under the Licensing of Businesses Law, in the individual licence granted to the business.

§4. Collection and Haulage

104. Collection of solid waste is the responsibility of the local authority under the powers granted to it.[248] Each local authority also has the power to promulgate bylaws to expedite the removal of solid waste.[249] In practice, most towns and cities have passed such bylaws. These bylaws also include provisions forbidding the unlawful dumping of solid waste, except in the containers and areas provided for that purpose. The bylaws forbid removal and haulage of solid waste by anyone other than the local authority or its agents. Most local authorities have bylaws for the separation of waste at source, others have promulgated bylaws forbidding the use of plastic containers on beaches.

§5. Waste Disposal

105. In 1993, the country decided to opt for integrated solid waste management, copying the term as it is used in European countries. The government decided that a certain portion of Israel's solid waste would be recycled, a portion would be incinerated and used as an energy source, and the remains would be land filled under properly authorized landfill sites.

Looking at the statistics from 1993 to 2020, it is clear that, integrated solid waste management has not been implemented. Reports from 2020 show that only 22% of solid waste from local authorities is recycled. The government has succeeded in reducing the number of unregulated landfill sites and has created large sites in different corners of the state in order to make them logistically amenable to the local authorities. The programme designed by the Ministry of Environmental Protection was carried out without major legislation.[250] In fact, the only regulations for solid waste disposal were those requiring that a landfill site forbid the use of burning on the site.[251]

In an attempt to move forward from concept to actual implementation, the Ministry's integrated waste management plan was given the approval of the National Planning and Building Board in the form of a solid waste management master plan. Two of the main outcomes of the plan are a tipping fee and a tyre recycling law.

---

247. *See*, e.g., K.T. 5733, 1647; K.T. 5733, 11.
248. Municipalities Ordinance (New Version), 1 L.S.I. (NV) 247.
249. Exemplary Bylaw for Local Councils (Sanitation and Removal of Nuisances), 1972, K.T. 1220.
250. Regulations for the Abatement of Nuisances (Prevention of Unreasonable Air and Olfactory Pollution from Garbage Dumps), 1990, K.T. 5250,386.
251. *Ibid.*

An update of the Cleanliness Law imposes a tipping fee on the waste which is land filled according to the type of waste. The purpose is to reflect the true price of land filling, thus encouraging local authorities to recycle and reuse waste as an economically viable alternative. The funds collected are returned to local authorities or the private sector for the purpose of establishing recycling and recovery systems.

§6. Solid Waste Landfill Sites

106. Beginning in 1993, the Ministry of Environment embarked on a programme of reducing the number of solid waste landfill sites in Israel.[252] This programme was initiated because studies showed that most of the 500-odd solid waste sites were not designed properly, resulting in environmental and health nuisances.

In order to reduce the number of sites, the Ministry used a three-pronged approach. Criminal suits were filed against mayors of several cities operating sites under primitive conditions. Second, the national plan for solid waste landfills was given priority treatment. Third, the Ministry published tenders for the operation and maintenance of national sites to replace some of the sites that were being closed down. The Ministry has successfully overseen the construction and operation of five large national landfill sites, where solid waste is handled in the proper sanitary landfill manner, reducing the problem of groundwater pollution and production of methane gas.

Unfortunately, the closure of the hundreds of unregulated waste disposal sites does not prevent continued environmental degradation. The sites require rehabilitation in order to prevent leachate infiltration from polluting soil and water.

§7. Recycling

107. In June 1993, the Knesset passed the Law for Collection and Removal of Solid Waste for Recycling.[253] This framework legislation enables the local authorities of Israel to prepare the groundwork for recycling. The law permits local authorities to distinguish between types of solid waste containers and proposes bylaws on collection and removal of solid waste for recycling, and prohibits using a recycling container for any other use. The law empowers the Ministry of Environmental Protection to force local authorities to carry out their duties under the law if they fail to do so voluntarily.

With the law's passage, three main obstacles arose to its implementation. The first is inherent in all solid waste recycling programmes: there must be an 'industry' for collection and reuse. Israel, unfortunately, is a small country which has not developed that industrial base, therefore, the economic incentive for recycling is lacking. Without this incentive, the local authorities refused to pass the necessary local legislation to require recycling.

---

252. S. Gabbay, *The Environment in Israel* 91 (Jerusalem: Ministry of Environment 1998).
253. S.H. 1422, 116.

The second obstacle was that the law placed the burden of purchasing special recycling bins and collection of those bins on the local authority, while it failed to take into consideration that Israel's local authorities have no budget for this programme. The third obstacle arose within the government itself. When the Ministry of Environmental Protection prepared regulations to force the local authorities to create a recycling programme, the Ministers of the Interior and Treasury objected. They argued that the economic burden could not be justified by the programme. As a result, a leading environmental NGO filed a case in the Supreme Court to force the publication of regulations.[254] The Supreme Court decided in favour of the NGO and declared that the regulations will be published. The proposed regulations require local authorities to design and implement a recycling programme that reduces the amount of solid waste by a certain percentage, over a certain period of time.

Regulations were published in 1998, requiring the following: each local authority is required to report to the Ministry of Environmental Protection the amount of solid waste it produces annually. Second, the law requires a more significant reduction in the amount of solid waste produced to encourage recycling. Finally, the local authorities are to set timetables or deadlines for the reduction of solid waste over the coming years. Unfortunately, the regulations have not been enforced to the full and a major reason for this is that the Ministry of Environmental Protection has not created the industry required for purchasing recycled materials. In spite of this, recycling in Israel has increased from 10% in 1998 to 22% today. But this is far from the European standard for recycling and far from the goal set by the Israel Government of a 50% reduction by 2020. The local authorities failed to meet these regulations. A suit was filed against several local authorities and the Ministry of Environmental Protection in order to speed up the process.[255] The Strategic Plan for the Treatment of Waste has set a recycling target of 51% by 2030, but it appears doubtful that this goal will be met.

The recycling efforts have concentrated on the following areas. First of all, there has been increased use of organic waste for the production of compost for agricultural use. Second, Israel has continued its recycling of paper and cardboard, so that today approximately 34% of all paper in Israel is recycled. Third, the Tire Disposal and Recycling law requires producers and importers to recycle all used tires. The law is one of the first in Israel that invokes the principle of the cradle-to-grave producer responsibility, placing responsibility for the environmental impact of a product on the producer or importer. Finally, there is the recycling of used oil (both engine oil and cooking oil), plastics, building waste and backyard waste.

However, only 6% of plastic is recycled. In 1999, the government successfully had a bill passed for the recycling of glass and plastic drinking containers. The law compels retailers of drinking containers of more than 100 millilitres and less than 1.5 litres to require a deposit and return the deposit as paid when the bottle is returned. The bottles are to be collected by an association for recycling created by

---

254. Bagatz 7099/95, *'Adam Teva V'Din' v. The Minister of Environmental Protection and the Minister of Interior* (not published).
255. Bagatz 8623/99, *Adam Teva V'Din (The Israel Society for Environmental Defense) v. The Ministry of Environmental Protection and 261 Others* (not yet published).

the drink manufacturers. The law is modelled on similar laws in Europe, but implementation in Israel is very weak In addition, the public has found that they are purchasing bottles with a 30 agorot (ILS 0.3) deposit with no chance of getting their money back unless they make a trip to the supermarket where they purchased them. Some businesses refused to accept refundable containers or limited the amount they will accept. This is a poor example of government inadequacy in the face of the real problem of solid waste and litter

In order to address these weaknesses, the law has been amended four times over the past decade. The amendments include an ILS 1,800 fine for refusal to accept deposit containers and require supermarket chains to receive up to fifty containers a day per person. More importantly, the law now puts the responsibility for collecting and recycling containers of 1.5 litres and larger on the manufacturers and importers. The amended law includes obligatory quarterly recycling reports and direct fines on producers and importers for non-compliance with collection and recycling targets. *The Packaging Management Law*. The 2011 law attempts to reduce packaging waste and increase recycling by imposing direct responsibility for collecting and recycling packaging waste on the manufacturers and importers themselves. The law covers a wide range of packaging materials, including paper, glass, cardboard, plastic, metal and wood. Manufacturers and importers are required to recycle 60% of the total weight of the packaging of the products they sell or import. *The Electrical and Electronic Equipment and Batteries Law*. The 2012 E-Waste law provides a framework for recycling electronic and electrical equipment and batteries. Like the Packaging Management Law, responsibility for the collection and recycling/reuse of electronic devices is given to the manufacturers and distributors. The goal of this law is to reduce the amount of e-waste, prevent it from reaching landfills and dumps, and mitigate the negative environmental and health effects of these products.

108. Law Banning Free Plastic Bags in Supermarkets. In 2016, a law came into effect that would end the free distribution of plastic bags in supermarkets. In an agreement reached with the Minister of Economy, the law requires supermarkets to charge 10 agorot (USD 0.03) per bag. The owners of the major supermarket chains signed an agreement with the Minister of Environmental Protection to distribute seven reusable shopping bags to every household in Israel for free. The funds collected are transferred to the Ministry of Environmental Protection's Cleanliness Fund. Initially, the fee will be charged only in supermarket chains, but the Minister has the right to expand the law to other businesses as well. The fee is only charged on shopping bags (with looped handles), not smaller bags that come in direct contact with food. According to a report from the Ministry of Environmental Protection, in 2021, large supermarkets sold 501 million plastic bags, a reduction of 71% from 2016 when the law came into effect.

§8. LITTER

109. The government has successfully legislated the prohibition of littering through the Maintenance of Cleanliness Law, 1984.[256] This law attacks blight from litter, both on private and public property, by making it a crime to dump litter, building waste, or abandoned vehicles anywhere. At the same time, the law authorizes local authorities to declare a vehicle 'abandoned' after taking proper procedures. Once the procedural period has lapsed, the local authority tows the abandoned vehicle to a recycling centre.

A government vehicle-scrapping programme began in 2010. Owners of private vehicles twenty years or older that are still running and with a valid registration licence are paid ILS 3,000 upon delivery of their vehicles to authorized scrapping sites. The programme was an overnight success but has been frozen several times due to budget constraints. The programme was renewed on 3 November 2013 with a budget of ILS 5 million. On that day, the entire budget was used up, with 1,500 vehicles scrapped. Despite the positive public response, the programme has not been renewed.

The law also establishes a fund for cleanliness projects. Regulations under the law require manufacturers of drink containers, other than milk or milk products, to pay a duty per drink container into the fund annually.[257] These regulations create an inter-ministerial committee to regulate the receipt and expenditure of monies under the law. The law also has an educational aspect. It requires drink manufacturers to stamp their products with a distinctive seal, which states that littering is prohibited. It further authorizes the Minister of Environmental Protection to empower members of the general public with the right to notify the police of violations of the littering law. The members of the public so empowered are called cleanliness trustees. Those notifications are then forwarded by the police to the littering party with a request that a fine be paid for littering.

In 1997, the Knesset updated the Maintenance of Cleanliness Law with a series of amendments.[258] The amended law contains four major changes. First of all, there is a definition in the law which includes the term litter 'waste' such as skins or hides, tires and trunks of trees. This definition was amended in order to meet the new change also adopted in the law, which enables a local authority to create special sites for discarding garden trimmings, tires, and automobile scrap. The second major change relates to the fund which was created in the original law for clean-up projects. The original law limited the use of money from the fund to clean-up projects only. The new amendment enables the use of the fund for the protection of the environment, including cleanliness and preventing litter of solid waste. The fund can also be used for recycling and preventing unsightly signs and billboards.

The new penalty clause raises the fines and jail sentences as determined in the law and it also allows a court to punish a driver for littering a highway by taking

256. 38 L.S.I. 190.
257. K.T. 5746, 411.
258. S.H. 1622, 132. along Israel's roads as well as preventing violation of the Dangerous Substances Law of 1993. The law further states that being punished under the law by being required to pay a fine does not pre-empt payment of an additional amount into the Cleanliness Fund. The third major change refers to the punishment section of the law.

away his/her driving licence. The fourth major change enables the Minister of Environmental Protection to order the clean-up of a littered site at the expense of the person who caused the filth.

The enforcement mechanisms were further expanded by the 2008 amendment as part of the 'Polluter Pays' law. This includes empowering the courts to levy fines equal to the economic benefits attained by the polluter. In addition, maximum fines and imprisonment terms were increased, and powers to impound vehicles involved in polluting were given to Ministry inspectors.

An additional aid to the reduction of litter along Israel's highways can be found in the Public Health (Prevention of Nuisances) (Removal of Plastic Sheeting) Regulations, 1993.[259] These regulations are aimed at the agricultural sector, which uses plastic sheeting and tunnels for growing fruits and vegetables. The regulations require farmers using plastic sheeting to remove them from their fields, once they are no longer needed, to an authorized solid waste dump or a recycling centre. It is forbidden to burn the plastic. The regulations set out punishments for those who fail to meet their requirements.

§9. Medical Waste

110. The Ministry of Health regulations for the handling of hospital waste make a distinction between three major types of waste.[260] The first is defined as 'dangerous medical waste', which includes substances which contain antibiotics, medications and similar types of dangerous medical substances. The second type of waste is defined as 'cadaver waste', which could be waste from parts of human or animal bodies which can arise from medical treatment or experiments in medical laboratories. The third major type of waste is general hospital waste. The regulations require that a hospital creates separate containers for medical waste, cadaver waste and general waste, which occurs during the day-to-day operations of the institution. These containers are to be kept separate and their treatment after use is also to be kept separate. In addition, the regulations forbid the pouring of certain wastes, including dangerous medical waste, into the sewage system.

The hospital is required to sort the various types of waste in order to have them transferred to proper sites for disposal once they have been collected in their proper containers.

§10. Enforcement and Control

111. With the passage of the Maintenance of Cleanliness Law, there has been a reduction in littering due to active enforcement. Credit for enforcement goes to the Ministry of Environmental Protection, and the members of the general public who volunteer as cleanliness trustees. Each year approximately 2,000 new trustees are registered. In 2012, about 1,000 trustees filed at least one report.

259. K.T. 5493, 295.
260. K.T. 5848, 1101.

An additional reason for the law's effectiveness is that it is simple to enforce. Anyone throwing litter from a car can be identified by his/her licence plates. Cleanliness trustees or police officers need only notify the licensing authority that they spotted litter being thrown from a vehicle. This is sufficient for a summons to be issued against the driver of a moving vehicle from which the litter was thrown. Courts do not hesitate to fine those littering, and most litterers caught prefer to pay a fine rather than go to court. Similar to parking tickets, this idea of fines rather than criminal action has been instigated in eight other environmental laws as well.

There has been some enforcement of the storage facility requirements for solid waste under the Planning and Building Law and the Licensing of Businesses Law. The problem here is in the realm of toxic or problematic waste. Even more difficult to enforce is the actual disposal of solid waste by local authorities.

For years, the Ministries of the Interior and Health cajoled the local authorities into better housekeeping measures to prevent nuisances and 'spontaneous' fires at solid waste landfills. In the last ten years, with pressure from the Ministry of Environmental Protection, efforts have been made in two areas to improve the disposal of solid waste by local authorities. The first is through proper planning. There is a national plan for siting solid waste dumps so as to reduce their visual effect and potential pollution of groundwater. Second has been the untiring demand of the Ministry of Environmental Protection to require proper sanitary landfill measures to reduce nuisances on-site. The regulations forbidding the burning of solid waste added enforcement powers to the Ministry of Environmental Protection to further reduce nuisances at landfill sites.[261]

Despite these efforts, Israel needs a comprehensive law for treatment and disposal of solid waste. The National Plan for Disposal of Solid Waste is no substitute for legislation. Furthermore, individual treatment of sanitary landfills has not been successful in preventing pollution of soil and groundwater.

Several cases have been brought by the Ministry of Environmental Protection for illegal disposal of solid waste, both against individuals and local authorities. More recent cases have successfully convicted not only a town or a village but also found the town officials personally responsible.

The fines for convicted polluters have also increased, in line with the Law for Environmental Protection (The Polluter Pays) 2008 (*See* paragraph 50 The Law for Environmental Protection (The Polluter Pays) (Amendment of Laws)). The law increased fines for illegal dumping of garbage as described in the Cleanliness Protection Law to ILS 226,000, or about USD 64,000.

261. Prevention of Nuisances (Prevention of Unreasonable Air and Olfactory Pollution at Landfill Sites), 1990 (KT 5250, p. 386, 22 Feb. 1990).

Chapter 5. Soil Pollution

§1. Pollution by Chemicals

112. One of Israel's more serious problems is the pollution of the soil by chemicals, especially pesticides and herbicides. Studies show that the pollution has reached groundwater sources, and earlier studies showed the existence of pesticides and herbicides in the food chain.

At first glance, one finds a crisscross of legislation aimed at preventing pollution of the environment by chemicals and direct health effects on humans. Unfortunately, this crisscross is similar to a lattice with sufficient gaps between the bureaucratic splays to cause concern. This chapter, however, will not deal with the legal framework to prevent direct effects of toxic substances on the population of Israel, but discuss that subject as it relates to the prevention of soil pollution.

Israel is a small country engaged in intensive agricultural development. The use of intensive agricultural methods, combined with Israel's compact size, limits Israel's capacity to neutralize the effects of soil pollution. There are no wide-open spaces where soil pollution has no impact on water supplies. This requires extremely protective legislation and enforcement regarding what goes on and into its soil.

Since 1956, Israel has had a Law for the Protection of Plants.[262] This law has enabled the Minister of Agriculture if he/she deems it necessary to prevent the spread of pests to: (1) forbid the transport of plants; (2) prohibit or limit the import of plants; (3) prohibit or limit the production and sale of plants; (4) regulate the sale, distribution, production and import of chemicals intended for the extermination of pests, and set standards for such chemicals.

In the same law, the Minister is authorized to regulate the use of any chemical for the extermination of pests if he/she determines them to be dangerous to man, animal or plants. There is no mention in the law of soil pollution, nor is the Minister empowered to regulate chemicals with long-term effects on the soil.

In 1967, the Minister of Agriculture issued regulations to regulate the sale of chemicals used in any one of the following processes: to regulate growth, prevent disease or defoliation, or control thinning or destruction of pests.[263] The regulations require every person intending to sell a chemical, to which one or more of the above applies, to submit the product for licensing. The licensing process entails submitting data on the toxicity of the chemical, its effectiveness and its impact on the environment, including its degradation qualities. The head of the Department of Plant Protection may require additional data, if needed, to determine the effectiveness of, or the danger inherent in, a product. The regulations require that each product approved be so labelled as to state its effectiveness, toxicity and antidote. No label may be changed or amended without the approval of the head of the Department of Plant Protection in the Ministry of Agriculture.

262. 10 L.S.I. 75.
263. Regulations for Plant Protection (Arrangement of the Sale of Chemical Devices), 1967, K.T. 2628.

In addition to labelling requirements, plant protection regulations require manufacturers to properly package and store their products to prevent harm. The regulations further forbid repackaging of any other material in a package previously used for pesticides. Finally, it forbids the use of pesticides and herbicides except on those plants, and against those pests, as stated on the product's label.

Soil pollution by farming can be one of the most destructive elements to the environment. Not only can it cause problems in the immediate environment, but it can also affect groundwater, air, and the food chain. Israel has moved in the direction of sustainable agriculture but not nearly as fast as the European programme, 'Common Agriculture Policy' or CAP. Israel has conducted studies on integrated pest management. In the Beit Shean Valley, Kibbutz Sde Eliyahu commercially raises beneficiary natural enemies for sale to farmers as an alternative to chemical pesticides. In addition, the organic food market in Israel has developed rapidly in the past few years. It still accounts for only 1.5% of Israeli agriculture overall, and 15% of agricultural exports. In 2004, a law was passed regulating the labelling and testing of organic produce.[264] Israel has regulations for pesticide residues, which are enforced by the inspectors of the Ministry of Agriculture.[265]

113. The Department of Plant Protection in the Ministry of Agriculture does not have sufficient staff for proper enforcement of the laws and regulations set out above. It depends on the services of plant advisors, who operate under the auspices of the Ministry of Agriculture, but whose major job is to increase agricultural yields, not protect the environment. As a result, the ministry has actually done little to prevent soil pollution from pesticides and herbicides. It has carefully enforced the introduction of pesticides and herbicides and labelling requirements, but there has been little or no enforcement of the environmental-protection-oriented provisions of the law.

Ministry of Environmental Protection inspectors oversee the use, storage and handling of pesticides, as part of their authority under the Hazardous Substances Law of 1993. The law requires a poison permit for all businesses dealing with poisonous materials. The ministry's inspectors investigate citizen complaints, supervise the storage of pesticides and herbicides and oversee the usage of these potentially harmful materials.

Until recently, farmers were expected to pay for the proper disposal of unused pesticides and herbicides. This was very expensive, dissuading farmers from obeying the law. The Ministry of Environmental Protection initiated a free programme for collecting unused agricultural chemicals. Smaller amounts are brought to regional collection sites, while larger amounts are collected at the farms. The programme indicates a significant change in tactics by the ministry officials, who know that enforcement and punishment have limited effectiveness and that spending a small amount on prevention can save large amounts otherwise spent on environmental clean-up.

264. Law Regulating Organic Produce, 2005.
265. Regulations for Animal Diseases (Prevention of Biological Residues), 2000.

§2. POLLUTION OF THE SOIL BY SEWAGE

114. In addition to the direct application of chemicals, soil pollution occurs from the use of sewage water for irrigation. Israel reuses large quantities of sewage for irrigation under regulations promulgated by the Ministry of Health in 1981.[266] These regulations set stringent standards for the purification of water to be used in irrigation. In addition, the regulations limit the type of plants that may be so irrigated. For example, cotton and dry alfalfa or other products not eaten by man may be irrigated with purified sewage. The regulations do not relate specifically to soil pollution, but they require the removal of toxic substances and other materials that could build up in the soil.

115. *Brownfields*. Over the past few decades, the world has been shocked by the number of instances where large chemical companies abandoned a site which was later used as a residential area. One of the most famous of these cases is the Love Canal case. The Hooker Chemicals and Plastics Company used a 16-acre site near Niagara Falls, New York, for the disposal of over 21,000 tons of various chemical wastes. The site was subsequently used for the building of a school and homes. In the case of the Love Canal, the United States responded with regulations to find and clean-up the polluted sites. The major laws were the RCRA, the Resource Conservation and Recovery Act (42 USC section 6901. 1976. Amended 1984) and the *Comprehensive Environmental Response Compensation and Liability Act* (CERCLA). These two acts gave birth to the concept of the cradle-to-grave legislation whereby a chemical substance was followed from its original place of manufacture or import to its final destination in order to prevent extensive soil pollution in the United States. In addition, the Super-Fund amendments to CERCLA authorize money to find former landowners of abandoned sites, clean-up these sites and sue the perpetrators of pollution.

Israel has followed this legislation for years, but other than reading about the American experience, Israel has not followed suit with comparable legislation. Indirect legislation which applies to pollution of soil in Israel can be found in the Licensing of Businesses Law, the Planning and Building Law, the Water Law and other similar acts. These acts forbid pollution in general but do not require clean-up of a specific site once it has been polluted. Nor has there been legislation passed

---

266. Public Health Rules (Purification of Sewage for Irrigation), 1981, K.T. 1357. *See also* Public Health Regulations (Standards for Sewage), 1992, K.T. 1033, Public Health Rules (Standards for Wastewater Quality and Rules for Wastewater Treatment), 2010. regulations is the responsibility of the Ministry of Health. There has been criticism, however, as to the lack of continual monitoring of purified sewage used for agricultural use. Heavy metals found in purified sewage have led to a demand that industrial waste be pre-treated or separated from household waste. This would enable purified household sewage only to be used for irrigation. In 2010, regulations were promulgated to rectify this situation, with stricter and wider standards, as well as stricter guidelines for testing, control, publication and reporting. The regulations contain separate standards for wastewater to be used for the irrigation of crops. The regulations also set deadlines for implementation by individual wastewater treatment plants, but many WWTP's have not met these deadlines.

requiring a search of polluted sites for brownfields or the requirement for the perpetrator of the act to be found and prosecuted. One of Israel's largest polluting factories happens to be government-owned and it has caused a brownfield situation in the heart of the country. The company's sites in Jerusalem and Ramat HaSharon were abandoned, leaving thousands of hectares polluted with chemicals that were found on the site. In a case brought against the government for clean-up, the government was asked to do everything in its effort to prevent the transfer of the site to an innocent party until the site was cleaned up.[267] The government did take it upon itself to clean-up the site, but this is the exception to the rule, pointing out that the rule is that businesses can abandon sites in Israel without being required to clean them up. However, there has been active enforcement of the Dangerous Substances Law against existing sites in order to prevent soil pollution and abandon sites with chemicals in the soil. In addition, the Ministry of Environmental Protection has effectively used the Planning and Building Law to prevent building on sites where there are known chemical deposits. The initiator of a plan needs planning permission to build on a site, and unless a study is done to determine that no soil pollution has occurred in the soil, the Ministry will not allow the entrepreneur to build on the site. The result is, therefore, that in spite of the fact that Israel has not adopted legislation specifically for soil pollution, it has found a method of preventing new buildings on sites that are polluted using the Planning and Building Law as a vehicle for enforcement.

A survey of the contaminated lands in Israel, ordered by the Ministry of Environmental Protection, identified hundreds of contaminated sites. The total cost of assessment, treatment and future contamination prevention is estimated at ILS 9.8 billion.[268] The survey was ordered in accordance with the proposed Environmental Protection Law (Prevention of Soil Contamination and Treatment of Contaminated Soils) from 2008.

The area of lands suspected to be contaminated is 4069 dunams, comprised of: army bases and security industries (35%), industry (30%), tank farms and refineries (15%), gas and fuel stations (15%), and other sources (5%).[269]

Due to the lack of land for building in the centre of the country and the shortage of apartments, pressure on the government will inevitably result in the rehabilitation of these lands.

116. Ground and Water Pollution from Gasoline Stations. The Water Authority and the Ministry of Environmental Protection promulgated regulations in 2006 and 2010 to protect water sources from pollution caused by fuel leaks.[270] The regulations require constant monitoring and planned action in the event of a fuel leak that endangers a water source. But the regulations only require reporting to the assigned

---

267. High Court of Justice, Case No. 3485/00. Israel Union for Environmental Defence against Israel Military Industries. *See also* para. 74.
268. M. Shecter, et al., LDD Advanced Technologies, Estimated National Costs to Survey and Treat Contaminated Lands, Final Report-Public Tender No. 13/09, May 2014.
269. *Ministry of Environmental Protection, 'In the Environment for You', Second quarterly report (2016),* pp. 7–8 (Hebrew).
270. Water Regulations (Prevention of Water Pollution) (Fuel Lines), 2006; Water Rules (Treatment of Water Pollution from Fuel), 2010.

water quality authority if more than 1 cubic metre of fuel leaks, an amount that can contaminate vast amounts of water. Recent regulations were promulgated to cut the risks of fuel leaks by detailed instructions for building and operating fuel lines, and procedures to be followed in case of a leak.[271] But in spite of the regulations and activities of the Water Authority and Ministry of Environmental Protection, in 2010, the Water Authority drilled forty-eight additional testing wells, exposing twenty new sites where fuel pollution was detected in the groundwater. In recent years, ten wells that provide drinking water were found to be contaminated with fuel from gas stations at a distance of up to 400 metres from the wells. About 350,000 litres of fuel were pumped out of the aquifers in 2010. At seventeen sites, the treatment of groundwater continues.[272]

271. *Ibid.*
272. G. Reshef, H. Gal & S. Alhanani, *Activities of the Water Quality Branch of the Water Authority Concerning Fuel Pollution: Summary of 2010 Activities* (Israel Water Authority).

Chapter 6. Noise Pollution

§1. Introduction

117. Noise pollution is handled legislatively in much the same way as air pollution, as discussed in Chapter 2. The major piece of legislation protecting the environment from unreasonable noise is the Abatement of Nuisances Law, 1961, also known as the Kanowitz Law. In addition, noise may be controlled through proper planning under the Planning and Building Law and under specific statutes relating to vehicle and aeroplane or airport-generated noise.

§2. The Abatement of Nuisances Law

118. The Abatement of Nuisances Law (the Kanowitz Law) was discussed in Chapter 1 as it connected with general environmental laws. Here, the law will be analysed from the standpoint of noise pollution protection.

The Kanowitz Law is unique in the annals of Israeli legislation. Not only is it Israel's first piece of 'environmental' legislation, but it also includes within its framework a unique legal apparatus. For example, the law is a hybrid. It enables civil suits by private citizens, and criminal suits by the State as well as private citizens against a polluter. Private criminal suits, one should note, exist by law in Israel, provided the complainant first makes an application to the Attorney General regarding his/her intention to bring such a suit. In environmental matters, criminal suits often serve as a stronger deterrent than civil suits.[273]

A further unique contribution of the Kanowitz Law is its expansion of tort law. Under Israel's Torts Ordinance, a suit against a polluter causing a 'public nuisance' – that is, a polluter causing a nuisance to the general public – can be brought to court by the private citizen only if that citizen has suffered monetary loss. This burdensome restriction was removed in the Kanowitz Law, making it easier to bring a suit in tort against a large polluter.

Second, the law contains provisions to ease the plaintiff's burden of proof in a civil suit. If the plaintiff succeeds in proving that the polluter has violated a regulation under the Kanowitz Law, the burden of proof then shifts, and it is incumbent upon the polluter to then show that although he/she has violated a regulation, he/she did not disturb the plaintiff – a somewhat impossible task.

Finally, the law has another unique aspect. It brings the provision of Israel's Licensing of Businesses Law in line with Kanowitz's regulations. This is done by requiring that every licence issued includes at a minimum, the regulations promulgated under the Kanowitz Law.

The law opens with a declaratory statement: no one will cause unreasonable noise pollution if it disturbs or is likely to disturb a person in the vicinity or passers-by.

---

273. *Israel Union for Environmental Defence v. Haifa Chemicals* 000183/01 Haifa District Ct.

What is unreasonable noise pollution? The law fails to answer this question. Instead, it places the burden on the Minister of Environmental Protection to define this term in regulations.

In addition to regulations, the minister administering the law is empowered to issue specific instructions to individual polluters, ordering them to take certain steps to prevent a violation of the law. These instructions may be stricter than the regulations promulgated under the law. They apply to individual factories and their administrators. These individual orders are comparable to performance orders issued in other countries. They include specific instructions against a polluter, ranging from the type of fuel to the use of a log book.

The Kanowitz Law forbids loud or unreasonable noise that causes or may cause a nuisance. Without proper regulations, the law would hardly be an improvement over the common law or general rules of negligence incorporated in the Torts Ordinance. The ministers responsible for implementing the law – Health and Interior originally, but now Environment too – recognized this fact in 1966 and published regulations prohibiting certain types of noise, except from transportation, at certain hours of the day or night in specific neighbourhoods.[274]

The first set of regulations recognized the right of the average citizen to peace and quiet during the afternoon 'siesta' hours and during the night. In fact, the regulations create absolute liability for one causing noise during these hours, with no requirement that noise reaches a measured decibel level. Types of noise forbidden include singing, shouting, playing a musical instrument, radio or television, etc. This prohibition applies if the noise is in a residential area and the noise is created in a residence, outside or in another structure with the windows and doors open.

The regulations, although primitive, are easily enforced by the police and are, therefore, essentially effective. Except on permitted holidays, most residential celebrations quiet down at the hour appointed in the regulations. Yet, the regulations are not effective in other situations: noise in mixed-usage neighbourhoods, noise from industry in general, and noise created during the day.

Therefore, in 1977, the Ministers of Interior and Health published regulations to control the level of noise from all sources, except transportation noise.[275] These regulations introduced the decibel as a measuring device for acceptable noise levels. Noise tests are performed in the complainant's home with doors and windows open. The regulations guarantee every resident of Israel a right to quiet at a certain noise level during the day and night, according to the area in which he/she lives. Hospitals and schools are designated as quiet areas, and industrial zones are designated as noisy areas.

These regulations were upgraded to include impulsive noise, background noise, and noise travelling within one's building.[276] Israel has, therefore, regulated permitted noise levels during certain hours of the day and night according to the make-up of the neighbourhood.

---

274. Regulations for the Abatement of Nuisances (Prevention of Noise), 1966, K.T. 2264.
275. Regulations for the Abatement of Nuisances (Unreasonable Noise), 1977, K.T. 716.
276. K.T. 5750, 1006.

The next set of regulations published were those to reduce noise pollution from building sites.[277] This is an extremely irritable form of noise pollution because it may occur in any neighbourhood. The regulations established emission levels and require owners and operators of the building equipment to use only that equipment which reduces noise to a designated decibel level. Noise tests are performed in proximity to the equipment and not at the home of the complainant. Regulations also limit the hours for using large building equipment for excavation, construction and demolition work in residential areas.

Additional noise regulations control alarms, air conditioners, car horns and animals.[278] New regulations limit the hours for major causes of noise in residential areas, including renovations and repairs, the usage of building engineering equipment and the usage of noisy gardening equipment. Leaf blowers are now prohibited in residential areas as well as the installation of new car alarms.[279]

An amendment to the Licensing of Businesses law and subsequent regulations require that there be a noise-metre in banquet halls to monitor the level of noise and notify when the noise exceeds standards set in the law.[280] Failure to install the noise-metre means that the hall owner will not be able to get a business licence. The regulations require the noise-metre to be connected to the sound system, causing the power to the system to be cut off when the noise level reaches an average of eighty-five decibels for ten seconds. Similar regulations were promulgated for discotheques.[281]

Other regulations limit and control noise from quarries[282] and aeroplanes.[283] The law allows monetary fines, similar to parking tickets, to be imposed for twenty-nine different types of noise violations.[284]

§3. The Planning and Building Law

119. The Planning and Building Law empowers the Minister of the Interior to publish regulations to reduce noise through proper building codes. This can be done in several ways. First, the Minister could define in regulations the type of building construction materials required to reduce noise within buildings. Second, he/she has the power to publish regulations requiring the use of plumbing materials that reduce the transfer of noise between neighbouring apartments. Further, he/she could publish regulations to define minimum distance requirements from roads to buildings

277. Regulations for the Abatement of Nuisances (Unreasonable Noise from Building Equipment), 1979, K.T. 3992.
278. Abatement of Noise Regulations (Prevention of Noise), 1992. K.T. 5474, 8.
279. Abatement of Noise Regulations (Prevention of Noise), 1992 as amended in 2011.
280. Licensing of Businesses law, para. 2F, Licensing of Businesses Regulations (Installation of Noise Metre in Banquet Halls and Outdoor Reception Areas), 2006. K.T. 6508, 1076.
281. Business License Regulations (Installing a Noise-Metre in Discotheques), 2014 K.T. 7407, 1622.
282. Abatement of Nuisances Regulations (Prevention of Air Pollution and Noise from Quarries), 1998.
283. Airplane Noise, Regulations of Airplanes (Noise from Airplanes) (Amendment), 1992. K.T. 2156, 1399 as amended in K.T. 5459, 1345 (1992).
284. Criminal Procedure Order (Finable Offences-Prevention of Noise) 2000.

in order to reduce transportation noise. Unfortunately, the Minister has published only one regulation to reduce noise at the planning stage: to require a minimum width in wall construction.[285]

120. For transportation noise, Israel has adopted EEC regulations for new motor vehicles, tested the same way for noise as for air pollution. Similar EEC regulations have been adopted for used vehicles; some cities have adopted bylaws for environmental quality and prevention of nuisances that include sections on noise prevention from vehicles. The planning commissions have adopted a standard for the planning and building of new roads to reduce noise from traffic. The standard, however, has not yet been converted to a formal regulation, but it serves as a guideline for planning approval.

121. Finally, noise from airports and planes is controlled in two ways. Airport noise is controlled under the Planning and Building Law, including control of noise for landing and take-off. Second, aeroplanes must meet international noise level standards adopted by the international community.

In the decision by the National Planning Council to enlarge the Ben-Gurion International Airport, the airport authority was required to meet the noise contours developed for the reduction of noise around the site of the existing airport. As a result, the Airport Authority was required to compensate landowners if the noise affecting a person's property reached levels exceeding the permitted level as designed in the noise contours. Furthermore, the Airport Authority was required to conduct meetings and develop programmes for schools to explain environmental problems, including problems as a result of noise. This requirement was implemented in order to increase the public's awareness of environmental problems and as part of internalization of airport noise problems in the Airport Authority itself. In addition, the master plan requires that for take-off and landing, certain operational restrictions be put in place, and forbids the use of certain types of aeroplanes which cause more noise than others. These aeroplanes have been labelled Type One, Type Two and Type Three, depending on the amount of noise they generate, and the regulations require that only quiet aeroplanes be used during certain hours of the day. Finally, the Airport Authority has allocated millions of shekels in order to provide acoustic protection for schools which are located near the airport and are eligible for acoustic treatment.

§4. Enforcement

122. Enforcement of measures to prevent noise pollution is as follows: Airport noise is controlled by monitoring stations located around the Ben-Gurion airport. There have been no reported cases of criminal fines levied against offending aircraft, probably due to the fact that the monitoring stations are manned by the staff of the airport. Other airports have no monitoring devices and are a constant source of public complaints.

285. K.T. 5730, 1841.

Vehicle noise is only controlled at the annual licensing test for vehicles, but the test is not conducted to determine noise levels. It is aimed to remove items from vehicles which have deteriorated through use, like exhaust pipes and mufflers, and this, in turn, reduces noise pollution.

The only effective enforcement mechanism against noise pollution has been through the Kanowitz Law. This law, as mentioned previously, contains both criminal and civil remedies. On the criminal side, enforcement has depended on the quality and staffing of local authorities because the police do not have the capability of carrying out noise measurements. On the civil side, there have been numerous suits, mainly injunctions, to prevent noise in residential neighbourhoods.[286] The most important of these suits reached the Supreme Court, which has made the following determinations:[287]

- It is irrelevant who located first, the person causing the noise or the one suffering from it. Each individual has the right to the use of his/her property, free from unreasonable noise.
- It is irrelevant that the polluter would suffer economic harm by reducing noise pollution. This is true even if the polluter is a large factory and the plaintiff is a poor old man. The Supreme Court of Israel has not accepted a balancing of conveniences test once noise pollution has been found to occur.[288]
- Finally, even with the passage of noise regulations based on decibel levels, one may sue for noise pollution without having to prove, scientifically, a violation of the Kanowitz regulations.[289] It is sufficient to show that the noise created was unreasonable under the circumstances. In short, regulations of noise levels stated in decibels do not prevent general nuisance suits because, in the words of the Supreme Court, not everyone walks around with a decibel metre.

In 1995, the Supreme Court resolved a question of compensation to a landowner for noise which resulted from the building of a highway near his home. The landowner argued that he was entitled to compensation under the Planning and Building Law for the taking of his property due to the noise levels which would be incurred after building the road. In the law courts, the landowner received compensation for the confiscation of property, while at the Supreme Court level, the Justices debated the merit of the claim as well as the amount of money advocated. In their final analysis, the Supreme Court held that the plaintiff would be entitled to compensation, but under the narrow guidelines of the Planning and Building Law. This law, which was the basis for the plaintiff's suit, allows compensation for damage to land use and not to the person or the environment. Therefore, the Supreme Court remanded the case to the lower court, requiring it to determine the exact value of compensation allowed for the noise created by the new road.

286. *See*, e.g., Civ. App. 186/52, *Hotel Aden v. Garzon*, P.D. 8, 1121; Civ. App. 436/60, *Ezri v. Klein*, P.D. 15, 1177.
287. Civ. App. *44//76*, *ATA v. Schwartz*, P.D. 30 (3) 785.
288. *See* D. Kretzmer, *Judicial Conservatism v. Economic Liberalism: Anatomy of a Nuisance Case*, 13(3) Is. L. Rev 298 (1978).
289. Crim. App. 151/84, *Israel Electric Co. v. First*, P.D. 39 (3) 1. *See* discussion, A. Rosenthal, *Measuring Noise: Reaching an Optimal Judicial Policy*, 20(1) Is. L. Rev. 74 (1985).

At first glance, the case appears to be a reversal of Supreme Court opinions prior to the decision, which gave a clear call for a right to quiet. On the other hand, upon closer inspection, the ruling, in this case, was made in the context of the Planning and Building Law and not the Kanowitz Law. One finds, therefore, that the court case does not change the general rule, supported by the Supreme Court, that Israeli citizens have a right to quiet in their homes.[290]

290. The Local Planning and Building Commission for Jerusalem against Gilad Bar-Ali. Civil Appeals, No. 1188/92, 463 (1995).

Chapter 7. Radiation

123. Israeli law covers the subject of radioactive substances from four vantage points: mining, the workplace, the planning and building of a nuclear power plant and the siting of cell phone antennas. The laws' provisions basically cover the major problems of exposure but do not as yet have specific instructions concerning high-tension wires, radio transmittal and radar stations.

§1. Mining

124. As in some other areas of environmental protection in Israel, Israel's law covering the mining of radioactive minerals is an ordinance dating from the British Mandate.[291] The ordinance prescribes the conditions for extracting radioactive materials. Radioactive material is broadly defined in the supplement to the law. It includes uranium or thorium and their derivatives as well as a host of other minerals.

No one is permitted to mine for a radioactive substance unless he/she has been previously licensed by the Minister of Defence. Once mining begins, monthly reports of mining progress are to be delivered to the Minister of Defence. Once a radioactive substance has been discovered, its use in Israel, export or disposal is to be determined by the Minister of Defence.

§2. The Workplace

125. The control of radioactive substances in the workplace, including ionizing and non-ionizing substances, is covered by two major pieces of legislation: the Pharmacists Ordinance and the Worker's Safety Ordinance. The Pharmacists Ordinance is not limited to licensing pharmacists. Through its provisions, the Minister of Health has been given broad powers to control the use, sale and distribution of any chemical substance he/she lists in the supplement to the ordinance. The supplement lists radioactive substances and their derivatives as a 'chemical substance' controlled by the ordinance.

Following the listing of radiation, that is, ionizing and non-ionizing, as a substance or subject covered by the Pharmacists Ordinance, the Minister of Health published regulations controlling work with such materials.[292] The regulations cover both ionizing and non-ionizing radiation as well as radioactive instrumentation. It is forbidden for anyone to work with a radioactive substance or a machine producing ionizing or non-ionizing radiation without a permit from the Minister of Health. A person so authorized to act must work according to the terms of the permit. Licences for use are limited to five years unless cancelled previously by the Minister of Health.

291. Radioactive Materials Ordinance, 1947, P.O. I 261.
292. Pharmacists Regulations (Radioactive Elements & Byproducts), 1980, K.T. 992.

The regulations specifically forbid the unauthorized disposal of a radioactive substance on land, water and in the air. By order of the Minister of Environmental Protection, all radioactive waste must be hauled to the Centre for Dangerous Substances at Ramat Hovav, discussed in the next chapter. It is also forbidden to dilute a radioactive substance without permission.

In addition to the general health regulations published under the Pharmacists Ordinance, the Minister of Economy (today the Economy Minister oversees commerce, industry and labour) has published regulations under the powers granted by the Workers' Safety Ordinance.[293] These regulations control the use by workers of machines producing ionizing radiation, however, the use of machinery which produces non-ionizing radiation is not covered by these regulations.

The purpose of these regulations is to reduce the exposure of workers to ionizing radiation in the following ways. First, the regulations set out permissible levels of exposure. Second, they require a workers' safety officer, who is knowledgeable in the field of measuring radiation and who understands the dangers of exposure to radioactive materials. The safety officer determines the safety devices necessary for use in the workplace. It is the responsibility of the employer, however, to protect his/her workers from exposure by taking the following steps: appointing a safety officer and supplying him/her with the necessary data to carry out his/her job; supplying protective and measuring devices where necessary; publishing instructions for safety; reporting accidents or dangerous events to the Labour Inspectorate.

The author has been involved in Israel's largest class action suit against the Nuclear Research Facility in Dimona on behalf of some seventy-five workers who claimed to have contracted cancer as the result of exposure to radiation and other chemical substances at the plant. This case has exposed the Nuclear Research Facility to inspection by the government, and they have been found wanting in their previous monitoring and testing devices. The case originated in a Supreme Court case, which was filed by the author in 1992.[294] The case filed on behalf of the Nuclear Power workers was entitled *Shimon* Dinina versus the State of Israel, the Atomic Energy Commission, ATC, etc. Jerusalem District Court 323/93, 1993 and Estate of the Deceased Haim Klein and Others against the State of Israel, Atomic Energy Commission and Others. Jerusalem District Court 20058/95. Civil Action 198/95, 212/95, Jerusalem 1995.[295]

§3. Planning and Building

126. In addition to the Planning and Building Law discussed previously, Israel has a special regulation relating to the planning and building of a nuclear power plant. The regulation empowers the Prime Minister to build and operate a nuclear

293. Work Safety Regulations (Workers in Ionizing Radiation), 1981, K.T. 1057.

294. The Roof Organization for Workers of the Nuclear Research Facility versus the Minister of Labour and the Minister of Health, Bagatz 2917/92 (1992).

295. R. Laster & C. Somech, *Scientific Panels for Determining Health Effects Among Radiation Workers at Israel's Nuclear Research Facilities*, Environmental Health Perspectives, 105, Supplement 6 (December 1997).

power plant. It is assumed, however, that this regulation does not abrogate the Planning and Building Law's requirement for the preparation of an EIA.[296]

§4. Enforcement and Control

127. Enforcement and control of the laws dealing with radioactive substances is the responsibility of the Minister of Economy, the Minister of Environmental Protection and the Minister of Health. The three ministers have established departments for ensuring compliance with the regulations as published. As for the enforcement of the regulations, the measurement of radioactive exposure has been delegated to a branch of the Atomic Energy Commission which has the necessary monitoring devices to do such measuring. Environmental monitoring is carried out in very few parts of the country, due to lack of resources. In addition, there is supervision of medical use of radioactive materials. But there is still a need for better control and supervision of radioactive waste from hospitals and industry.

128. Non-ionizing Radiation. The Ministry of Environmental Protection has the authority to set exposure thresholds for non-ionizing radiation. It has adopted a twofold limit: one for short-term exposure, and one for continuous and long-term exposure. A major problem to public health is the numerous base stations for cellular phones. Some of these were erected without a permit, resulting in a crisis of faith among the public. Rushing in to fill the gap, the Mayor of Herzliya moved to establish regulations for the siting of base stations. The Knesset responded favourably and in 2006 passed the Non-Ionizing Radiation Law, with the purpose of protecting the public from non-ionizing radiation. The law requires obtaining a permit before erecting any new antennas, which will be given only after all efforts have been made to limit the exposure of people in the vicinity, and a report on the amount of radiation from the antenna has been presented to the Ministry of Environmental Protection. Once in use, the antenna's radiation must be measured annually with a report sent to the Ministry. The law also requires cell phone companies to compensate local authorities sued by their citizenry for exposure to cell phone base stations.

Non-ionizing radiation regulations require the information supplied to the Ministry of Environmental Protection to be published on the Ministry's website and updated at least once a month. Also, a report describing the inspections and general oversight of non-ionizing radiation sources will be presented yearly to the Knesset Interior and Environment committee. As of 2010, the Ministry of Environmental Protection's Division of Noise and Radiation Abatement has installed a system developed by an Israeli company that allows the Division to track all third-generation cellular antennae operating in Israel.

Two national plans were passed to regulate antennas that emit non-ionizing radiation. They take into account safety considerations as well as planning and aesthetics. Both plans require a safety permit as prescribed in the Non-Ionizing Radiation Law from the Ministry of Environmental Protection. The plans give priority to placing new antennas on existing antenna poles. Only if this is not possible will a new

296. Notification of Supervision over Commodities and Services (Nuclear Plant), 1974, K.T. 280.

antenna be allowed to be erected. The plans also encourage a wider network of small antennas in built-up areas, based on the assumption that this will lower radiation levels in urban areas, minimize visual scarring, and encourage a more just dispersion. Before any antenna is erected, the public, and especially those people living in close proximity, must be notified and given a chance to be heard.

Plan 36B for larger antennas requires proper zoning before a building permit may be given. Plan 36A for smaller antennas (with a safety range of less than 10 square metres) does not contain any special zoning rules, except forbidding antennas on coastal beaches. In order to encourage smaller antennas, Plan 36A includes a speedier and limited permit process for smaller antennas that have a safety range of less than 3 metres (12 metres if in an open area), as well as requiring 100% compensation for any resulting economic harm.

Israel does not have a law that delineates standards for magnetic radiation from high-voltage electric lines. Instead, the Ministry of Environmental Protection has adopted the World Health Organization guidelines for twenty-four-hour exposure: up to 1,000 milligauss (mG) for magnetic fields and up to 5,000 volts per meter for electric fields.

The Ministry of Education has published rules governing the exposure of students and teachers to non-ionizing radiation in schools.[297] Exposure is largely a result of the twenty-first-century technologies used for teaching, including Internet and Wi-Fi, projectors, laptop computers and tablets, as well as student usage of cell phones. These rules include radiation testing before and after installation of equipment, educational programmes for students and teachers to raise awareness, limiting the usage of WIFI according to age groups, and distancing charging stations from the classrooms.

297. *Rules of the Director General of the Ministry of Education*, 3.6–11, 8 Jul. 2013.

Chapter 8. Other Sectors

§1. Toxic Substances

I. Introduction

129. Israel has no single example of comprehensive legislation controlling toxic substances from cradle to grave. The operative legislation dealing with toxic substances is, for the most part, a mixture of legislation aimed at a certain aspect of the use of toxic substances with patches applied later to cover environmental gaps. As will be seen, the legislation has serious shortcomings and needs revision.

II. Pharmacists Ordinance (NV) 1981

130. As its name implies, the Pharmacists Ordinance was originally created in order to license pharmacists and supervise their handling of pharmaceuticals. A major tenet of the law is to require pharmacists to keep a logbook recording possession of poisonous substances. The law forbids anyone, other than a pharmacist, from handling the sale or distribution of poisons without a licence. The law empowers the Minister of Health to determine by regulation the definition of poisons to be supervised. Yet, the law defines 'poison' as any substance the Minister of Health lists in an appendix to the law. This, in effect, enables the Minister to control the use of any substance in Israel.

In 1972, the Minister of Health exercised the power granted to him under the Pharmacists Ordinance and promulgated regulations dividing poisons into three categories: agricultural, industrial and medical.[298] For each category, the Minister determined the type of poison to be registered in the poisons logbook and the manner of logging required. An agricultural poison is defined as any substance used in agriculture listed in an appendix to the regulations. A medical poison is defined as a poison used for diagnosis, treatment, relief or healing as listed in the appendix. An industrial poison is any poison used in industry, crafts, research, teaching, business or household use listed in the appendix. At the same time, the regulations require proper licensing and packaging of poisons. But unlimited power is often burdensome and ineffective. In fact, the law basically serves as legislative regulation of the pharmaceutical profession on the one hand, and as a labelling and packaging law on the other, for certain chemical substances.

III. The Dangerous Substances Law, 1993

131. Early in 1993, the Ministry of Environmental Protection convinced the Knesset to pass a new bill to protect the environment from toxic and dangerous

---

298. Pharmacists Order (Classification of Poisons, History and Possession), 1972, K.T. 272.

substances. The bill, entitled The Dangerous Substances Law 1993,[299] is not, however, an all-encompassing statute as one would expect from environmental legislation. Basically, the law divides responsibility between the Ministry of Environmental Protection and the Ministry of Health. It does this by transferring certain powers granted to the Ministry of Health under the Pharmacist's Ordinance (NV 1981)[300] to the Minister of Environmental Protection. One must admit, however, that the transfer of power could have been carried out in a more elegant manner.

As stated in paragraph 129 *supra*, the Pharmacists Ordinance delineates the Minister of Health's powers to supervise 'poisons'. This is in keeping with the knowledge available during the law's passage in the 1930s. Second, the law enables the Minister of Health to regulate the sale, distribution and handling of 'poisons' through licensed pharmacists. The Dangerous Substances Law uses the same formula as the Pharmacists Ordinance. It opens by defining a dangerous substance as 'a poison or a harmful chemical'. The law does not, however, define what is a poison or a harmful chemical. It simply refers the public to a list of 'poisons' and 'harmful chemicals' attached as appendices to the law. The Minister is not bound by any constraints in adding or detracting a poison from the appendices. The Minister has already used his power to add poisons to the list. He amended the list of poisons in regulations published in 1963 and again in regulations published later the same year.[301]

The law forbids anyone from handling a dangerous substance without a licence and in accordance with its terms. A licensee must maintain a register of the sale and purchase of each dangerous substance. The law gives almost unlimited power to the Minister of Environmental Protection to control dangerous substances. The Minister is authorized to publish regulations for 'the handling and use of dangerous substances, their production, export, import, packaging and sales thereof, transport, warehousing and possession'.[302]

It was expected that with the publication of the Dangerous Substances Law, the Ministry of Environmental Protection would use this framework legislation to make order out of the chaotic supervision of dangerous substances that exists in Israel. Instead, the Minister simply added an additional bureaucratic hoop for manufacturers and distributors of dangerous substances to jump through. One of the few regulations promulgated under the new law forbids the import or export of dangerous substances unless the importer or exporter meets the listed conditions under the regulations.[303]

Instead of using the power granted to him under the Dangerous Substances Law, the Minister has exploited the power invested in him under the Licensing of Businesses Law. Under this law, the Minister of Environmental Protection promulgated important regulations in 1993 for factories producing dangerous substances.[304] These regulations require a manufacturer of a dangerous substance to be prepared

299. S.H. 1408, 28.
300. D.M.I. New Version 35, 694.
301. K.T. 5762, 1035.
302. K.T. 5762, 1044.
303. K.T. 5612, 1152.
304. Regulations for Licensing of Businesses (Dangerous Factories), 1993, K.T. 1052.

in the eventuality of an accident occurring on the premises. Preparation includes compiling a dossier with data on dangerous substances on the premises, their potential for danger, types of accidents that can occur, and the methods for handling such accidents. The regulations also require the manufacturer to report once a year to the licensing authority, about the types of dangerous substances on the premises or any changes in operational procedures.[305]

The Minister of Environmental Protection, in 1994, published regulations prohibiting the import or export of dangerous solid waste without receiving permission from the Ministry.[306] One holding a permit must report to the Ministry the amount of dangerous solid waste imported or exported.[307]

The Minister of Environmental Protection has also used the power vested in him to promulgate regulations for the use and control of containers for pest extermination, used by the general public.[308] These regulations are what one would normally call labelling regulations. They require that a person selling or distributing a container containing a dangerous substance used for pest extermination be required to label the container in such a fashion that it explains the type of dangerous substance in the container, its use, misuse and emergency use. In addition, the label must state that one using the substance not in accordance with the regulations is endangering his/her health. An inter-ministerial committee has been set up to approve the import, sale and distribution of such containers.[309]

The Dangerous Substances Regulations, Disposal of Radioactive Waste (2002)[310] require those persons who have radioactive waste in their place of business to dispose of such waste according to the regulations. They require that no one will dispose radioactive waste, liquid or solid, except at a designated site. The site is at the Atomic Energy Commission Plant in Dimona. Furthermore, the regulations forbid the burning of radioactive solid waste or the emission of radioactive solid waste to a sewage outlet.

Other regulations promulgated by the Ministry of Environmental Protection bring Israeli legislation in line with the Montreal Protocol on Substances that Deplete the Ozone Layer. These regulations restrict the production, consumption, import and export of substances that deplete the ozone layer. The regulations contain an exemption clause, which sets a predetermined quantity of controlled substances for critical use.

In addition to the above regulations, the Plant Protection (Regulating the Import and Sale of Chemical Substances) Regulations (1994), promulgated by the Ministry of Agriculture, also regulate dangerous substances. These regulations require importers to submit a dangerous substance to an inter-ministerial committee for approval before the substance can be imported or sold in Israel. An application for

305. *Ibid.*, at s. 5.
306. Regulations of Dangerous Substances (Import and Export of Dangerous Solid Waste), 1994, K.T. 1152.
307. *Ibid.*, at s. 4.
308. Regulation of Dangerous Substances (Registration of Pest Extermination Substances), 2002, K.T. 1285.
309. K.T. 5633, 257.
310. KT 615, 420.

approval by the committee must show that the substance is effective as well as discuss its negative impact on the environment. The committee may accept or reject the substance, and its decision may be appealed in court.

132. Until 2016, pest exterminators were regulated under the Ministry of Health business regulations. In reaction to fatal accidents, the regulations were replaced with primary legislation, the Law for Regulating Pest Exterminators, 2016.[311] According to the law, exterminators must have the appropriate training and a licence from the Ministry of Environmental Protection. The law establishes four levels of licences and criminal penalties for infractions.

IV. The Plant Protection Law, 1956

133. The Plant Protection Law was discussed earlier in the chapter on soil pollution. It enables the head of the Department of Plant Protection in the Ministry of Agriculture, as advised by an inter-ministerial committee, to permit or prohibit a pesticide or herbicide. Yet again, as in the Pharmacists Ordinance, the law has two aims, and in this case, they are inconsistent. On the one hand, the law requires the head of the Department of Plant Protection to exterminate pests and increase agricultural yields by the use of chemicals. On the other hand, he/she is to be aware of the dangers inherent in the use of pesticides and prevent the introduction of dangerous or ineffective products into Israel.

As stated earlier, the law has been used effectively in limiting the import of dangerous or untested pesticides approved elsewhere in the world. It has not been effective, however, in reducing pesticide use, residues, waste and disposal.

V. The Civil Defence Law, 1951

134. The Civil Defence Law[312] is an inventory statute. It enables the Minister of Defence to require anyone to report to him details of a dangerous substance held by that person. The Civil Defence (Announcement of Dangerous Substances) Ordinance of 1995 requires all those possessing dangerous substances to report the type and quality in their possession to the Civil Defence authorities. In order to determine what substances are to be reported, the Ministry of Defence has published, in regulations, a list of dangerous substances, updating the previous list which appeared in the regulations of 1989. There is no correlation between this list and the list published under the Pharmacists Ordinance Regulations published by the Ministry of Health, and the Dangerous Substances Regulations published by the Ministry of Environmental Protection.[313]

311. *Law for the Regulation of Commercial Exterminators*, 2016, S.H. 2531, p. 548.
312. 5 L.S.I. 72.
313. K.T. 5765, 889.

VI. The Ports Ordinance

135. The Ports Ordinance contains provisions for the control of shipping, handling and loading dangerous substances in a port.[314] A dangerous substance is defined as any substance appearing in the appendix to the regulations or any substance which the Port Director has determined to be dangerous, considering the special circumstances of his/her particular port facilities. The ordinance requires a ship's captain to notify the Port Authority that he/she is carrying a dangerous substance thirty-six hours before he/she enters the port. The ship's captain must also certify that the dangerous substance is properly packaged and labelled according to the Inter-governmental Maritime

Consultative Organization IMCO codes. All ships carrying dangerous cargo are to anchor at a place as directed; the cargo is to be removed, handled, stored and transported under the supervision of the Port Authority.

VII. Licensing of Businesses

136. Under the Licensing of Businesses Law, the Minister of Health is empowered to regulate businesses in order to ensure proper sanitary conditions. The Minister of Environmental Protection is also empowered to regulate businesses to ensure protection of the environment.

Using the power granted under this and other laws, the Minister of Environmental Protection has issued regulations regarding disposal of toxic substances.[315] These regulations define toxic substances as inflammatory, explosive, corrosive or poisonous substances with a United Nations number as defined in the appendix to the Services and Commodities Control Law, 1962. The regulations require that such substances be removed from the premises and transported under proper conditions to a site established in northern Negev for the handling and neutralization of dangerous substances. This site is known as Ramat Hovav.

In recent years, the issue of location of dangerous substances in close proximity to residential areas has been raised. The problem has worsened with the rapid expansion of many cities. The Ministry of Environmental Protection is now in the process of developing a standard national policy concerning separation between dangerous substances and the general population.

The most glaring example of this is the ammonia tanks currently located in Haifa Bay. The Ministry of Environmental Protection spearheaded a government decision to move the tanks to a new production facility in the Negev by 2017 when the current poison permit expires. The tanks endanger the lives of hundreds of thousands of Haifa residents. The Haifa Chemicals Company did not comply with the government's decision, claiming that removing the ammonia tanks would result in the firing of 1,500 employees. The City of Haifa went to court and was awarded a court order to close the ammonia tanks. A court appeal by Haifa Chemicals was rejected,

314. Ports Regulations, 1971, K.T. 306.
315. Regulations for the Licensing of Businesses (Disposal of Dangerous Waste), 1990, K.T. 22.

with the court confirming the total removal of the ammonia tanks. A new plant for ammonia production is planned in the Negev desert area.

Another aspect currently being tackled is the effects of earthquakes on storage facilities for dangerous substances. The Ministry of Environmental Protection has published guidelines for factories storing dangerous substances that require engineering reports and plans for minimizing damage in the event of an earthquake.

VIII. Asbestos

137. Asbestos was widely used in Israel until recent years, chiefly in making roofs and other asbestos cement building products. An asbestos cement factory was established in Nahariya in western Galilee in 1952 and was closed down in 1997. But throughout the lifetime of the plant, asbestos waste had been dumped in several areas of western Galilee. As public awareness of the dangers of asbestos grew, residents began demanding a solution. In spite of several government decisions, the asbestos waste has not been cleaned up. In 2011, the Ministry of Environment began a five-year project for identifying, removing and disposing of the asbestos waste in western Galilee at a cost of about USD 83 million, half of which will be the responsibility of the plant owners.

138. The Asbestos Law. In 2011, the Prevention of Hazards from Asbestos and Harmful Dust Law was approved. The law bans the use of asbestos in new products and requires a phased removal of friable asbestos (asbestos not locking into cement or another material) in industry and public buildings within ten years. Non-friable asbestos, found mainly in roofs, will require proper maintenance in public buildings, including painting, mapping and registration. The law also requires regulation of the licensing of asbestos workers and permit requirements for asbestos work.

IX. The Workplace

139. Control of dangerous substances at the factory is also the responsibility of the Minister of Economy (formerly Trade, Industry and Labour). Under the Labour Inspection (Organization) Law 1954, the Minister has promulgated regulations to require employers to notify their workers regarding health or safety dangers in the workplace.[316] This requires the employer to instruct the workers on the proper use of any device or substance which could be injurious to their health. It also requires an employer to notify his/her workers of the introduction of any new dangerous substance in the workplace. Finally, if an employer conducts a test in the workplace for a dangerous substance, he/she must notify the employee of the results of the test.

316. Organization of the Supervision over Work (Notification of Information and Instruction to Workers) Regulations, 1984, K.T. 4666. Tests are to be conducted in accordance with the Organization of the Supervision over Work (Environmental Monitoring & Biological Monitoring of the Workers with Harmful Substances) Regulations, 1990, K.T. 5309.

The above regulations do not define the term dangerous substance; each employer is to make the determination of what is dangerous to his/her employees. The Ministry of the Economy has, however, published several types of regulations regarding specific substances considered dangerous. The first type is a total ban of substances considered carcinogenic for which substitutes are available.[317] This regulation requires the employer to get special permission to use the substance. The second type of regulation sets permissible levels for exposure to certain known carcinogens.[318] The Minister of Health has published regulations protecting workers from ionizing radiation.[319] The Minister of Economy has published regulations protecting workers exposed to the following dangerous substances: heavy metals,[320] organic and phosphorus-based pesticides[321] and aromatic dissolved carbon.[322] These regulations set out health and safety requirements for workers working with these dangerous substances.

The interaction of environmental health and safety has come to the forefront in several leading cases in Israel. The first of these are cases dealing with asbestos exposure which at first attracted attention due to the huge number of asbestos workers who contracted asbestosis from working at the Isasbest plant in Naharia. After the first wave of cases filed by workers against their employer, a new wave appeared comprised mainly of citizens living near the plant, who suffered from asbestos-related disease as a result of environmental contact. One of the major victories for the green NGOs was the case against the siting of a building at a formerly abandoned asbestos waste dump in Naharia.[323] In this particular case, the city of Naharia intended to build a park for children on an abandoned asbestos waste dump, and the city's efforts were stymied by public action and finally by a decision of the District Court.

Another court case connecting environmental health and safety involved the Haifa Chemical plant near the Kishon River. There, Haifa Chemicals, a well-known polluting facility, was sued by the Israel Union for Environmental Defence (explored in the previous chapter on water pollution). It has now come to light that several workers at the Haifa Chemical plant contracted asbestosis and other diseases due to the use of asbestos in the plant with poor or little supervision. Finally, several incidences of fire occurred in the warehouses operated by Haifa Chemicals and a State report shows a complete disregard for all rules and regulations during the operation and maintenance of these warehouses.[324] An additional instance occurred in the pollution of groundwater from chemicals from the Tadiran plant in

317. Work Safety (Prohibition of Work with Certain Carcinogenic Materials), 1984, 415.
318. *See*, e.g., Work Safety (Occupational Safety and Health for Workers Working with Mercury), 1985, 504; (Asbestos) K.T. 5744, 722, K.T. 5751, 133.
319. K.T. 5763, 126.
320. *Ibid.*, 441.
321. *Ibid.*, 192.
322. *Ibid.*, 450.
323. *Medinat HaYiladin v. Isasbest and the District Planning Court.*
324. Committee appointed by the Minister of Environmental Protection to Investigating the Fire at Haifa Chemicals, February 2003.

Ekron. In that plant, some eighty-five workers in the nickel battery department contracted diseases related to exposure to nickel and chrome.[325] Later on, these substances were also found in the groundwater near Ashdod. A similar case of exposure to harmful chemicals occurred at the Israel Military Industries plant in Ramat Hasharon.[326] All these cases point to a need for coordination between the Ministry of Environmental Protection, the Ministry of the Economy, the National Health Service Department of Industrial and Medical Doctors, and the Ministry of Health.

X. Non-agricultural Pesticides

140. Under the Services and Commodities Control law,[327] the Minister of Health has issued regulations licensing the sale and production of pesticides presumably for household use because agricultural use is covered in the Protection of Plants Law. These regulations enable the Minister of Health to prevent the sale or production of any pesticide unless the pesticide has first been approved by the Ministry. A person requesting a licence for sale and production must present material to the Ministry on the effectiveness of the pesticide and other data as requested, including its toxicity to humans. Unfortunately, no system has been developed nationally for the collection and safe disposal of pesticides and their containers after usage.

XI. Transportation

141. The Transport Services Law of 1997 and its 2001 regulations regulate the transportation of dangerous substances and largely correspond to the UN Recommendations on the Transport of Dangerous Goods – Model Regulations (The Orange Book).[328] All transported hazardous substances are marked according to the Globally Harmonized System of Classification and Labelling of Chemicals (GHS).

The law is aimed at raising the level of safety for commercial vehicles and those providing haulage services, as well as protecting the environment. No one may operate a hauling service without a permit and in accordance with the terms of that permit. The law further enables the inspector of transportation to require those working in the hauling field to be properly trained for their duties and those transporting dangerous substances to receive special training.

In addition to the law and regulations, there is an inter-ministerial committee for dangerous substances, which must approve appropriate transportation routes for dangerous materials to avoid or reduce community exposure in case of an accident. This committee has approved internationally approved markers for trucks carrying dangerous substances.

---

325. Report by Y. Yakku & Oded.
326. High Court of Justice, Case No. 3485/00. Israel Union for Environmental Defence against Israel Military Industries.
327. Order for Supervision of Commodities and Service (Devices to Exterminate Pests Dangerous to Man), 1962, K.J. 1097.
328. *Israel National Report-Chemicals, UN Commission on Sustainable Development*, 2010.

XII. Evaluation

142. Looking at the legislation, one immediately grasps the problem. There is an abundance of laws and regulations, many overlapping, while some areas are left uncovered. Each law defines dangerous substances with no relation to other laws on the subject. The legislation is not environmentally orientated. For the most part, its original purpose was to ensure the proper use of dangerous chemicals and registration of those using or selling such products. There is also no provision for the reduction of dangerous chemicals and pesticides in the environment or neutralization of chemicals or dangerous substances. Even the regulations for disposal of dangerous substances are cryptic and may prove very difficult to implement. The criteria for registration of chemicals are broad; thus, they probably fluctuate in practice as those registering chemicals change attitudes or jobs. There is also no tracing mechanism in the statutes due to a lack of coordination nor is there a community 'right to know' requirement for storage, production and disposal of dangerous products.

As can be seen from the above, the creation of the Ministry of Environmental Protection in 1989 and the passage of the Dangerous Substances Law of 1993 have had a significant impact on the treatment, storage, transportation and disposal of dangerous waste. The mere fact that the Ministry controls the use of dangerous solid waste at the plant site has clearly improved the situation regarding the handling of solid waste. In addition, the Ministry's joint regulation with the Ministry of the Economy requiring a manufacture safety data sheet is a step in the right direction for environmental health and safety methods which will work together. Furthermore, the Ministry's regulations for compiling a file for each industry about the emergency measures to be taken when there is a spill or an accident concerning dangerous substances are of major importance in a country as small as Israel. The new regulations for disposal of radioactive solid waste and the amendments to the other regulations produced by the Ministry of Environmental Protection for disposal of solid waste at the facility for solid waste disposal have also reduced the danger to the environment in the handling and disposal of solid waste. Major problems, however, still remain. The concentration of hazardous substances at the Ramat Hovav site, the National Centre for Dangerous Solid Waste, has led to a never-ending source of problems. During its years of operation, the site has suffered from explosions, accidental fires, leaking into groundwater and an untold number of mishaps. According to reports, these mishaps have not led to serious environmental danger, but the reports themselves leave questions to be answered especially concerning the pollution of groundwater in the southern part of Israel. In addition, the radioactive site at the Atomic Energy Centre near Dimona has been kept under secret lock and key for years so that no one really knows what the potential environmental effects are of this site.

There is no coordination between the different lists of dangerous substances that appear in Israeli laws. Also, the laws regulating the usage of most chemicals (outside of pesticides, cosmetics, food additives and medicines) put the burden of proof on the Government. In other words, so long as a chemical does not appear on a list of dangerous substances in one of the above-mentioned laws, its usage is not controlled. The Government does not have the resources to test new chemicals effectively, so by the time a chemical appears on a list, it may well be already in use.

In Europe, the precautionary principle has guided new chemical legislation. REACH, the new European law for registration of chemicals transfers the burden from the Government to the manufacturers and distributors to evaluate the hazards and risks of chemicals and to prove a chemical is safe for usage. This must be done before a chemical can be marketed. A single registry provides easy access to information, and one registry process ensures uniformity in testing, usage and production of chemicals.

Under pressure from the OECD, Israel has agreed to reform its legislation concerning testing and registration of chemicals.[329] In addition, Israel's large chemical manufacturers export many of their products to Europe, bringing them under the governance of European laws in any case.

143. Enforcement. Finally, not enough emphasis can be placed on the fact that there are too many authorities and far too many ministries involved in the handling, operation, transportation and disposal of solid waste. The situation has been criticized over the years by the Comptroller's office, but no one seems to pay heed to the Comptroller's criticism.

It is clear that the Ministry of Environment cannot enforce the Dangerous Substances Law with the personnel at hand. It often uses the district and local environmental authorities for enforcement powers. Yet, these authorities are independent of the Ministry of Environmental Protection. Second, there seems to be no cross-fertilization between the Ministries of Health, Labour and the Environment, where together they could pinpoint hot spots for dangerous substances.

As mentioned earlier, all dangerous substances are to be disposed of at Ramat Hovav, a plant located in the Negev for the receipt of dangerous substances. The plant is miles away from the sectors producing dangerous substances. Therefore, although the idea of creating a plant for the storage and disposal of dangerous substances is laudable, the distance factor creates difficulties in the transportation of dangerous substances.

Third, reports show that less than 70% of the dangerous substances which are to be shipped to the national site for disposal of dangerous substances at Ramat Hovav actually reach that site. This means that a great number of dangerous substances on the list are being deposited somewhere in the natural environment. Furthermore, there have been repeated problems at the Ramat Hovav site itself.

The Army evacuated two units stationed near the site, due to complaints of the effects of the site on the health of the soldiers. It has come to the attention of the public that the Ramat Hovav site has ordered an incinerator for burning organic waste. The various NGOs that attacked the original purchase of the incinerator have now met with the operators of the Ramat Hovav site and the Ministry of Environmental Protection, in order to ensure that the incinerator so purchased will actually improve the quality of the environment, rather than cause environmental degradation.

A real challenge to the Ramat Hovav site hovers as the army is relocating a large number of army bases from the centre of the country to a site near Ramat Hovav.

329. Israel Ministry of Environmental Protection, *Israel's Position with Regard to OECD Council Acts and Other Relevant Instruments in the Field of Environment*, March 2010 pp. 31–32.

Air pollution studies found the site to be outside the acceptable range. In 2004, the government decided to reclaim the site and make the necessary environmental improvements by 2010. In response to a petition to the High Court of Justice, an environmental impact statement that includes possible exposure of soldiers and health impacts was presented. The regional planning committee gave the plans their approval on the condition that the remaining environmental pollution is treated. In 2015, the first army base was opened at the site.

§2. Rational Use of Energy

I. Introduction

144. Israel uses energy sources, as do all other industrial countries, for power plants, household and industrial use, transportation, desalination and irrigation. Israel has attempted to reduce its dependence on oil and coal by exploiting the sun. With a population hovering around 8 million people, it is estimated that 90% of the homes heat water most of the year by glass solar collectors. Solar water heating is mandatory in new residential buildings up to nine stories *high.*[330]

In 2010, electricity was produced from the following fuel sources: coal-61%, fuel oil-0.9%, natural gas-36.6%, and diesel fuel-1.5%.[331] By 2019, the sources of fuel for electricity production had changed to 66% natural gas, 7% renewable energies, and the rest coal and other fuels.[332] Due to Israel's large offshore gas reserves, the country has greatly increased its energy independence.

Israel has built several small solar electric plants, mainly in the Arava Desert and the Dead Sea regions. In 2011, the first commercial solar field, covering 20 acres of the Arava desert, was constructed at Kibbutz Ketura. It is expected to produce 4.95 megawatts. A second field at Ketura, covering 133.4 acres, was completed in 2015. In March 2011, the government published two more tenders to market land for solar energy initiatives involving photovoltaic electricity generation and expected to supply 15 megawatts of electricity.[333]

The Ministries of Energy and Agriculture & Rural Development will examine the production of electricity from solar energy on active agricultural land of an area of 1,800 dunams in a pilot programme.[334] It hopes to benefit Israeli agriculture by maximizing farmers' profits, preserving agricultural land and combining agricultural activities with promoting energy goals and preserving the environment.

Industrial plants consuming a minimum of 300 tons of crude oil or its equivalent per year, or a minimum of 1 million kilowatt-hours of electricity per year, are

330. Planning and Building Regulations (Request for Permit, Conditions and Fees), 1970, K.T. 1841.
331. *Israel Environment Bulletin, Israel Ministry of Environmental Protection*, Vol. 43 (March 2017), 19.
332. Ministry of Energy and Infrastructure, The Structure of the Energy Sector in Israel. 6 Jun. 2021.
333. Israel Ministry of Energy and Water Resources. https://www.gov.il/en/departments/topics/electricity_and_renewable_energy (last visited 30 Oct. 2019).
334. Ministry of Agriculture and Rural Development, Press Release 11 Jan. 2022.

required to hire energy conservation officers.[335] The officers are linked with the Ministry of National Infrastructures, Energy and Water Resources to work out measures for conservation.

During the 1980s and 1990s, the IEC shifted the source of energy for its fossil fuel power plants from oil to coal. During this period, all new power plants were built with the capacity to burn coal instead of oil. This has resulted in a reduction in the amount of air pollution. The coal purchased contains less sulphur than oil, and all new power plants are required to install electrostatic precipitators. In the late 1990s, the IEC began converting its coal-fired plants to natural gas, resulting in a large reduction in air pollution. Due to the discovery of natural gas reserves off the coast, this trend is increasing.

The Ministry of National Infrastructures, Energy and Water Resources has expended resources in trying to find alternate sources of electric power production in the following areas: the Ministry has explored the possibility of pumped energy storage along the Dead Sea Region due to the tremendous difference in heights at the edge of the Dead Sea. Israel has two wind farms, the larger of which supplies 6 megawatts/hour of electricity. Finally, the Ministry is working on the use of pumped air, similar to pumped storage, for the production of energy. All of the above uses are considered environmentally friendly and will reduce the emission of sulphur into the atmosphere, and not just in Israel. Unfortunately, they comprise a tiny amount of Israel's total energy usage.

145. The government has published several decisions to encourage the development of renewable energy sources, with limited success. For example, the government decided that by the year 2020, 10% of Israel's energy needs will be provided by renewable energy sources.[336] But that goal was not met. Recently, a plan has been put into action to buy power from small-and medium-sized solar facilities, mainly on the rooves of industrial and agricultural buildings at a subsidized price in order to encourage their construction. The government has also set a goal for a 20% reduction in energy demand through improved energy efficiency.

The Ministry of National Infrastructures, Energy and Water Resources has looked into the building of a nuclear power plant for the production of energy. Since the Chernobyl and Fukushima disasters, however, there has been a public debate about the inherent dangers of such a power plant and the Ministry has not yet defined its goals on this issue. At present, Israel has no nuclear power plants for the production of energy.

II. Energy Legislation

146. The Energy Enterprise Law, 1996. The major thrust of government legislation in the last several years has been two-fold. The government has encouraged

335. National Energy Authority Regulations (Supervision of the Efficiency of Energy Use in Enterprises), 1981, K.T. 488.
336. *Government Decision No. 3484* from 17 Jul. 2011.

competition in the production of energy, while it is requiring energy conservation.[337] All large energy users are now required to prepare a study showing measures to conserve energy. The study is to be updated once a year. In addition, factories with large energy requirements must appoint an employee to be responsible for promoting the efficient use of energy. This employee prevents energy waste, supervises maintenance procedures, measures energy use, records types of fuel and trains personnel in energy conservation.

The most ambitious piece of legislation in the field of energy was published in 1996, titled the Energy Enterprise Law. Section 1 of this law sets out its aims as follows: to organize the activities in the field of energy for the benefit of the public, ensuring availability, quality and efficiency, while creating conditions for competition and reduction in costs. This is a bold statement which most countries would be proud to produce in their legislation but would find difficult to implement. The law sets out chapters for licensing and supply of energy and probably the most innovative section of the law is a regulatory body composed of members of the public who are to set tariffs for energy charges, while at the same time creating a framework for service to the public. The energy law enables companies other than the IEC to create and produce energy which will then be sold to the Israel Energy Corporation at a price set by the public licensing authority.[338]

147. The Sources of Energy Law, 1989. This law was passed with the purpose of regulating energy sources, ensuring they are used efficiently and reducing energy usage. Several regulations were promulgated in order to reach these goals including regulations enabling fines to be levied on individuals and industries that do not meet the required standards.[339]

A law was recently passed that exempts the sale of electricity by small-scale solar energy producers from paying income tax.[340]

III. International Rational Use of Energy

148. In the agreement between Israel and the Hashemite Kingdom of Jordan, section 19 defines the general principles for cooperation in the use of energy. These principles include cooperation in the development of solar energy. This cooperation has already found fruit in the cooperative venture for solar energy in the Gulf of Aqaba and Eilat. In addition, further agreements ought to be signed between the two countries, once these agreements have been ratified by both sides. Regarding the Palestinian Authority, the agreement has not defined clearly the rights and responsibilities over energy use. Part of the agreement, however, is section 15, which

337. Sources of Energy (Undertaking a Study to Find the Potential for Energy Conservation) Regulation, K.T. 5763, 1099 and Energy Sources (Supervision of Efficient Use of Energy) Regulation, K.T. 5764, 10.
338. S.H. 5766, 208.
339. Regulations for Administrative Infractions (Administrative Fines-Energy Sources), 2004.
340. *Law to Encourage Investment in Renewable Energy (Tax Breaks for the Production of Electricity from Renewable Sources)*, 2016.

makes a determination about gas and fuel containers. This section requires the Palestinian Authority to build and site gas and fuel containers in such a fashion, as to not cause a negative effect on the environment or safety factors in Israel or Israeli settlements. The section requires the Palestinians to use standards for the protection of the environment that have been developed in America, Britain or Israel.

Part II. Nature Conservation and Management

Chapter 1. Monuments and Landscapes

§1. Monuments

I. Antiquities

149. Israeli law distinguishes between antiquities and buildings of historical significance. Antiquities, protected under the Antiquities Law of 1978, are defined as any 'object, whether detached or fixed, which was made by humans in or before the year 1700 of the Common Era, which is of historical value, and the Minister (of Education and Culture) has declared to be an antiquity'.[341]

150. The law declares that any antiquity discovered becomes the property of the State, as well as the ground in which it was discovered. The law requires anyone discovering an antiquity, other than one licensed at an archaeological dig, to notify the head of the Antiquities Authority within fifteen days of the discovery. Any person carrying out land works who discovers an antiquity must notify the Antiquities Authority and cease operating for fifteen days unless he/she receives notice from the Antiquities Authority that he/she may continue his/her work. If the Director of Antiquities halts work on the land permanently, the owner or occupier will be compensated by the State for his/her loss.

The law also has separate provisions for archaeological digs, sale and export of antiquities, collectors and sites. Each phase is carefully regulated by the Antiquities Authority, on the one hand, to preserve antiquities, and on the other to protect the purchaser. Archaeological sites are operated under a licence, the holder of which is required to report periodically to the Antiquities Authority. Dealers in antiquities are also licensed and are required to have a special licence for the export of antiquities.

The law authorizes the Director of the Antiquities Authority to declare a place to be an antiquity site. This declaration is published in the *Official Gazette* and in the Land Registry, and notification is given to the District Planning and Building Commission. Once such a site has been declared, a person may not carry out works on the site without written permission from the Director of Antiquities. The Antiquities

341. 32 L.S.I. 93.

Authority Law established an Archaeological Council comprised of sixteen representatives from the government, museums and the academic world.[342] The Council's main function is to set policy and approve the Authority's budget.

Harming antiquities or an antiquities site is punishable by a prison sentence or fine. A person found in an antiquities site with digging tools is assumed to be attempting to unearth antiquities unless they can prove otherwise.[343]

The law provides ample protection for antiquities and encourages the exploration and discovery of antiquities. Criticism has been levelled at the Antiquities Authority for poor maintenance of declared sites. Apparently, the Antiquities Authority archaeologists find searching, uncovering and publishing findings a greater challenge than 'passive' protection.

II. National Sites

151. The National Parks, Nature Reserves, Historical Sites and Monuments Law protects historical sites that are not antiquities.[344] The law defines a historical site as that building or group of buildings, including their surroundings, which are of national historical importance in the development of the founding of the modern State of Israel. This period is normally considered to begin around 1870. The Ministry of the Interior is empowered to list those sites deemed worthy of national historical importance. Once a site is listed and approved under the Planning and Building Law, no one may alter or destroy the site without permission from the Ministry of Environmental Protection, the Planning Board and the Knesset Committee on the Environment. Protection of national sites is *granted* by law to the local authority or to the Nature and Parks Authority.

The Planning and Building Law 1991 amendment requires every local planning commission to set up a subcommittee of the local planning committee for national sites.[345] The subcommittee must prepare a list of sites worthy of preservation due to their 'historical, national, architectural or archaeological importance'. Once such a list is prepared, the sites may then be submitted to the planning commission for approval as preserved sites. Such a site may not be changed without the approval of the planning commission and in accordance with the preservation plan.

Once a site has been so designated, its owner may make only those changes to the site as provided in the preservation plan. This in essence reduces the owner's control over his/her own property. If the owner then claims damages for the resulting reduction in property value, the local authority may either pay compensation to the owner or, if the local authority has no money available, it may amend or cancel the designation plan.

The amendment enables an owner of a preserved site to get a tax benefit for preserving his/her home. However, if the local planning commission finds a preservation site to be in a state of disrepair, it may require the owner to repair the site to

342. Antiquities Authority Law of 1989, para. 6.
343. Antiquities Law of 1978, para. 38.
344. The National Parks, Nature Reserves, Historical Sites and Monuments Law of 1998.
345. 47 L.S.I., unpublished; S.H. 5751, 164.

keep it in its designated preserved state. If the owner fails to make the necessary repairs, the local authority may then expropriate the property, according to the rules set out in the amendment, and repair the property according to the plan.

152. Implementation of the National Sites Amendment to the Nature Reserves, National Parks, Historical Sites and Monuments Law has been disappointing. Unlike the Antiquities Law, which has existed in some fashion since the British Mandate, the National Sites Amendment has no tradition of enforcement. Second, unlike the Antiquities Law, the National Sites Amendment requires positive action in the form of planning and compensation. Finally, developing background studies, declaring, planning and preserving a historical site requires work, coordination and money. Often, the lack of resources to compensate owners of national sites dooms the process of preservation at the outset.

In fact, since the law's passage, few sites have been designated, while numerous sites have been bulldozed and replaced by newer buildings. Efforts by the public in the last few years have succeeded in focusing attention on national historical sites and this, in turn, has been somewhat effective in conserving some sites. Ambitious plans are underway in Tel Aviv and Jerusalem to protect historic buildings. The National Council for Historic Sites also adds its insight to the struggle for preservation. Yet to date, planning boards refuse to recognize the importance of protection and Israel is losing a heritage worth preserving for the next generation.

§2. LANDSCAPES

I. In General

153. Landscapes are not protected by a specific law in Israel. They are protected, however, under the Planning and Building Law and the Law for National Parks, Nature Reserves, Historical Sites and Monuments (*see* above). Under the Planning and Building Law, planning commissions are empowered to set aside land because of its natural beauty. A national plan for certain landscapes has been passed under the Planning and Building Law. In addition, cities and municipalities are entitled to set aside certain areas for their landscape value, and this has been done at various locations.

But Israel's growing population and rising standard of living have resulted in developers continuously pressuring the planning authorities to authorize additional construction in the little open space still left in the centre of the country.

154. National Outline Plan 35 is an attempt to put into practice the theory of sustainable development. It combines building, development and protection. Its purpose is to provide solutions for building and development while protecting open spaces for future generations. The plan emphasizes the principle of contiguous open spaces that include extensions along streams and rivers and the protection of nature, farming, vistas and history. An additional principle is emphasizing development within existing cities and limiting 'suburbanization', promoting public transportation, and giving preference to development in the Negev and Jerusalem.

The plan consists of statutory instructions and maps as well as recommendations of policy measures which should be taken into account in decisions made by government authorities to assure the achievement of its planning goals.

155. After a long legal struggle, in 2009, the Supreme Court upheld a plan to build an apartment complex next to a seasonal lake in the city of Netanya. The lake fills up with winter rains and dries up in the spring. The area contains the third-largest concentration of the Coastal Iris (in Latin *Iris atropurpurea*) in the world. The Court held that the planning authority took into account the lake, and its plant and animal population when accepting the plan. Since the original plan was to build on most of the lake, the final plan was a compromise that even the Nature and Parks Authority accepted. The presiding judge declared that the appellant's request for a total ban on construction in the area of the lake was extreme and unrealistic.

II. Billboards

156. Israel is unique in its protection of the highway landscape. A highway is defined as any road connecting two populated areas. In 1966, the Knesset passed a law prohibiting the siting of billboards along highways unless the billboard met certain criteria.[346] In 1979, an amendment to the law was proposed to limit the number of billboards along inter-city highways. At first, it was contemplated to require billboards to be set at a certain distance from the highway, but the American experience proved that limiting distance meant larger billboards at a greater distance. It was, therefore, decided to prohibit any billboard 'visible' from an inter-city road. Signs on business establishments along highways were permitted under strict conditions, but no general advertising signs are now permitted if they are visible from Israel's highways.

In spite of the law, large billboards were posted along the 20-kilometre freeway which runs through the heart of Tel Aviv. In 2008, a petition from an environmental group resulted in the Tel Aviv District Court ordering the billboards taken down. The Roads (Affixing of Signs) Law was amended by the Knesset to allow the billboards to return. The focus of the argument in the Knesset was not the environment and visual pollution, but road safety.

Regulations allow businesses to post one billboard on their property, with size, distance and location strictly controlled.[347]

A 1999 amendment to the law permits certain uniform signs which advertise sponsorship of roadside clean-up and maintenance.[348] The usage of this amendment has been negligible.

Enforcement of the law is carried out by the Department of Public Works. The Department supervisors give notice to a person placing a billboard visible from a highway, and if he/she fails to remove it within the time allotted, the Department supervisor does so at the owner's expense.

346. Roads (Affixing of Signs) Law, 1966, 20 L.S.I. 4.
347. Roads Regulations (Signs), 1980, K.T. 4103.
348. Roads (Affixing of Signs) Law, para. 5(5).

What has become much more of a nuisance is the posting of temporary signs and stickers advertising small businesses and events. In 2003, an appeal to the District Court in Tel Aviv upheld a lower court decision fining a couple under the Roads (Affixing of Signs) Law and the Maintenance of Cleanliness Law.[349] They posted hundreds of signs along inter-city roadways, advertising the sale of their home. After ignoring several warnings, the Court fined them ILS 210,000 and required them to sign an ILS 350,000 guarantee not to repeat the offence for three years.

III. Quarries

157. Israel has taken steps to rid the country of scarred landscapes from abandoned quarries. In 1973, the Knesset amended the Mining Ordinance to create a mechanism for reclamation of abandoned quarries.[350] The law empowers the Minister of Commerce to create a fund for the reclamation of abandoned quarries from the fees paid by quarry owners and operators. Once a mine inspector finds a quarry, or a part thereof, worked out, he/she notifies the operator to submit a reclamation plan. In those instances where the mine has already been abandoned and the quarry has ceased operations or its owner is insolvent, the Nature Reserves Authority may reclaim the quarry with financing from the Reclamation Fund.

Implementation of the amendment to reclaim quarries got off to a poor start after the passing of the law because the Ministry of Commerce failed to pass regulations creating the mechanism for payment into the Reclamation Fund. Only five years after the law's passing were the amendments promulgated, activating the law. Another problem in enforcement was the fact that the Fund contemplated reclamation of existing and future quarries. In the beginning, there was not enough money in the Fund to reclaim already abandoned sites. A third problem was the scope of the law. It covers only particular types of mining operations – sand, dirt, aggregates – but does not cover the mining of phosphates within its provisions. On the whole, however, the law has been successfully implemented. Since its passing, 223 quarries have been reclaimed through the fund.

In 2003, two government ministers took ILS 300 million from the fund and transferred them to the general government account, managing them as part of the general government budget. A successful claim to the Supreme Court by the IUED and the Union of Quarry Materials Manufacturers in Israel returned the funds to the Quarry Reclamation Fund. The Court held that the fund has a specific source of funding and a specific purpose. Money paid into the fund is meant for reclaiming quarries, and for that purpose alone.[351]

An interesting use of the law was applied by the Shikma B'sor Drainage Authority. The Drainage Authority requested permission to reclaim damaged Wadi beds with money from the Reclamation Fund. Proper use of this vehicle enabled the Drainage Authority to reclaim several seasonal streams in the Negev.

---

349. Roads (Affixing of Signs) Law, 1966, 20 L.S.I. 4, Maintenance of Cleanliness Law 38 L.S.I. 190.
350. 27 L.S.I. 210.
351. High Court of Justice, Case Nos 7526/03 and 890/03, *Israel Union for Environmental Defence v. Economics Minister*, Mr Silvan Shalom.

Chapter 2. Parks and Nature Reserves

§1. Introduction

158. Israel has been blessed with a law for the creation of national parks and nature reserves since 1963.[352] The law was revised in 1992 and then in 1998 and is now called the National Parks, Nature Reserves, Historical Sites and Monuments Law of 1998. The law defines a national park as any area which is to be used for public recreation in nature or to preserve assets which have historical, archaeological, natural or landscape value, whether they remain in their natural setting or have been placed in the setting to be used for these values and which the Ministry of the Interior has declared to be a national park. A nature reserve is defined as any area where there is protected wildlife, plants, land, caves, water or landscape which are of interest to science or education and are to be protected from any unwanted changes in their natural state or their biological composition or during their development and which the Minister of Environmental Protection has declared to be a nature reserve. A historical site is defined as a building or any group of buildings, including their surroundings, which have national or historical importance in the development of the State of Israel and which the Minister of the Interior has declared as a national site. A monument is declared as any monument site dedicated to the soldiers of the Israel Defence Forces who fell in order to protect the State of Israel.

§2. Authorities Established to Execute the Law

I. Introduction

159. The Law for National Parks, Nature Reserves, Historical Sites and Monuments creates a Council for National Parks, Nature Reserves and National Sites. The Council is composed of government representatives, representatives of local authorities, persons from scientific and public bodies interested in natural science and members of the general public. The Council is appointed by the government, according to the recommendations of the Minister of Environmental Protection. The Council serves as an advisory body to the Authority. It also serves as an advisor to the Minister of Environmental Protection, who is charged with implementing the law's provisions, including those provisions related to the designation of natural assets to be protected, as discussed later. The law establishes the method, through proper planning, for the creation of a national park and nature reserve.

There can be no national park, nature reserve, historical site or monument without the approval of Israel's planning authorities. Under the Planning and Building Law, the planning commissions are empowered to designate the location of these sites, and only upon the approval of the designated site can the Minister of Environmental Protection or Interior so declare the site a park, reserve, historical site or

352. National Parks, Nature Reserves, Historical Sites and Monuments Law, 1998.

monument. At one time, the Planning and Building Law, and the National Parks, Nature Reserves, Historical Sites and Monuments Law were under the administrative authority of the Minister of the Interior. Since the creation of the Ministry of Environmental Protection, the authority over these two laws has been split. Only time will tell the effect of this dichotomy.

II. Nature and Parks Authority

160. The law created a Nature and Parks Authority to manage the national parks and nature reserves of Israel. It is designated as an independent government organization and has the right to sue and be sued. As an independent body, it oversees the operation of the national parks and nature reserves system. This entails actual implementation of bylaws for the protection of parks.

III. Protected Natural Assets

161. In addition to the authorities mentioned above, the National Parks, Nature Reserves, Historical Sites and Monuments Law creates a mechanism for the protection of singular natural assets. A natural asset is defined as an animal, plant or inorganic object which the Minister of Environmental Protection deems in need of protection. If the Minister of Environmental Protection finds a natural asset of value outside a nature reserve requiring protection, he/she may designate such an asset as a natural asset. This prevents anyone from removing, selling or destroying the natural asset. Some are protected in certain regions, while others are protected wherever they may be found. In 1979, the Minister used the powers given under the law and drew up a list of protected assets, which was replaced by a newly revised list in 2005.[353] The law has been utilized successfully in Israel to protect certain animals and plants. The law's provisions have been augmented by efforts to educate the public, especially the young, about the value of protecting natural assets. The young, in turn, will educate their parents concerning the value of these *protected* animals and plants.

But while the law protects animals and plants, it does not protect their habitats or ecosystems.

IV. Enforcement and Control

162. Since the law's passing, 66 national parks and 190 nature reserves have been approved by the Minister of the Interior, covering 20% of Israel's land mass. However, most of these are situated in the desert region of the country, with only 3% of the Mediterranean region designated as nature reserves and parks. More than 200 additional proposed nature reserves and national parks are in various stages of

353. Declaration of National Parks, Nature Reserves, Historic Sites and Memorial Sites (Protected Natural Assets) 2005.

the approval process. These parks and nature preserves were designated under the National Master Plan for National Parks, Nature Reserves and Landscape Reserves as recommended by the National Planning Council and approved by the government in 1981. The Nature and Parks Authority has enforcement powers and is supported by inspectors who rigorously enforce the law within the confines of a park or nature preserve. Inspectors also do not hesitate to enforce the law for the protection of natural assets outside the confines of a park or preserve, although their powers are limited.

Chapter 3. Wildlife and Animal Protection

163. In the previous section, it was noted that the Minister of Environmental Protection is empowered to protect a natural asset even outside the confines of national parks and nature preserves. Regulations under the law list numerous plants, animals, fish and corals, which are to be protected. In addition, Israel has a specific law for the protection of animals, designated the Wild Animals Protection Law, 1955.[354]

A wild animal is defined under this law as a mammal or fowl not accustomed to living with a man. The law empowers the Minister of Agriculture to designate in regulations those animals which may be hunted, and those which are pests. An animal not so designated for hunting or as a pest is a protected animal under the law. A proposed amendment to the law designates all wild animals as protected unless otherwise noted.

The law also sets out 'humane' provisions for hunting. It is forbidden to hunt with the following 'weapons' or methods of hunting: blinding, poisoning, drugging, hunting in a motorized vehicle, etc. Further, the Minister is empowered to define the limits of the hunting season. He has done so, in regulations which were issued in 1976.[355] These regulations set the length of the hunting season and the permitted hours of hunting as well as those animals designated as game animals and those designated as pests. The list of game animals is short and includes hares, wild ducks, wild pigeons and coots. Pests are rodents, bulbuls, larks and nutrias. According to the regulations, all hunters are required to be licensed. The regulations are more restrictive for those hunting game animals than for those listed as pests. For both categories, however, there are restrictions as to seasons, periods, and types of weapons used. Israel is a party to the Convention on International Trade in Endangered Species of Wild Fauna and Flora (CITES) and has adopted its own national legislation to ensure its implementation.[356] This law is also used to prevent the introduction of invasive species.

164. Animal Protection. Since 1994, Israel has passed several laws protecting the welfare of animals. The Animal Welfare Law forbids the torture and abuse of animals.[357] Conviction of animal torture carries a maximum penalty of three years imprisonment. Regulations require animals that are kept for non-agricultural purposes to have reasonable living conditions.[358]

354. 9 L.S.I. 8.
355. Regulations for the Protection of Wild Animals (Forbidden Areas), 1971, K.T. 1250.
356. Declaration of National Parks, Nature Reserves, Historic Sites and Memorial Sites (Implementation of the Convention on International Trade in Endangered Species of Wild Fauna and Flora) (Protected Species), 2004.
357. Animal Welfare (Protection of Animals) Law, 1994.
358. Animal Welfare Regulations (Animal Protection) (Kept for Non-Agricultural Needs), 2009.

An amendment from 2002 outlaws cosmetic surgery on animals, including the cropping of ears and tails. Other laws and regulations control animal licensing and inspection, exhibitions and animal experimentation.[359]

The Law for Regulating Supervision of Dogs, 2002, requires all dogs aged 3 months or older to have a licence. Dogs considered dangerous breeds will only be licensed if their owners have third-party insurance. The law requires the Minister of Agriculture to develop methods for limiting the dog population (but without harming any dogs).

Israeli law does not give an animal legal standing, and it may not be a side in a legal proceeding. But a public petitioner can bring suit in the interests of an animal.[360]

359. Regulation of Dogs Inspection Law, 2002; The Animal Welfare (Animal Protection) (Exhibitions, Shows and contests of Animals) Regulations, 2001; Animal Welfare (Animal Experimentation) Law, 1994; Nature Reserves (Arrangements and Behaviour) Regulations, 1979.

360. High Court of Justice Case No. 466/05 *Reis v. National Planning Council; Gil Johananoff, Animal Law in Israel*, Nevo Publishing, 2009, p. 108.

Chapter 4. Agricultural Resources

§1. Introduction

165. Israel's founding fathers had a strong ideological attachment to agriculture. The State was founded on the premise that Jews should be able to work the land, something previous generations were forbidden to do in some other parts of the world. Therefore, one finds numerous articles of legislation for the protection of agriculture, agricultural products and methods of production.

§2. Soil Protection

166. The Water Law declares agriculture to be one of the six permitted uses of water. The law further protects agricultural interests by creating an advisory Water Board, a majority of the members of which are from the agricultural sector. In addition to the Water Law, Israel has laws aimed at preventing damage to the topsoil to protect agricultural land: the Sand Erosion Ordinance, 1922;[361] the Soil Erosion (Prevention) Ordinance, 1941;[362] and the Drainage and Flood Control Law, 1957.[363]

167. The Sand Erosion Ordinance permits the Chief Forestry Office to prevent agricultural land from being damaged or covered by sand.

The Soil Erosion (Prevention) Ordinance empowers the Minister of Agriculture to publish regulations for the prevention of soil erosion. Such regulations were passed in 1960, and they empower the Head of the Department for Soil Protection and Drainage in the Ministry to protect agricultural land from erosion. The Department Head has the authority to determine the proper method of land use, including cultivation and grazing, to prevent erosion. This power is rarely used because the Conservation Authority, discussed below, has not been established.

The law also enables the creation of a Soil Conservation Authority, the purpose of which is to initiate and establish enterprises for the protection of land and the prevention of soil erosion. To date, three authorities have been created, under the auspices of the Shikma Besor Drainage Authority, Lower Jordan Drainage Authority and the Kinneret Drainage Authority.

168. The Drainage and Flood Control Law was a pioneering effort to protect Israel from the ravages of flooding and soil erosion. The law creates a National Drainage Council to set policy and enables the Minister of Agriculture to create National and District Drainage Authorities. Using his power, the Minister has created Drainage Authorities throughout the country. Originally, there were twenty-six Drainage Authorities but this number was reduced in 1997 to eleven, operating along catchment basin lines.

361. *Laws of Palestine* Vol. II, 1314.
362. P.O. I, 37.
363. 12 L.S.I. 5.

The Authorities are political bodies, made up of elected officials in the designated district. The Minister of Agriculture so defined the geographical boundaries of the Drainage Boards to give agricultural interests majority representation on each Board. The only areas not managed by a Drainage Board in Israel are the lower portion of the Yarqon River near Tel Aviv, where the Yarqon River Authority operates and the lower Kishon River in Haifa where the Kishon River Authority operates.

The Drainage Boards are required to prepare a plan for their region to prevent flooding and soil erosion. The Boards have done so and, for the most part, have carried out their responsibilities. Israel is fortunate to have an efficient Drainage Board system, which acts to keep erosion and flooding to a minimum.

169. Coastal cliffs. The central part of Israel's coastline, roughly between Ashkelon and Hadera, contains many 10- to 30-meter calcareous sandstone cliffs. These unique cliffs, which afford beautiful views of the beaches and sea, are crumbling and retreating eastward endangering both people and property in Israel's most populated area. The government passed a decision to protect the cliffs, with a budget of ILS 0.5 billion. The Ministry of Environmental Protection, together with the Ministry of the Interior, led the way for the creation of National Plan 13/9/A for Israel's Mediterranean coastal cliffs, approved in 2015. In 2013, the Mediterranean Coastal Cliffs Preservation Government Company Ltd. was created in order to take responsibility for all coastal cliff issues, including planning and implementation of coastal protection, maintenance and monitoring.

§3. Protection of Animals and Plants

I. Animals

170. The Minister of Agriculture has direct control over the production and breeding of plants and animals. One of several laws for the regulation of animal growth is the Improvement of Agricultural Production (Livestock) Law, 1952.[364] The Minister of Agriculture is empowered, under this law, to enact regulations for the improvement of animals and to forbid and restrict or control the following: breeding, sale or production of animal semen, artificial insemination, penning of animals and health standards for growth and insemination. Regulations under the law have been passed applying to dairy cattle, goats and bees.[365]

364. 6 L.S.I. 34.
365. Regulations for the Improvement of Agricultural Production (Livestock), (Cows & Regulations for the Improvement of Agricultural Production (Animals), (Bees), 1968, K.T. 1527. Regulations for the Improvement of Agricultural Production (Animals), (Goats), 1957, K.T. 1513. Milk), 2001, K.T. 480.

II. Plants

171. The Protection of Plants Law, described earlier in the section on pesticides, vests the Minister of Agriculture and the Head of the Department of Plant Protection in the ministry with exceptional authority to protect plants. The Minister may make regulations coordinating the growth, transfer, sale, export and import of plants in order to prevent plant pests. He/she may also promulgate orders for the import and use of production methods, including hormones. Using his power, the Minister has passed regulations to protect plants against disease,[366] as well as to prevent the unauthorized transfer of weeds by requiring that such weeds be destroyed and not used for animal feed or compost.[367] Israel also has a series of legislative acts dealing with the production of plants and plant products for export.

172. Botanical Gardens. The Law for Botanical Gardens, 2006, gives the Minister of Agriculture the power to declare botanical gardens for the preservation and display of plant species. The law creates a Council for Botanical Gardens to advise the Minister comprised of representatives from government and non-government agencies, academia and the public.

366. *See*, e.g., Regulations for the Production of Plants (Prevention of the Spread of Sclerotium Rolfsil), 1960, K.T. 1363; (Sale of Cotton & its Transportation), 1962, K.T. 156.
367. Regulations for the Protection of Plants (Prevention of the Spread of Wild Weeds), 1953, K.T. 1430.

Chapter 5. Forests and Trees

173. About 8% of Israel is forested. Israel has what one would call woods, rather than actual forests. Yet semantics aside, trees and forests are cherished by Jewish and Israeli cultures, in both ancient and modern times. The most prevalent Hebrew word for forest, '*ya'ar*', is mentioned more than forty times in the Bible.[368]

The Ottoman Empire, which ruled the region for 401 years, had an anti-forest legacy based on tax practices that discouraged tree planting, and vast areas of trees were cut down to be used for fuel.[369] When the British arrived in the region during World War I, their vision of a land flowing with milk and honey, with babbling brooks and large shady forests as depicted in European art was dashed.[370] Like the early Zionist settlers and philanthropists, their picture of the region was based on a Northern European vision of dense, conifer-based forests. In order to 'fix' the situation, the British Mandatory Government embarked on a comprehensive forestry programme. They passed legislation that defined forests in spatial terms, designating areas that would someday become forests and protecting the few areas that already were forested. The British forestation programme complemented the JNF's forestry programme already underway. The JNF is a non-profit organization founded in 1901 by the Zionist Congress to purchase and develop land in Ottoman and British Palestine, and subsequently in Israel. Over the last century, the JNF has planted extensive forests totalling 240 million trees throughout Israel and manages these forests for the public.

The Woods and Forest Ordinance of 1920 was legislated by the Mandatory government in order 'to protect forests and to produce and manage special places for forests'.[371] An updated and detailed version of the Forest Ordinance was passed in 1926 and eventually became Israel's major piece of forestry legislation.[372] The law empowers the Minister of Agriculture to declare areas that are not private property as protected forest areas. The Forest Ordinance also provides for the protection of private forests, if required according to the Minister of Agriculture. The Ordinance contains a long list of activities that are forbidden in forest areas without a government permit.

The Forest Ordinance protects trees everywhere, not just in public forests or on public land. No tree over 2 meters tall and with a trunk larger than 10 centimetres in diameter may be cut down, removed or transplanted without a permit. Forest Ordinance regulations contain an extensive list of trees that are specifically protected without regard to size. The list is comprised primarily of trees that are found in nature, rather than those grown for agricultural purposes.

Within Israel's cities, trees provide shade from the sweltering summer heat, lessen air pollution and lower temperatures. The few old trees that have survived are a window to the past. In order to protect urban trees and promote urban tree

368. A. Tal, *All the Trees of the Forest* 12 (Tel Aviv: Kibbutz Hameuchad Publishing House, 2014).
369. S.E. Cohen, *The Politics of Planting*, The University of Chicago Geography Research Paper No. 236, 45–46 (University of Chicago Press 1993).
370. D. Schorr, *Forest Law in the Palestine Mandate: Colonial Conservation in a Unique Context*, in *Managing the Unknown* 71–90 (U. Luebken & F. Uekoetter eds, New York 2012).
371. *Woods and Forest Ordinance*, 1920; *Palestine Gazette*, 15 Oct. 1920.
372. *Forest Ordinance*, 1926, *Palestine Gazette*, 16 Dec. 1925.

planting, in 2015 the Tel Aviv District Planning and Building Committee approved a policy document for trees. The main recommendations include marking and signage for trees of special importance, allowing building work only at a safe distance from the roots of mature trees, giving preference to leaving mature trees in situ, shading a minimum of 30% of parking areas with trees and planting trees to cover a minimum of 40% of public spaces. While not legally binding, it is expected to influence the Committee's discussions and decisions, especially concerning the fate of trees in areas designated for building.[373]

The Forest Ordinance was amended as part of the 'Polluter Pays' law, allowing heavier penalties for environmental harm. Significant harm to the environment can be punished by up to three years imprisonment, and harm that results in economic gain for the violator can be punished by a fine equal to the economic gain.

The law for National Parks, Nature Reserves, National Sites and Memorial Sites gives the Minister for Environmental Protection the power to declare specific natural resources, including trees, as singled out for special protection, either in specific areas or in the entire country. The designated ministers have used these powers to create lists of protected natural resources, including lists of protected trees.[374]

In 1995, the Israeli government passed National Outline Plan No. 22 for forests and forestation, and for the protection of both ecological and human needs.[375] According to the Plan, forests and woodlands are part of Israel's landscape and play an important ecological role, while the public needs open spaces to enjoy nature near where they live.

The Plan classifies and delineates forest and afforestation formations, guiding their preservation, cultivation and integration into the overall planning system.[376] The plan declares 1.6 million dunams of land (160,000 hectares) as forest – either existing forests or areas designated to become forests.

Plan 22 states that forestation activities will be carried out while protecting the diverse natural vistas and environments. It allows for additional lands to be forested in line with the Planning and Building law. Detailed plans will be prepared to delineate the different planned uses of forests, the forestation activities planned, access, paths and exact boundaries. This will be done not only for planned or planted forests but also for natural forests.

Plan 22 does not provide total protection for forests against development. The planning and building authorities can change the declared usage of an area from a forest to an area designated for development. Therefore, in recent years, the Ministry of Agriculture has decided to declare all the forest areas listed in Plan 22 as protected forest reserve areas, under powers granted by section 3 of the Forestry

---

373. T. Rinat, *Tel Aviv District Goes to Battle for the Planted*, Haaretz Newspaper, 25/12/2015 (Hebrew).
374. *Declaration of National Parks and Nature Reserves (Protected Natural Resources)*, 1971; *Declaration of National Parks, Nature Reserves, National Sites and Memorial Sites (Protected Natural Resources)*, 2005.
375. National Outline Plan 22 is now part of National Outline Plan No. 1, which came into effect on January 1 2020.
376. M. Kaplan, *National Outline Plan for Forests and Afforestation NOP22*, Policy Document, Jewish National Fund, Jerusalem 2011, p. 10.

Ordinance.[377] Declaring forests as forest reserves gives them a status equal to nature reserves, thus preventing any activity that may cause harm, including building and development.

Several forests listed in Plan 22 have also been designated nature reserves under National Plan No. 8 for National Parks, Nature Reserves and Landscape Reserves.

Israeli policy designating the purpose of forests has changed over time. Since the late 1800s, the JNF and the Israeli government, following in the footsteps of the British Mandatory government, saw the planting of forests as a way of redeeming the land. They wanted to make the desert bloom, drain the swamps and create jobs. Forests were seen as something manmade, to be managed with intensive human intervention. A typical forestry project began with bulldozers levelling the land, followed by a heavy dose of herbicides so nothing but the tree saplings would grow. Planting a single variety of trees in rows made for easy planting and access.

Environmental groups disagreed with this view, seeing forests as ecologically biodiverse areas as well as green spaces for the public to enjoy. In the year 2000, the IUED petitioned the Supreme Court sitting as the High Court of Justice against the government and the JNF for their environmentally harmful policies, without preparing the required development and forestry plans.[378] The Court grouped forests together with any other building project, in that it needs to have planning approval. The court held that 'any and all plantings of forestlands were illegal unless they received prior approval from the relevant regional planning commission. For this to happen, forests need to be based on very detailed plans that specify what trees will be planted, how the forests will look, and what activities they support'.[379] These plans must be open to public scrutiny.

Today, government forestry policy views forests as multi-purpose, with scenic, ecological, social, touristic and economic objectives. The Supreme Court has supported this view, finding the provision of forests and green spaces as a public purpose of supreme importance.[380]

174. In addition to the Forest Ordinance, there are laws dealing with damage caused to forests by grazing. The Shepherd's Ordinance empowers the Minister of Agriculture to control grazing throughout the country. No one may graze animals in unauthorized areas. In addition, the Plant Protection (Damage Caused by Goats) Law of 1950 enables the Minister of Agriculture to limit the number of goats one may own in a certain area.[381] The law controls the number of goats in order to prevent uncontrolled grazing and the resulting destruction of forests and plants.

---

377. D. Yorista, *Press Release No. 469/10*, Israel Ministry of Agriculture, 16 Sep. 2010.
378. Case No. 288/00 and 4438/98, Supreme Court sitting as the High Court of Justice, *Israel Union for Environmental Defense et al. v. Min. of Interior et al.*
379. A. Tal, *All the Trees of the Forest* 195–196 (Kibbutz Hameuchad Publishing House 2014); Case No. 288/00 and 4438/98, Supreme Court sitting as the High Court of Justice, *Israel Union for Environmental Defense et al. v. Min. of Interior et al.*
380. Case No. 7579/07, *Supreme Court sitting as the High Court of Justice, Said Dahamsha v. Israel Land Authority;* Case No. 4067/07, *Supreme Court sitting as the Court of Appeals, Mahmoud Halil Abed Alfatah Jabrin and others v. the State of Israel.*
381. 4 L.S.I. 181.

175. Enforcement of the above legislation is carried out by the Ministry of Agriculture with assistance from the Israel Lands Authority, the JNF and the Nature Reserves and Parks Authority. Forests are carefully planted and controlled by the JNF, and fires are kept under control by the Nature Preserves Authority and the JNF. Overgrazing, which caused damage to forests in the 1970s, has been virtually stopped after stiff enforcement measures were taken by the Nature Preserves Authority under the Damage by Goats Law. Grazing is still used as a tool for limiting forest fires. In addition, the use of a single variety of trees has also been stopped by the JNF, and there is now planting of various types of trees in Israel's forests. This change in policy occurred after the IUED filed a suit against the JNF for overzealous use of pesticides to reduce undergrowth.[382] During the hearing on the motion, the JNF promised the court to become more ecologically inclined and this attitude was adopted.

382. High Court of Justice 288/00, *Israel Union for Environmental Defense v. Minister of Interior et al.*, P.D. 55(5) 673.

Chapter 6. Fish Resources

176. Israel has only one freshwater lake and a few streams available for fishing. It does have, however, a lengthy coastline along the Mediterranean Sea. Early legislation protecting Israel's fish stock was instituted during the British Mandate, and it has not been changed to a great degree since then.

The Fisheries Ordinance of 1937 enables the Minister of Agriculture to license fishermen who fish in inland or coastal water.[383] One not licensed is prohibited from fishing. The Ordinance also specifically prohibits the use of certain devices to catch fish, for example, dynamite and poisons are strictly forbidden. The Minister of Agriculture is empowered by the ordinance to issue regulations controlling fishing in Israel and its coastal waters. Subsequent regulations forbid fishing in certain areas and with certain types of nets. Certain species of fish and underwater animal and plant life are also protected under the Nature Reserves Law and appropriate regulations.

The Ministry of Environment together with the Ministry of Agriculture have passed a reform to allow growing fish near or in streams but reducing their footprint on stream quality. The reform has as yet to go into effect due to a disagreement between the government and the fish farmers.

383. P.O. Suppl. I, 157.

Chapter 7. Subsoil and Minerals

177. Israel is not blessed with many natural resources in its subsoil. There are quantities of copper and sufficient quantities of phosphate and salt, yet Israel has no commercial quantities of precious metals and oil. This changed when in 2009 and 2010 large amounts of natural gas were discovered off the coast of Israel under the Mediterranean Sea. Israel has become, for the first time, an energy exporter.

With the discovery of natural gas within Israel's Exclusive Economic Zone (EEZ) in the Mediterranean – the marine area between 12 and 200 nautical miles from Israel's coast, just beyond the country's territorial waters – arose the question of which law shall be applicable in that space. As one of only a few countries, Israel until recently has not clarified the legal circumstances that apply to its EEZ. Introduced already in 2013 but adopted in 2017, the *Marine Areas Law* officially defines the EEZ and makes Israeli law applicable to these maritime areas. The applicability of Israel's environmental protection laws to offshore exploration activities for natural gas is one important result.

Israel's Mining Ordinance governs mining, and the Water Law protects substrata and groundwater.

The Mining Ordinance of 1925 creates the position of Mining Officer in the Ministry of Development.[384] No one may mine or investigate mining without a licence. The licence designates the area to be investigated and the materials to be mined. Once a mineral has been discovered, it belongs to the government and may not be removed or sold without permission. The law further states that a mining project does not include a right to water found under the surface or in a stream.

178. Oil and Gas Exploration and Production. In Israel, the Petroleum Law from 1952 and Petroleum Regulations from 1953 regulate oil search and production. But the law does not contain any mechanisms for environmental regulation and control, including the protection of water sources. The Ministry of Environmental Protection has prepared initial instructions for regulating oil and gas drilling on land. But these instructions have no legal standing.

In 2012, the Energy and Water Minister promulgated regulations circumventing the previously required planning and building process for oil and gas exploration wells.[385] The new regulations also set time limits for committee discussions, environmental expert reports, and deciding objections and other decisions. The regulations include a requirement for an environmental assessment that will detail the possible environmental harm to water sources, land, air, sea, natural assets and landscapes, and recommendations for limiting the possible negative effects.

179. Fracking. Fracking, or hydraulic fracturing, is the process of removing natural gas from underground shale deposits by blasting them with a mixture of water, sand and chemicals at high pressure. This allows the gas to flow out to the well head. The major environmental concerns are the large amounts of water used in the process and the potential pollution of groundwater.

384. *Laws of Palestine*, Vol. I, 903.
385. *Petroleum Regulations (Permission to Deviate from the Planning and Building Law)*, 2012.

The process of fracking is different from conventional oil and gas drilling, but in Israel, they are all regulated by the same laws and regulations. The Water Law forbids polluting of water sources and allows the Water Authority to carry out all actions required to oversee and protect water sources. But this law alone will not protect Israel's water sources from potential harm.

In 2014, the Jerusalem District Planning and Building Committee rejected a plan to build a pilot fracking facility in the Judean lowlands. The project would have heated the underground shale to 350°C, and if successful would have led to a full-scale commercial operation. Most of the objections centred on the unknown environmental impact of the project. An additional proposed fracking project in the Golan Heights by the same company has been temporarily halted by the High Court of Justice, following a petition by the IUED and local residents.

180. In earlier chapters, we discussed the duty of owners to reclaim mines and quarries. We also discussed water rights and the protection of the soil. It should be further noted that drainage, including from the subsoil, is also controlled under the Drainage and Flood Control law, discussed in the chapter on water pollution.

Chapter 8. Biodiversity

181. All of the above laws have only recently been looked at as parts of an overall plan to protect Israel's ecosystems, often taken for granted and abused. In compliance with the Convention on Biodiversity, the Ministry of Environmental Protection published a National Biodiversity Plan, which includes a broad and comprehensive action plan for conservation and management.[386] This plan, together with the 2003 government decision for sustainable development, provides a blueprint for the government and the Knesset to follow.[387] The plan is being implemented primarily through the planning and building laws, and national and regional master plans.

Initiatives have also been taken at the local level. For example, the city of Jerusalem published an urban nature survey that lists urban sites with high biodiversity indicators. This survey is part of the Countdown 2010 initiative of IUCN. The survey will be used to give legal protection to urban areas with biodiversity considered imperative to protect.

386. Israel's National Biodiversity Plan, Ministry of Environmental Protection, Policy and Planning Division, January 2010.
387. Strategic Plan for Sustainable Development in Israel: Government Decision No. 246, 14 May 2003.

Part III. Zoning and Land Use Planning

§1. Introduction

182. The effectiveness of land use planning in Israel to protect the natural and physical environment has been discussed previously, in chapters where relevant. This chapter will not repeat what has been written but will explain the environmental protection relevancy of planning law in Israel.

§2. The Planning and Building Law, 1965

183. The nature of planning in Israel is that the planning commissions or boards are to envision and regulate growth and plan for the future. When the Planning and Building Law was passed in 1965, it required the local and district planning boards to prepare outline plans within the time period designated in the law. None of the boards met this time requirement. Even today, some local outline plans date from the British Mandate, having been amended or modified but not overhauled. The Planning Commissions' failure to meet this prerequisite and plan well ahead of events puts a crimp in the entire planning process. Most of the plans contain no clear environmental guidelines. The result is that planning continues on a piece-meal basis. What comes up for review is discussed, but not always within a planned environmental framework. This gives rise to political and entrepreneurial pressure on the planning boards, who then have no planning cover under which to retreat, so they acquiesce under the demands of this pressure.

Theoretically, the law is to work as follows. At each planning level, local, district and national, there are to be outlined plans. These plans are to be visionary and not necessarily physical. By this is meant, for example, that the planning authorities not only decide the siting of an airport but also the air lanes for the entrance and exit of aeroplanes, insofar as they have an impact on physical planning.

The National Planning Council is empowered by the law to plan population distribution. This, in principle, should guide the growth of cities and towns. Furthermore, the National Planning Council is authorized to approve plans for Israel's water resources and other natural resources as well as power plants, dams, nature reserves, national parks, airports, etc., that, if used properly, could improve the basic environment of the State.

As one moves down the hierarchy from the National Planning Council to the district and local commissions, planning power becomes not only more specific but critical to environmental protection. District planning commissions are empowered to site industrial projects and residential units as well as parks in a district plan. Local planning boards may require environmental controls in the business and industrial units to be built so as to prevent environmental nuisances. The siting of roads, transmission lines, and quarries are all within the jurisdiction of the planning boards, including their proper construction and operation to prevent nuisances.

In 1995, the Planning and Building Law underwent a major revision, which is entitled The Planning and Building (Amendment No. 43) Law of 1995. This amendment intended to give more independence to the local planning authorities. It also had the intention of reducing the time from application for planning permission to actual approval by the planning commission.

Finally, the law creates a new window for appeals from planning decisions to the Administrative Courts, which are located in the District Courts of Israel, instead of the Supreme Court.

It must be stated that the amendment leaves sufficient room for the previous operation of the Planning and Building Law to continue as it has historically. There have also been provisions provided in the law for a member of the Ministry of Environmental Protection to be present on both the District Planning Commission and the subcommittee of that commission which reviews planning appeals. The law further attempts to set time limits for planning board decisions, including decisions regarding EIAs. These time limits may be extended, however, in extenuating circumstances.

In summarizing this major amendment to the Planning and Building Law, it must be said that the initiators of the law had in mind reducing bureaucracy, as well as cutting the time periods involved in the approval of plans. The overall approach of the amendment is efficiency, as set out in time limits for approval. Efficiency, however, is not necessarily a function of the planning boards. It is also a function of the planners themselves, and those submitting requests to the planning commissions. Therefore, there may be no efficiency gained as a result of the changes in the Planning and Building Law. There may, however, be less regard for environmental concerns under the illusion that environmental concerns take up time to review and discover. Alongside these institutional 'environmental' amendments to the law, one finds that from time to time, the government cannot resist amending the law to reduce deliberation in planning by speeding up the process. This occurred during the large *aliyah* (immigration) of immigrants in the 1990s. It occurred again in 2004, with an amendment aimed at speeding up the approval of national infrastructure plans: airport, rail, power stations, etc. These national projects are the ones that need the most careful deliberation but the government cannot be bothered with such trifles.[388]

In 2010, the government proposed a new planning bill, aimed at taking away power from the planning committees and long-term zoning plans and putting it in the hands of government functionaries. Among its many proposed changes, the bill allows the Interior Ministry to set up special planning sub-committees independent of the National Planning Council. With Israel's small size, rapid development and growing population, there is a need to maintain a cautious approach to planning in order to leave future generations open spaces. The manner in which the planning

388. S.H. 1544, 450.

reform bill was drafted raises a red flag. It was written behind the closed doors of the Interior Ministry and the Prime Minister's Office, with little input from the public or planners. Despite its massive size (nearly 250 pages), the bill was reviewed for only twenty-one days before coming before the Knesset for its first reading. The bill passed its second and third readings and became a law in 2014.

There has been a rapid increase in individual planning of homes, under a plan approved by the National Planning Council. This plan, #38, allows individual homeowners to add additional floors to their homes with minimal approval by the local authority. As a result, numerous entrepreneurs have taken advantage of this new tool to revamp city centres, at the expense of the neighbourhood, infrastructure and communication.

§3. Environmental Impact Statements

184. In keeping with other countries of the world, Israel decided in 1982 (since revised in 2003) to enact legislation requiring the preparation of environmental impact statements or assessments for certain plans. As in other countries, Israel chose the legal mechanism most suited to its legal system. In America, the environmental impact statement process was triggered at first by government monetary involvement. In Israel, the impact statement process is part of the planning process, as described below.

First of all, the introduction of the process required no legislative change. It operates under regulations published by the Minister of the Interior under his/her power to implement the Planning and Building Law. The regulations create the office of the Environmental Advisor appointed by the Minister of Environmental Protection. It defines an environmental impact statement as a document covering the connection between a proposed plan and the environment where it is to be implemented, including assessments as to forecasted or anticipated impacts on the environment and specific actions of the means necessary to prevent negative impact. In other words, the impact statement not only connects the proposed plan to its environmental impact but also requires the planner to state those means necessary to reduce or prevent negative impacts.

The impact statement process goes into effect in one of the following situations. It is a required part of the planning process for power plants, airports, seaports, oil refineries, toxic waste sites or dumps, and drying areas of the sea or the sea itself. For airport landing strips, jetties, national water supply arteries, dams and reservoirs, sewage purification plants, mining and quarry sites, solid waste dumps and industrial plants sited outside industrial areas, it is required only if the National or District Planning Commission decides, after making a determination, that the planning scheme for these projects will have a significant impact on the environment, exceeding local limits. Plans that require an EIA in accordance with regulations enumerated in some national, regional or local master plans contain regulations with EIA requirements. EIAs are currently incorporated into the regulations of national master plans on roads, railways, power stations, coasts, waste disposal, immigrant absorption, quarries, and others. Finally, if a representative of any ministry sitting on any of the Planning Boards finds that a plan has a potentially significant environmental impact or is within an environmentally sensitive area, he/she not only may require the preparation of an impact statement for that plan but also a review of the sensitivity of the environment in which the plan is proposed and its exposure to pollution, degradation or risk.

185. The environmental analysis is to be done according to the guidelines prepared by the Environmental Advisor to the Planning Commission and approved by the Commission. It must include a description of the environment existing prior to the proposed plan, the reason for the preference of the site chosen and alternatives, a description of activities planned in implementation of the plan, an assessment of the environmental impacts and those means necessary to prevent negative impacts and suggestions for the plan's provisions, and conclusions and recommendations for integration in the 'regulatory' provisions of the plan.

Once an impact statement has been prepared, the Planning Commission reviews its findings as part of the planning process. This review is limited in time and at its conclusion, the Planning Commission must comment on the impact statement and determine those environmental measures which must be incorporated into the plan, if approved. There is no requirement that if the impact statement shows negative impacts the plan should be rejected.

Even prior to the enactment of the 1982 regulations, the impact statement process was followed for the siting of power plants and major sewage purification plants. With the passage of these regulations, the process has become an integral part of the planning system.

In 2014, the Ministry of Environmental Protection objected to the proposed route of the planned railway line from Tel Aviv to Eilat. The Ministry was successful in obtaining a ruling in the Southern District Planning Committee that Israel Railways must complete an EIA to study both the implications of the proposed route and the transport of hazardous materials by train. For example, the proposed route would have trains carrying hazardous materials pass through the centre of the city of Beer Sheva.

§4. Highways (Toll Roads)

186. A similar approach, but in legislation unrelated to planning and building, is represented by laws for the construction of two highways in Israel, which are paid for by tolls. The first law is entitled the Toll Road (The Israel Land Highway) Law 1995.[389] The second is entitled the Toll Road (The Carmel Tunnel) Law 1995. Both laws enable the government to set up a mechanism for levying tolls on the new Trans-Israel highway and the tunnel recently built in the Haifa area under the Carmel Mountains. There has been much criticism of the two roads, although they are quite different in scope. The Carmel Tunnels have undergone environmental review and were found to have little effect on the immediate quality of the environment in the vicinity of the tunnels. They may have an overall environmental effect if they

389. S.H. 1545, 490.

increase traffic in the Haifa region, which they very well may do. Therefore, their overall environmental effect will be to degrade the quality of the environment. On the other hand, studies were done, plans approved and construction completed.

The Trans-Israel Highway, however, never had an environmental impact statement done for its entire length. In fact, the road was built in stages and EIAs were completed for each stage separately. An attempt by Israel's NGOs to require that an overall EIA be made for the entire road was rejected by the Supreme Court.[390]

This rejection put a serious crimp on a comprehensive review of the entire road. There is no question, however, that the Trans-Israel Highway has a degrading effect on the quality of the environment.

First of all, it has channelled resources from public transport to private. Second, it cut a swath through large wilderness areas and farmland. Third, it has begun creating urban and suburban areas outside of the central urban areas of Israel at the expense of agricultural land and open spaces. Finally, it now requires the construction of additional access highways. The environmental groups in Israel who fought the construction of the central highway had little effect in getting the government to reduce the scope of the concept. In fact, a second phase of construction was recently completed, adding an additional 10-mile segment to the highway's northern end. The Israel Union for Environmental Defence (IUED) unsuccessfully appealed to the High Court of Justice to delay construction until other alternatives could be assessed. In 2016, an additional segment was added on the southern end, reaching northern Negev. Plans are moving ahead to extend the toll road to northern Galilee and southward past Beer Sheva.

390. S.H. 1545, 493.

Part IV. Liability

187. Israel inherited its legal system from the British. Yet, unlike under the common law system, the British Mandate powers adopted a Torts Ordinance to govern the system of compensation for torts in Israel. This ordinance was redrafted into Hebrew in the form of a New Version in 1968 and is now called the Civil Wrongs Ordinance (New Version).[391] Under the Ordinance, actions for negligence have been categorized.

The Ordinance permits actions for damages against private individuals and public servants. It permits actions against joint and several tortfeasors. Actions against employees are deemed the responsibility of the employer if the employer authorized or ratified the act, or the act was committed by the employee in the course of his/her employment. Actions may be brought not later than seven years from the day on which the cause of action occurred. The day on which the action occurred is defined as the day when the damage occurred or the day on which the damage was discovered. There is a provision, however, that if the damage was discovered more than ten years from the day on which it occurred, then action will be barred. This provision causes special problems for victims of exposure to dangerous substances. In cases of exposure to radiation or asbestos, for example, damage may not be discovered medically until more than ten years after the exposure occurred. At that time, action would be barred. This anomaly in the law has been recognized by legal scholars and legislation is being prepared to remedy the situation.

188. Most actions for environmental damage arising under the Civil Wrongs Ordinance are brought under the nuisance section of the law. The Ordinance defines a nuisance as either a public or a private one. A public nuisance 'consists of an unlawful act, or omission to discharge a legal duty, where such act or omission endangers the life, safety, health, property or comfort of the public or obstructs the public in the exercise of some common right'. A private *nuisance* consists of any person so conducting himself/herself or his/her business or so using his/her immovable property materially to interfere with the reasonable use and enjoyment of the property of another person.

A suit for a public nuisance may be brought by the Attorney General of Israel or his/her representative. A suit for a public or for a private nuisance may be brought by a private individual only if he/she has suffered pecuniary damage. This dichotomy reduces the effectiveness of a private individual or public organization using the Civil Wrongs Ordinance to protect the natural environment.

---

391. 367 2 L.S.I. (NV) 5.

The Kanowitz Law, discussed in detail in the Chapters on air and noise pollution, did away with the dichotomy. The law enables a private individual to bring suit against an environmental nuisance brought on by air, noise or olfactory pollution even if the plaintiff has not suffered pecuniary damage. This is the only law which enables such a suit, however, in the environmental law field. There are other laws, discussed previously in the sections on ocean pollution and litter, which require clean-up costs of the pollution to be borne by the polluter.

Part V. Juridical Actions of Individuals

Chapter 1. Introduction

189. A natural adjunct of the environmental law system in Israel is the practice of law before courts and administrative bodies. Practice of law in the environmental law area before the courts does not differ from practice in other areas. Israel is blessed with excellent judges and well-defined procedural norms of practice.

A large portion of environmental law is practised before administrative agencies. Yet, if one asked the Israeli legal practitioner if he/she practised before administrative agencies or tribunals, he/she would act as if he/she did not understand the question. This is because Israel has no orderly practice of administrative law, and not until 1992 was the country graced with an Administrative Law Act.[392] Practice before administrative agencies is often informal, yet there are laws which establish administrative tribunals, create norms for filing objections and delineate procedures for formal hearings.

392. The Administrative Courts Law, 1992, S.H. 90. The law's provisions apply to the following environmental laws: The Water Law, 1959, The Local Authorities (Sewerage) Law, 1962, The Antiquities Law, 1978.

Chapter 2. Administrative Remedies

190. The practice of administrative environmental law in Israel centres around two major areas. The first is the appearance before committees statutorily created. The second is before tribunals especially created to adjudicate environmental problems.

191. One finds statutory committees in a number of laws with environmental attributes. If one looks at the Law for the Prevention of Sea Pollution from Land-Based Sources, 1988, one finds that the law empowers the Minister of Environmental Protection to form a committee composed of representatives of several ministries to act on requests to permit dumping into the sea. Regulations promulgated under the law define the manner in which requests are to be submitted to the committee, the timetable for the committee's decisions, the scope of the committee's decisions and limitations on the committee's decision-making powers.[393] The regulations are silent on the right to appeal the committee's decisions. The regulations do not require the committee's meetings to be open to the public, nor is a member of the public a member of the committee.

192. A similar type of process is found in the Law for the Protection of Plants. Under this law, the Minister of Agriculture is empowered to create a committee of three to hear appeals from the decisions of the Head of the Department of Plant Protection of the Ministry of Agriculture. For the purposes of this chapter, these decisions relate to the introduction of pesticides or herbicides. If the Head of the Department of Plant Protection rejects a request for use, the applicant has a right to appeal to an appeals committee. The law does not require the Minister of Agriculture to appoint an inter-ministerial committee or a committee of experts; he/she is free to choose any three individuals. In regulations, the Minister of Justice has prescribed rules for the operation of the appeals committee.[394] These rules delineate the procedure for filing appeals, including background material to be filed and a timetable for filing. The regulations also determine the manner in which the committee makes its decision and notifies the appellant. The regulations do not prescribe rules for appeal from the decision of the appeals committee.

193. A different approach to the above committees can be found in the Water Law. Within it is created a Water Tribunal, similar to a Water Court. The Water Tribunal is composed of a District Court Judge, who serves as Chairman and two laymen from a list prepared by the Minister of Agriculture and approved by the Water Board. The Water Tribunal sits as an appeals court in the District Court of Haifa. The Water Tribunal is empowered with the same powers as a District Court, within its province.

The province of the Water Tribunal is set out in the Water Law. It hears appeals from decisions of the Water Authority in the area of water supply, water quality and

---

393. Regulations for the Prevention of Sea Pollution from Land Based Sources, 1990, K.T. 250.
394. Regulations for the Protection of Plants (Procedural Rules Before the Appeals Committee), 1967, K.T. 474.

water pollution. The majority of appeals to the Water Tribunal relate to questions of supply, cost and damage to water supply systems. The Tribunal, however, also hears cases on the right to water,[395] water pollution[396] and flooding.

194. A third example of administrative environmental law is that of the Planning Commission. The Planning and Building Law, 1965, sets out methods for appeals from decisions and objections to plans. When a Planning Commission makes its decision, this decision may be appealed by one of two parties: the initiator of the plan or a governmental ministry. The public has no general right to appeal a Planning Commission's decision. The public, however, does have the right to object to a plan when it is submitted for Planning Commission approval and this objection may relate to any aspect of the plan. Who can object? The law states: 'anyone interested in land, building or other planning detail who sees himself injured by a proposed plan'. The Supreme Court has given this section a wide interpretation.

The law sets out how a plan is to be published and the method for objection. Objections are heard by the Planning Commission and not by a special appeals committee or tribunal. The hearing is to be open to the public and each objector is entitled to be heard. The law also enables environmental associations to file objections, not just aggrieved individuals. This right is limited, however, to those environmental associations listed in regulations published by the Minister of the Interior. Among those listed are the Society for the Protection of Nature and the Nature Reserves and Parks Authority.

395. For example, 105/02 *Administrative Appeal to the Water Tribunal-Ben Ezer v. Water Commission, Mekorot*, and the Yarqon River Authority on an unsuccessful claim to continue pumping water from the Yarqon River.

396. For example, 264/03 *Administrative Appeal to the Water Tribunal-Tadir Gan Metal Co. and Coor Metal Co. v. The Water Commissioner and the Ministry of Environmental Protection*, an unsuccessful appeal of a Water Authority pollution clean-up order.

Chapter 3. Judicial Remedies

§1. The Court System: An Introduction

195. Israel's court system is similar to that in other common law countries. There are three tiers of courts: Magistrate, District and Supreme. There are also special courts or tribunals, for example, Small Claims, Traffic, Labour (work-related and social security), religious courts (Jewish, Muslim, Druze, Christian) who have jurisdiction over matters of personal status, and others. The delineation between the tiers is by the seriousness of the crime or the amount of claim in dispute. Israel has no juries, and judges sit individually in most cases, with panels as the exception.

196. The Supreme Court of Israel has a unique role. It acts as an appeals court as well as an equity court for complaints against government action, more familiarly known as a '*Bagatz*', or the High Court of Justice. This latter role has been discussed previously but it is mentioned again because of its importance in the environmental law field. A few examples of *Bagatz* cases will serve to highlight the public's reliance on the *Bagatz* procedure in order to protect the environment.

197. In 1989, the United States government approached the Israeli government with a proposal to build a new transmittal station for the Voice of America radio service. The Israeli government looked at the project favourably, and the Americans proceeded to plan the station. A site was picked in the Negev, several kilometres away from the nearest farming community. The site, however, rested on a portion of a Nature Reserve and was near an Army installation. Objections to the site were raised by area residents. Their first appeal to the High Court of Justice failed because they argued that the plan should have been filed at the District Planning Commission level instead of with the National Planning Commission.[397] The Supreme Court rejected this argument and held that the Voice of America station had sufficient linkage to a national grid to be considered by the National Planning Council.

The plan was then brought before the National Planning Council for discussion. An environmental impact statement was prepared and discussed by the National Planning Council and the plan was approved. Again, the citizens turned to the High Court of Justice, arguing that the environmental impact statement was insufficient.[398] This time, the Court agreed with the residents. The Court remanded the plan to the National Planning Council with a directive to properly study the effects of the station on migratory birds and the army installations nearby.

A 2004 appeal to the High Court of Justice concerned the environmental effects of building the separation fence between Israel and the Palestinians on the government-approved route.[399] The claim was eventually rejected on the grounds

397. Bagatz 594/89, *Arava Tichona Area-wide Council v. National Planning Commission*, P.D. 44 (1), 558.

398. Bagatz 2324/91, *The Council for the Quality of Government in Israel v. National Planning Commission*, P.D. 45 (3), 678.

399. Bagatz 2056/04, *Beit Soreq Regional Council v. Government of Israel.*

that whatever route the fence takes will cause environmental harm, and the route and construction are being carried out in tandem with the Nature Reserves and Parks Authority.

But a similar case in 2015 was decided differently. The council and residents of the West Bank village of Battir together with the NGO Friends of the Earth Middle East (today known as EcoPeace) appealed to the High Court of Justice to stop the building of the separation fence through the town. They claimed that the fence would harm the ancient agricultural terraces and irrigation canals, which were declared a UNESCO heritage site in 2014. The Court decided to freeze the planned construction route.[400]

Another case concerned an amendment to the orders of the Planning and Building Law.[401] The appellants claimed the amendment is unconstitutional because they shorten the time an objection can be raised before the Infrastructure Committee, and thus, may harm the rights inherent under the Freedom and Dignity Basic Law. The Supreme Court rejected the appeal, and as part of their ruling declared that the right to a healthy environment cannot be derived from the Freedom and Dignity Basic Law. This is too wide an interpretation according to the ruling, and can only be guaranteed if and when the Knesset passes a Basic Law for the Environment.

In 2006, asbestos inspectors from the Ministry of Environmental Protection stopped working due to their inability to obtain insurance. An appeal to the High Court of Justice by the IUED and the Association for Quality of Life & Environment in Nahariya claimed this to be untenable due to the potential harm to the public.[402] In response to the lawsuit, the Treasury and the Civil Service Commission resolved the budgetary dispute, enabling the inspectors to return to work.

§2. Recourse to the Courts

I. Criminal Sanctions

198. Recourse to the courts is in one of three areas: criminal, civil and equity or justice. The environmental laws discussed in the preceding chapters all contain criminal sanctions for those violating their provisions. For example, one found guilty of water pollution may be fined and imprisoned for up to a year, and in cases of substantial environmental harm, for up to three years. Similar, but less drastic, provisions may be found in all environmental laws. There is, therefore, recourse to the courts for violations of environmental laws. Criminal cases are the province of the Attorney General or his/her representative. In some laws, there are provisions for private criminal actions. These laws include the Water Law and the Kanowitz Law, discussed previously.

400. Bagatz 7612/12 and Bagatz 8716/12, *Battir Village Council and 87 residents of Battir v. Military Commander in the West Bank.*
401. Bagatz 4128/02, *Israel Union for Environmental Defence (IUED) v. the Prime Minister of Israel.*
402. Bagatz 1336/06, *IUED and the Association for Quality of Life & Environment in Nahariya v. the Treasury*, Civil Service Commissioner and Ministry of Environmental Protection.

Until the 1990s, very few criminal cases were brought for violations of environmental law because the government was not forthright enough against violators. Furthermore, most major polluters of streams and rivers are municipalities, themselves governmental units. Therefore, criminal suits were brought only in extreme cases of pollution or as private criminal suits.

To help remedy this problem, the Knesset passed a law in 1997 for the purpose of protecting the environment and, in case of environmental damage, to return the damaged area to its former state.[403] The law increases methods of enforcement and allowable punishments in five different environmental laws and incorporates them as amendments in all five laws.[404]

As mentioned previously in the chapter on general law, the Polluter Pays Law has increased the maximum fines and prison terms allowed under thirteen different environmental laws and allows the court to impose even larger fines and prison sentences for crimes committed that cause or may cause severe environmental harm. It also allows the court to impose fines that reflect the damage caused and the economic benefits or profits gained from the act on top of any other fine imposed. The thirteen environmental laws amended cover air, water and soil pollution, solid waste, dangerous substances, and non-ionizing radiation.

Since the passing of these laws, the Ministry of Environmental Protection has put emphasis on enforcement. Nine regulations have been passed in several areas of environmental law which give the police the right to fine the offender on the spot.[405] These fines are similar to parking tickets and are given in lieu of an appearance in court. As a result, 19,667 'tickets' were given under the Maintenance of Cleanliness law in 2008, including fines for littering, legally posting signs and posters, and dumping building refuse and abandoned cars. Also in 2008, 1,568 reports were given for noise violations and 1,767 for air pollution violations from cars.[406]

There has been an increase in the number of court cases and higher penalties have been imposed on the violators of environmental laws. Over the last decade, the number of cases handled by the Ministry of Environmental Protection has increased from tens to hundreds. Frequently, injunctions are given to offenders to stop polluting and clean up environmental damage caused. The Ministry lawsuits, usually carried out by outside attorneys, representing the state in criminal proceedings, have a conviction rate of 98%. For example, in 2008, out of seventy-five court rulings, seventy-three cases ended in convictions. Judges have gradually recognized the importance of preserving the environment and punishing environmental offenders. Consequently, there has been a trend towards harsher punishment. Usually, fines are accompanied by a suspended sentence, where the offender signs a commitment to

403. Law of Environment (Methods of Punishment) (Amendments to Legislation), 1997.
404. Maintenance of Cleanliness Law, 1984; Abatement of Nuisances Law, 1961; Roads (Affixing of Signs) Law, 1966; Dangerous Substances Law, 1993; Public Health Ordinance, 1940.
405. For example, Criminal Procedure Order (Finable Offences – Prevention of Noise), 2000; Criminal Procedure Order (Finable Offences – Air Pollution from Vehicles on the Road), 2001; Criminal Procedure Order (Finable Offences – Maintenance of Cleanliness), 2000.
406. Ministry of Environmental Protection, Environment Bulletin Vol. 35 (September 2009), 21–26.

not repeat the environmental offence for a certain period of time. This obligation is assigned a high monetary value which the offender must pay if violated.[407]

Judges have also increasingly convicted not only the local authority or company itself but also its mayor or those holding senior management positions. Holding such persons liable is an essential step in deterring them from polluting and urging them to manage their entities in an environmentally friendly way. People tend to react more effectively when they, and not only the company or local authority, are held responsible for offences.

The District Court of Haifa has held managers and senior officials criminally responsible for behaviour that caused or contributed to environmental damage.[408] The District Court accepted various appeals from the Magistrate Court that sought to convict managers and impose punitive sanctions for *environmental offences*. In the Court's view, senior officials and managers have decision-and policy-making power, are responsible for budget, and are (also) responsible for the existence and removal of nuisances and environmental hazards.

Convicting them sends an appropriate message on behalf of the legal system and a warning to companies' managers to take their responsibility to avoid environmental damage seriously. Similarly, two managers were convicted together with their company for environmental offences of water pollution, dumping of hazardous waste and materials into the public domain and discharge of waste to the sea.[409]

'Putting liability solely on the authorities is not enough of a deterrent, it puts a financial burden on the public that has already suffered from the pollution, and this is instead of the person responsible for the treatment of pollution.'[410]

However, punishment is not as severe as in the United States, for example, where fines given to these individuals are higher and are often accompanied by a prison term, house-confinement arrest or community service hours.[411] Few cases in Israel have sentenced mayors and CEOs to prison terms or community service hours.

In the past, most judges felt inclined to give mild punishments to industries, so as not to punish its workers by causing unemployment. However, there has been a change in attitude, and judges have come to understand that they must also consider the harm caused to the environment. One illustration of such a shift is a decision from the Water Court in Haifa regarding industries polluting the Na'aman stream.[412] The industries requested a delay in stopping the flow of their sewage into the stream against the order issued under the Water Law. In response to this request, the Justice responded:

---

407. *See*, e.g., Rehovot Magistrates Court, Criminal Case No. 1165/99 *The State of Israel v. Royal Goose Inc*. The company director had been previously convicted and received a suspended sentence in the amount of NIS 80,000. In response to a violation of his obligation, the court invoked the suspended sentence in its entirety.

408. Haifa District Court Appeal No. 17/08/10261 *State of Israel v. Shemen Industries Ltd. et al.*

409. Haifa District Court Appeal 17/09/1003 *State of Israel v. Dor Chemicals Ltd. et al.*

410. The District Court of Nazareth, Criminal Appeal No. 1160/05 *Yitzhak Meron v. The State of Israel.*

411. *See*, e.g., *Tin Products Inc v. Lexington City Water*, South Carolina District Court, 5 May 2005; *United States of America v. BEF Corp and Elward B. Brewer*, US District Court for the Eastern District of Pennsylvania, 1 Apr. 2005.

412. Krayot Magistrates Court, Case No. 001880/04, *The State of Israel v. Milu-Off* et al.

> At first glance, these seem like technical requests, where the invisible threat is that rejecting the request will lead to many lay-offs and harm to the State's Treasury. This threat has succeeded for too long. It has turned all of our country's streams into open sewage channels and its ground into an accumulator of poisonous substances […]. As long as it is possible to save even a part of our country and return it to a condition that will allow healthy life, we must act. It is clear that this comes at a cost, just as there is a price for treating pollution.

Another indication of this shift can be found in two cases where the court rejected the compromise reached and gave the offender a harsher punishment, a first in environmental law cases.[413]

But there is still a serious lack of supervision in Israel. Not only is the general supervision of industry and local governments weak, but day-to-day supervision is practically nonexistent. One idea is for the various ministries responsible for different areas of the environment and the Water Commissioner to coordinate on-site, day-to-day supervision rotating every few months between various entities.

A system for evaluation and criticism must be created, whereby supervisors collect specific data regarding on-site occurrences, and entities should not be able to operate if they do not meet certain requirements. Supervision would help transform the enforcement of environmental laws into a proactive initiative rather than a reactive initiative. Prevention, rather than pursuing entities once a disaster has occurred, should be the objective. Moreover, tighter environmental supervision of businesses will change the mentality of businesses, forcing them to recognize the environment as an integral part of their business on which their success depends.

199. In order to better address the enforcement problem, legislators concluded that local authorities should take an active part in environmental enforcement. The Local Authorities Law (Environmental Enforcement-Authority of Inspectors), 2008, requires larger cities and towns to train inspectors to enforce sixteen existing environmental laws. Fines levied by these inspectors are paid to the local authority. Smaller towns have the option of taking part as well.

II. Civil Suits

200. As was discussed above in Part IV – Liability, civil suits in the environmental law field proliferate under the Torts Ordinance as nuisance actions. Numerous actions for damages or injunctions are brought before Israel's courts in the area of noise, air and olfactory pollution. The greatest number of suits are in the area of noise.

There are serious stumbling blocks to civil suits in the environmental law field in Israel. First of all, there is the normal problem of proof, with the burden on the plaintiff to prove that the defendant caused environmental damage. This problem is extremely difficult in cases of air pollution because there are no emission standards.

413. Nazareth District Court, Case No. 1160/05, *Yitzhak Meron v. The State of Israel*; Krayot Magistrates Court, Criminal Case No. 8753/02 *State of Israel v. Haifa Chemicals.*

Furthermore, except for air, noise and olfactory pollution under the Kanowitz law, a plaintiff must prove monetary loss. Third, Israel does not allow class actions in tort suits, nor will the courts allow an association for the protection of the environment to sue for the prevention of pollution in a pristine area arguing, for example, that its members hike in that area.

In order to remedy this situation, a law was passed by the Knesset: The Law for the Prevention of Environmental Nuisances (Citizen Suits), 1992.[414] The legislation enables a person to sue to prevent an environmental nuisance even if that nuisance does not cause monetary loss. The law also allows a non-profit association active in the environmental field to bring suit on behalf of its members against a polluter. Finally, the law creates the right of class actions wherever necessary against an environmental polluter. Yet, the law was modified in committee and allows actions only in suits for injunctions or mandamus. The Knesset rejected the concept of class action suits for monetary damages. The law has been used sporadically since its inception possibly because it provides for injunctions but not compensation. The definition of 'environmental nuisance' in the law has been expanded to include air pollution, noise, odours, water pollution, seawater pollution, solid waste pollution, pollution from dangerous substances, pollution from radiation, harm to the coastal environment, harm from asbestos, harm in a protected area, harm to a protected tree or any full-grown tree, harm to a forest or harm to a protected natural asset, and all when they are in violation of any law, order, plan, business licence or any other permit or licence, or that cause harm to human health or cause real suffering to a person.[415]

III. Enforcement Alternatives

201. Incentives. As previously mentioned, litigation is not the only ingredient to effective enforcement of environmental laws. A real turnaround cannot be based solely on fear of prosecution but requires proper supervision from the outset in order to prevent environmental offences from occurring, rather than reacting to them, and the development of a corporate culture where the environment is an integral part of the business's success. The bottom line for businesses, as well as local authorities, is they must allocate equal effort in creating and applying incentives in order to increase the incorporation of environmental awareness into their businesses.

Some countries offer incentives to industry and local authorities to encourage them to adopt a more environmentally friendly attitude in their business. There are several reasons, however, why such an approach is presently implausible in Israel, and alternative approaches to encourage industry and local governments are implemented.

First, the government does not have sufficient money to subsidize industry to improve the environment, but it has reduced tariffs on items that improve the environment. Second, there is no recognition of companies that invest in environmental projects.

---

414. 48 L.S.I, unpublished; S.H. 5752, 184.
415. Law for the Prevention of Environmental Nuisances (Civil Suits), 1992 s. 1. S.H. 2776.

The approach regarding local authorities is slightly different. Here, unlike in industry, the government has to subsidize, mostly in the area of solid waste pollution. One example is the Sewage Authority, which gives loans to local authorities. However, some areas with bad environmental conditions cannot even afford to pay back these loans. It is in these areas that the government must seriously think about subsidizing because the damage is not limited to local boundaries, but can affect the entire country.

Some local authorities also feel that they are unable to take on long-term responsibilities, such as investing in and operating sewage purification plants, and that, therefore, it is difficult for them to abide by certain legislation and standards. If and when the local authorities build such plants, they do so in adherence to the standards in place. However, if the Water Authority implements new standards requiring better water quality, as in 2010, abiding by these new standards might require additional investment by the local authorities.

202. Increased Flow of Information. In March 2005, an amendment to the Freedom of Information Act 1998 was passed, giving the right to freedom of environmental information. This amendment was introduced as a private members' bill and requires all government agencies to publish on their Internet site, or, in the absence of an Internet site, using other means, information regarding discharge to the environment. Prior to the amendment, there were some major laws, such as the Licensing of Businesses Law, that required companies to submit information to the government. There were also some bylaws requiring companies to report their emissions to local authorities. However, there was no obligation to report to the public. When presented, this amendment was a strong piece of legislation, and, as with many other environmental legislative proposals, was compromised in its environmental content.

203. Environmental Insurance. The benefits of environmental insurance are twofold: First, if environmental damage is caused, there will be someone to pay for its clean-up. Second, because the insurance companies will not want to pay for pollution clean-up, they will ensure that the entities they represent do not pollute by performing tests, checking pipes, etc. These companies will set a minimum baseline of environmental compliance.

204. Effectiveness Measurement. Legislation and regulations should not be created and enforced simply for the sake of doing so. Measuring their effectiveness is essential to understanding where improvements and changes must be made. Nevertheless, most environmental bodies in Israel do not use measuring tools to examine the success of enforcement.

The Ministry of Environmental Protection has an annual meeting where it reviews such topics as the success of its programmes and the number and kinds of cases filed in court. The Ministry has benchmarks for some areas, such as for air pollution and the number and kinds of cases brought to court.[416]

416. Interview with Rachel Adam, Deputy Legal Advisor, the Ministry of Environmental Protection, Jerusalem, 19 Sep. 2005.

Although this approach is a start, it is a weak one. Studies should be conducted before and after legislation is passed, or new enforcement mechanisms are introduced, in order to verify the degree of effectiveness. For example, only after international treaties relating to the environment are implemented as national law does the Ministry monitor the area covered by the legislation. No study is done before the implementation, and thus no prior data is available, severely weakening the Ministry's capability to measure progress in that area.[417] Less effective measuring tools prevent accurate measurement of environmental improvement and do not allow legislation to be used to its full potential by enforcement bodies.

205. Israel Securities Authority (ISA). The ISA was established in 1968 to protect the interests of the investing public. It requires corporations to disclose business and economic information and to enforce the laws and regulations when violations are discovered.

206. The Barnea Committee was formed to study the need for reform regarding the structure and the extent of information public businesses are required to submit. The committee published a report in 2001 in which it outlines suggestions for an overall reform of public companies' disclosure obligations.[418] Following their conclusions, the Israel Securities Authority adopted many of the recommendations, which were based on trends in the United States. Prior to these regulations, there was a more general obligation to report on environmental factors. These regulations are also general, but they are clearer and can no longer be ignored by public companies as they outline specific obligations.[419] They have also helped change several companies' environmental attitudes since they have to report to the State.

The Ministry of Environmental Protection has a cooperative agreement with the Israel Securities Authority which calls for the mutual sharing of information. This agreement is a helpful step in improved legislative enforcement because now when the Ministry suspects that a company has an environmental problem and believes it should be reported (because it is important information for the reasonable investor), the Ministry can turn to the Securities Authority, which verifies whether or not the company has reported the problem. If no report was filed, the Authority obliges the company to publish one. This violation is a criminal offence and reflects poorly on the company.

Although this relationship has not been sufficiently exploited, its use is increasing.

207. Voluntary Environmental and Social Reports. A non-legal trend has emerged whereby companies have voluntarily started issuing environmental and social reports. The two main reasons for this attitude are building the company's

417. Interview with Ori Livne, Director, International Relations Division, the Ministry of Environmental Protection, Jerusalem, 21 Sep. 2005.
418. Barnea Committee Report for the Renewed Study of the Reporting Model on the Business of a Company, Regarding Forecasts and Decrees.
419. Israel Securities Authority, Annual Report 2000, presented to the Minister of Finance and to the Knesset Finance Committee, April 2001, 86–88.

image and the belief that these reports increase the effectiveness of their processes and are financially beneficial. Hopefully, this attitude will spread to other Israeli companies.[420]

208. Environmental Impact Index. The Environmental Impact Index gives scores to Israel's largest publicly traded companies based on their impact on the environment and their compliance with environmental requirements and standards. It is designed to give investors a way to evaluate their exposure to financial risk due to a company's activities.[421] The 2014 list of forty-four publicly traded companies whose activities have a negative impact on the environment includes Paz Oil, Delek Group, Israel Electric Corp., Dor Alon and Israel Chemicals.

209. MAALA Stock Exchange Index. MAALA-Business for Social Responsibility is an organization whose objective is to promote social-environmental responsibility amongst businesses.[422] In 2005, the Tel Aviv Securities' Authority Stock Exchange allowed for an index called 'MAALA' that measures criteria in four central topics regarding companies' social responsibility, namely the environment, ethics, the workplace and human rights, and community investment. Forty-nine companies participated in the MAALA 2006 ranking, representing accumulated revenues of ILS 155 billion. Approximately 25% of the 350 largest companies in Israel currently participate in the rankings (a percentage similar to foreign markets). One of the major requirements for participating companies is to have a code of ethics. At 87% of the companies, the code of ethics is open to public scrutiny.

210. Companies with Foreign Interests. The implementation of an environmental corporate culture is more developed in Europe than in Israel, and therefore, those Israeli companies that want to manufacture, export or expand to Europe are required to take on such an outlook and abide by European environmental laws. Several Israeli companies have adopted the ISO14000/14001 voluntary international standards in the environmental field. These standards include environmental auditing, environmental performance evaluation, environmental labelling and life-cycle assessment.

211. International Treaties. Being a relatively young country, overwhelmed by security concerns, Israel does not prioritize the environment either domestically or internationally. As with most countries, although Israel has signed several international environmental treaties, the Ministry of Environmental Protection is frustrated as they do not have much say in the environmental policy signed in the international arena. Often the Foreign Minister and Justice Minister, who have other priorities, are those ratifying and implementing international conventions. There is also

---

420. The list of companies includes Nesher Cement, the Egged and Dan Bus Companies and the Israel Airports Authority.

421. *Ministry of Environmental Protection website:* http://www.sviva.gov.il/English/env_topics/Sustainable%20Development/EnvironmentalImpact-Index/Pages/Environmental-Impact-Index.aspx#GovXParagraphTitle2 (last visited 30 Oct. 2019).

422. MAALA homepage (Hebrew), www.maala.org.il (last visited 14 Apr. 2023).

an economic price for joining treaties which the Ministry of Environmental Protection, with its limited budget, is not always able to afford.[423] But environmental trends and concerns are increasingly global, and there has been an increase in Israeli ratification of international environmental agreements over the past decades.[424] As of 2011, Israel has ratified sixteen environmental conventions, six protocols, and two international environmental agreements, chiefly in the areas of biodiversity and nature, atmosphere, chemicals and marine protection.[425] Israel has signed a bilateral or multi-lateral environmentally related Agreement or Accord, a Letter of Intent or Declaration of Intent to work together, or a Memorandum of Understanding with at least thirty countries.[426] Israel recently signed a trilateral agreement with Greece and Cyprus for a regional readiness plan in the event of a sea pollution event as agreed upon in the Barcelona Convention for the Protection of the Marine Environment and the Coastal Region of the Mediterranean.

---

423. Interview with Ori Livne, Director, International Relations Division, The Ministry of Environmental Protection, Jerusalem, 21 Sep. 2005.
424. R. Laster & E. Choshen, *The Roots of Environmental Law and Administration in Israel* 91 (The Jerusalem Institute for Israel Studies, The Center for Environmental Policy, 2003) (Hebrew).
425. 401 Ministry of Environmental Protection: Ministry of Environmental Protection, International Relations Dept., Survey of Environmental Treaties Israel is a Party to, 20 Dec. 2010 (Hebrew).
426. https://www.gov.il/en/Departments/Guides/bilateral_relations_and_agreements?chapterIndex=2 (last visited 14 Apr. 2023).

Selected Bibliography

Becker, N. (ed.). *Water Policy in Israel*. Vol. 4 of 'Global Issues in Water Policy'. New York: Springer, 2013.

Bin-Nun, A. *The Law of the State of Israel*. 1990.

Frumkin, R. & D. Khenin. Vital Signs 2001, The Environmental Trends Shaping our Future,

World Watch Institute and the Heschel Center, Kvutzat Eretz V'Teva (published yearly) (Hebrew).

Gabbay, S. *The Environment in Israel*. Jerusalem: The Ministry of Environmental Protection, 2002.

Gouldman, D. *Legal Aspects of Town Planning in Israel*. Jerusalem: Institute for Legislative Research and Comparative Law, 1966.

Gvirtzman, H. *Water Resources in Israel*. Jerusalem: Keter Publishing, 2002 (Hebrew).

Kaplan M. *The Rivers of Israel: Policy and Planning Principles*. Jerusalem: The Ministry of Environmental Protection, 2004 (Hebrew).

Kendall, H. *Village Development in Palestine During the British Mandate*. London: Crown agent for the colonies, 1949, 115.

Laster, R. *The Legal Framework for the Prevention and Control of Water Pollution in Israel*.

Jerusalem Ministry of Interior, Environmental Protection Service, 1976.

Laster, R. 'Reading D: Planning and Building or Building and Then Planning'. *Law Review* 6, no. 7s (1973): 481.

Laster, R. 'Solid Waste Regulations for Waste Nuisances?'. *The Biosphere* 20, no. 6 (1991): at 15 (Hebrew).

Laster, R. & E. Choshen. *The Roots of Environmental Administration In Israel*. Jerusalem:

The Jerusalem Institute for Israel Studies, 2003 (Hebrew).

Laster, R. & E. Choshen. *Environment, Administration, and Law in Israel: The Central Administration*. Jerusalem: The Jerusalem Institute for Israel Studies, 2004 (Hebrew).

Laster, R. & E. Choshen. *Environment, Administration, and Law in Israel: Government Ministries*. Jerusalem: The Jerusalem Institute for Israel Studies, 2005 (Hebrew).

Ministry of Environment. *Environmental Quality in Israel*. The Ministry of Environment Annual Report (Hebrew).

Selected Bibliography

Air and Waste Management Association. Report of Activities for 2011-Legal Department, Ministry of Environmental Protection (Hebrew).

Shechef N, N. Halamish & Y. Alexandrov. *Soil Conservation Master Plan for Shikma-Besor River Basin*. Be'er Sheva: The Shikma-Besor Drainage Authority, 2013 (Hebrew).

Shnoor, B. *Toxic Torts*. Jerusalem: Nevo, 2011 (Hebrew).

Teclaff, L.A. *Water Law in Historical Perspective.* 1983.

Whitman, Joyce. *The Environment in Israel,* 4th ed. Jerusalem: Ministry of the Interior, 1988.

Index

The numbers here refer to paragraph numbers.

Index

Index

Index